T0305336

EXTINCTION EQUILIBRIUM

Economics for Generational Survival

Jefferson Frank

BRISTOL
UNIVERSITY
PRESS

First published in Great Britain in 2024 by

Bristol University Press
University of Bristol
1–9 Old Park Hill
Bristol
BS2 8BB
UK
t: +44 (0)117 374 6645
e: bup-info@bristol.ac.uk

Details of international sales and distribution partners are available at bristoluniversitypress.co.uk

British Library Cataloguing in Publication Data
A catalogue record for this book is available from the British Library

ISBN 978-1-5292-2636-2 hardcover
ISBN 978-1-5292-2637-9 paperback
ISBN 978-1-5292-2638-6 ePub
ISBN 978-1-5292-2639-3 ePdf

Cover design: blu inc
Front cover image: iStock/GeorgePeters
Bristol University Press uses environmentally responsible print partners.
Printed and bound in Great Britain by CPI Group (UK) Ltd, Croydon, CR0 4YY

FSC
www.fsc.org
MIX
Paper | Supporting
responsible forestry
FSC® C013604

To Yann

Contents

List of Figures   vi
List of Generations   vii
Acknowledgements   viii
Preface   ix

1   Introduction and Plan of the Book   1
2   Doing and Undoing Economics   21
3   The Long and Short of It   47
4   The Fed Did It   64
5   The Everything Bubble   88
6   Smart Motorways   101
7   The Future of Work   113
8   People and Robots   129
9   Universities   145
10   Housing   170
11   Let the Good Times Roll   186

References   202
Index   210

List of Figures

4.1	US monetary base	72
4.2	Money supply	74
4.3	The Phillips curve	77
4.4	Phillips loops	78
5.1	Market yield on US Treasury securities at 10-year constant maturity	89
5.2	Market yield on US Treasury securities at 10-year constant maturity: inflation-indexed	93
5.3	Wilshire 5000 Total Market Full Cap Index	94
5.4	Thirty-year fixed rate mortgage average in the US	96
6.1	Gold fixing price 10:30 a.m. (London time) in London bullion market, based in US dollars	103
6.2	US basic discount rate (discontinued)	106
6.3	US gross federal debt as percentage of gross domestic product	109
7.1	UK average pay in real terms	114
7.2	US median usual weekly real earnings for wage and salary workers, 16 years and over	115
7.3	UK trade union membership	118
8.1	US net domestic private investment and corporate profits after tax	139
8.2	US net domestic private investment, corporate profits after tax and gross private domestic investment	140
10.1	US House Price Index	180
10.2	UK annual private rents inflation rates	181

List of Generations

The UK National archives defines the generations as:

- Baby boomers – birth years 1946–1964
- Generation X – birth years 1965–1980
- Millennials – birth years 1981–1996
- Generation Z – birth years 1997–2012

The generation before the boomers, the 'silent generation', is now largely over 80, while the youngest members of their predecessor 'greatest generation' are now approaching 100. Generation alpha are the newest humans.

Acknowledgements

My 'greatest generation' father (Master's in Structural Engineering and Master's in Sociology) read through the entire manuscript and made a number of suggestions. He feels that you should skip over the Preface (unless you are an academic economist) and jump right into the first chapter.

I'd also like to thank my Editor, Paul Stevens, who encouraged me to 'express my voice'. This would have been a very different book without his input.

Preface

Academic economists don't usually write books. We are rewarded, in professional and self-esteem as well as promotions and pay rises, for our publications of highly mathematical articles in scientific journals. The Research Excellence Framework (REF) exercises, run about every five years by the funding bodies, rate departments in every subject at every UK university. The most important element is research output, judged by the list of publications submitted to the REF. As an example, for the 2021 REF the London School of Economics and Political Science (LSE) economics department submitted over 100 journal articles, two book chapters and no monographs.

Articles, to be published in top journals, need to be very focused and have just the right degree of originality. They cannot really challenge the conventional wisdom, since peer referees will be doing research in the area largely following the contemporary flow of thought and analysis. In general, this is perfect for developing 'normal science' (Kuhn, 1962). But it also means that vibrant debates on issues, both theoretical and policy, are limited.

Books and other policy forums used to provide an alternative channel. My PhD supervisor, James Tobin, author of *National Economic Policy* (1966), regularly debated with Milton Friedman, who wrote *Capitalism and Freedom* (1962) on their very different views of the world and optimal economic policy. Less conventional challenges were raised by John Kenneth Galbraith (*The Affluent Society*, 1958) and Joan Robinson (*Economic Philosophy*, 1962). One could read Keynes's *General Theory of Employment, Interest and Money* (1936) or Pigou's *Theory of Unemployment* (1933) to get conflicting views.

Academic economists would love to be able to affect the policy debate. The government sought to incentivize this by introducing *impact* to the REF. Instead of just submitting lists of articles, universities would also submit a few essays on how articles had *impacted* upon the real world. But this fails on two grounds. It doesn't take advantage of academics' intrinsic interests (particularly in a social science such as economics) in engaging in policy, but focuses upon providing an unnecessary and very indirect extrinsic motivation. Further, research is throwing a pebble into the water – the ripples spread out, merge with ripples from other stones, and tracing back to the original pebble (or academic article) is virtually impossible. It is, in general, far more productive to empower people by providing the channels for engagement. To take a different example of the same point, the government might best encourage electric car take-up if they made sure that there was a high-speed, readily available charging network through the country.

When I was a PhD student in macroeconomics and monetary economics, I would avidly read the testimonies of leading economists to US Congressional Committees. Parliamentary select committees could perform the same role, getting and publishing a wide range of testimonies from economists of widely different viewpoints. While this might be impeded by the current relative homogeneity of viewpoints within the profession, that sort of forum might in fact engender greater diversity of analysis and policy recommendations. We got into the current economic impasse by groupthink, and need more robust discussion of ways out. I was listening to an eminent economist explain that 99% of the profession favoured trade as free as possible, but he thought that maybe this underestimated the preference of voters to keep their job over getting shirts more cheaply. As with everything in economics, the weight of theory and evidence doesn't support 99% of economists having an unvarnished, unanimous view on trade or anything else. That's just not how economics (or science in general) works, as we'll discuss.

But all this was really to explain that this book comes a decade after my last monograph on general economic policy (Frank, 2014), although with co-authors I did write on the disastrous state of English universities in *English Universities in Crisis: Markets without competition* (Frank et al, 2019). The Coalition Government did not understand that markets need to be carefully constructed in the context of the particular good being provided – what works (although it turns out that it doesn't work) for a market for electricity won't work for a market for education. Except for that digression, like other academic economists, I had to focus on publishing mathematical articles in the scientific journals, since my department would not happily have taken the risk of submitting either book to the REF. That virtually no monographs are submitted to the Economics REF is an equilibrium – given that no one knows how the panel would react to books, no one is willing to take the risk of submitting one. Equilibrium is a fundamental concept in economics, not coincidentally appearing in the title to this book and the vital element running throughout the book.

It is rare that a decade of reflection doesn't change one's views, particularly since this decade was noteworthy in that the climate emergency and potential extinction moved to centre stage. My concerns about future generations – the proposed topic of the book – evolved from *equity* to *sustainability* to *survival*. In England, it's natural to frame almost every problem in terms of the housing market. So, let's go with that example to have a first look at understanding equity, sustainability and survival.

Equity across generations is reflected in the fact that young lecturers cannot currently buy the flat or house I could buy at that life stage, or anticipate ever buying the houses my generation of academics are living in now. According to the Office for National Statistics, in England the ratio of the median house price to median residence-based earnings has risen from 5.05 times in 2002 to 8.92 times in 2021. One could view those figures in many ways, but it's clear that there is an equity issue. Further, there are within-generation equity implications. A child of well-off parents may well be given a large deposit for a home. Those of the older generation who bought houses are sitting upon large capital gains, while renters of the same generation see their rent going up each year.

Sustainability (or rather its absence) can have different meanings. One is a planned decline in living standards. My generation can either explicitly or implicitly view their house as part of their pension, with the intention of downsizing when they retire. Their current standard of living (measured by the consumption of housing services) will, in a hopefully orderly way, change upon retirement. Related to this is someone who smokes. The consequences are easy to anticipate in terms of health issues, but an individual may still plan – implicitly or explicitly – to smoke and then face the consequential decline in health.

But sustainability concerns – particularly to an economist – might mean something else, that we are together as a society on a pathway that sooner or later must be found to be unrealistic or 'unsustainable'. Going back to housing, one could ask the question – if the next generation is unable to afford to buy my house when I want to downsize, who is going to buy it? If everyone is stretching to buy houses on the expectation that they will go up (relative to other goods and income) by 10% a year, at some point the market valuation of housing dwarfs everything else in the economy. By downsizing by just a little bit, in that world, I might double my disposable income. At some point people come to realize this and house prices crash.

Survival of my house is at question if, in Australia or California, it is overtaken by wildfires, or – in Florida – by hurricanes or flooding. While my own house burning because of a chip pan fire is a readily insurable risk, and my house can be rebuilt, the effects of climate are both economically uninsurable and do not necessarily allow for rebuilding of my house, the community or, in some cases, the country.

We generally – both as mathematical economists (because the mathematics is much neater) and as people – assume continuity, often not just in a variable but in its growth rate. If stock prices have been rising at an annual rate of 10% for several decades, we expect it to persist. Even for those who see unsustainable situations, determining a specific turning point is hard or impossible to do. 'Don't try to time the market' is basic investment advice. Contrary to subsequent claims by those who were taken by surprise, a fair number of economists saw the house price rises leading to the 2007 crash as being unsustainable, but didn't necessarily know whether the reckoning would occur in 2006, 2007, 2008, and so on. Further, because we've come to rely on being bailed out by the government or by the central bank, people weren't particularly worried about either a shift in economic fortunes or the timing of such a shift. They were right not to worry in the sense that, after a short-lived drop in prices directly during the financial crisis of 2007/08, the upward trajectory of house prices resumed. 'Stay invested' proved again to be sage advice, but it might not have been if the central bank had allowed the crisis to play out.

But continuity is not always a safe assumption nor even perhaps a desirable one. We want 18-year-olds, when they go off to university, to change dramatically, to develop independence and become in effect a different person (except to their parents, who will forever see them as children). We want stagnant businesses and organizations to blossom under dynamic new leadership or to shut down. The sandwich shop with stale bread and meagre fillings should close and make way for a better one. We don't want, after slavery in Britain was abolished in 1833, and in the US in 1865, to be facing the profound equality, sustainability and survivability issues that are still ongoing 150 years later. We don't want over-investment in housing – based upon government and central bank bailouts – to crowd-out productive investment in industry and the infrastructure, while simultaneously not providing adequate housing for much of the population.

Some economists and others still argue that global warming above 1.5 degrees is not an existential issue, that we can adjust to higher temperatures. Even if that were true (and it seems a rather *risky* wager to make on behalf of future generations), isn't it better to have the excitement of new technologies, new factories, new subjects in schools and universities, and drawing together to rebuild our world, than to wait and see how high the water rises – at that point, only emergency bailouts (literally, with pails of water) are available.

Looking over the last century, advances in technology were simply amazing compared to perhaps any other time in history. Televisions, automobiles, washing machines, computers at work and in the home, mobile phones, robots, aeroplanes, high-speed rail – the list goes on and on. In contrast, advances in policy have been sporadic (what seemed an inexorable march towards liberal democracy has been, at least temporarily, somewhat forestalled) and inadequate. Even in well-off countries, there is poverty, poor education for much of the population, drug addiction and overdose deaths – the list goes on and on, even without considering the global issues of continued wars and oppression, starvation and disease, and the climate emergency. Already, we've seen exceptional progress in bringing down the cost of production of batteries and solar panels. COVID vaccines were a further example of how we are best advised to play to our strengths – technology – and not our apparent weakness – economic and social policy. Vaccines were developed but we could not implement a system to ensure their complete uptake.

Where we've gone astray takes us back to the debates between Tobin and Friedman. I would suggest that Tobin won the arguments but Friedman won the politics. Friedman's world of deregulation, low taxation, free trade, flexible currencies has largely been put in place. Tobin reacted to the (at the time, viewed as radical to the point of crazy) proposals on flexible currencies by suggesting a tax on foreign currency transactions. The idea was that this might slow down what could otherwise be violent movements in the financial markets that would have real and serious effects on people's jobs and well-being. But even speed limits of that sort – much less guardrails – have not found favour in the political economy environment of the last four decades.

In Friedman's world as adopted in policy by Reagan and Thatcher, continued by 'left' parties led by Blair and Clinton, the guardrails were removed. If we had perfect markets and perfect policy makers, guardrails and constraints would limit discretionary policy in a potentially undesirable way. In the same way, the careful driver is unlikely to ever hit the guardrails on the highway. But in practice, our firms (notably the banks that are apparently but not in reality 'too big to fail') and policy makers are more like the adolescent racer who is constantly driving into the ditch and who always comes up with an excuse as to what 'exogenous shock' led to their predicament.

After 40 years with limited guardrails and speed limits, we find ourselves: in an existential ditch on the environment and climate change; in sustainability ditches with respect to house prices and inflation; and in equity and efficiency ditches on all levels of education, including universities, and with a continued failure to address racial and social inequities. It would be somewhat pointless to calculate just how moderate, sensible policies in all these areas over the last 40 years would have achieved our objectives at much lower cost. But that discussion – while it might guide us towards more rational policy making in the future – largely comes under the economic principle that 'bygones are bygones'. What are we going to do now, and quickly?

For the environment, we need a 'hell-bent for leather' approach to achieving net zero now, not in ten or 20 years, particularly as the evidence becomes clear that climate change is occurring even faster than predicted.

On equality, we need to jettison vapid approaches such as 'implicit bias training' or 'family friendly policies' and really address the institutionalized factors causing racial and gender inequality 50 years after the Equal Pay Act started the remedial process.

Taxes need to become progressive again and be set at levels that provide for first-rate public services. Corporations and other organizations should not be focused on 'maximizing shareholder value', which leads to economic inefficiencies as well as social inequalities, but instead on achieving beneficial outcomes for all their stakeholders – their workers, their consumers and their social environment, as well as their investors. In a world where we have massive needs for investment in net zero, it is simply daft to allow companies to buy back their shares rather than use the profits for investment.

Perhaps our most unconventional policy recommendations concern monetary policy and inflation. The monetary policies of the last 40 years – low and decreasing interest rates – have led to a massive monetary expansion and extraordinary asset price inflation. House prices are completely out of balance with incomes. The current inflation – by both monetarist and Keynesian theories of money – was an accident waiting to happen, consequent upon the level of monetary expansion. A perfectly sensible policy recommendation – espoused for example by Martin Wolf of the *Financial Times* – was that 'The Bank of England must have the courage of its conviction' (Wolf, 2023). That is, there should be a sufficiently tight monetary policy now, even at the cost of a recession, to bring inflation back down to target rates of 2%, as required by the law establishing the independence of the Bank of England. But that requires a belief that policy makers will start taking tough decisions, something not easily observed over the last decades.

Instead, for that reason but also because of the depth of the ditch we are in, we will argue for a different policy, for a controlled but substantial inflation that – provided interest rates are high enough to avoid further house price rises – eats away at the real values of the monetary stock, government debt and house prices, all of which are unsustainably high.

As for my next book, I'll be looking for a political economist to work with me on just how we got policy so wrong for so long. First, I need to work with colleagues to understand inclusive education (particularly at university level) and publish the results in mathematical economics journals in time for the 2028 REF.

London 2024

1

Introduction and Plan of the Book

This is a book about generations. It is about how economic policies over the last 40 years have 'sold the family silver'. The future has been impoverished to benefit the present. It is also specifically about Generation Z. This generation was born, according to the definitive US study of generations by Twenge (2023), from 1995 to 2012. They have begun voting and will shift the political balance. Older generations, sitting upon large capital gains in housing and stocks, will lose their dominance in determining policy. There will no longer be the strong political imperative in keeping interest rates and taxes low.

Generation Z needs to take control because their actual survival and not just their well-being is at stake. Their anticipated lifespans well exceed the period when the Earth – without drastic action – will become in large parts uninhabitable. Climate change has rapidly moved to the point where 40-degree days are likely to become common in England. There are wildfires in California and Australia, and hurricanes and unprecedented winter storms in the rest of the US. Wildfires in Canada have had severe effects on the breathability of air in New York City and other parts of the northern US. The climate emergency has reached the point of threatening extinction of many species, perhaps our own.

Fiscal and monetary policy will have to be re-thought. Governments will have to balance the books to avoid sharp rises in the interest rate. This means that there will have to be hard choices about rebuilding our education and health system, the social care system, the benefits system and infrastructure. To invest in the future or even to maintain reasonable public services, taxes will have to go up. Choices will have to be made between corporate and personal taxation, and whether or not to return to a progressive and redistributive tax system. Running deficits and printing money is no longer a sustainable option.

Monetary policy will have to make hard choices to rebalance the economy. The UK house price to income ratio of 9 to 1 is unsustainable even in the short run, as interest rates rise. The monetary authorities will have to decide whether to rebalance by having sharp house price falls to restore a normal ratio of 3 or 4 to 1, or to allow high inflation in earnings to catch up with house prices. Either will be more equitable to Generation Z, compared to current asset price levels.

There will have to be hard choices on population growth. We can no longer keep kicking the can down the road by population growth where the working age population is increasing to pay the pensions of the retired. As population grows, we stretch and strain the Earth's resources. Previously this was reflected in pollution and a diminished standard of environmental life, compensated in some ways by cheaper material goods and (because of low and stagnant wages) services. But now the choice poses the possibility of extinction, and – in that sense – population growth simply has to stop and be reversed. Pensions can be funded by physical investment or investment in human capital, or pensions can be reduced.

The saving grace in economic development over the last several decades has been technology. Everything, from high-speed railways and more efficient aeroplanes, to the spread of high-power and low-cost computers, to mobile phones, to cheap solar and wind power and the development of efficient batteries, has transformed our future economic potential.

In the same way, robots are to be embraced. Rather than relying upon cheap labour from population growth, expanding our pressure on the environment, it will be far better to have robots and artificial intelligence (AI) filling gaps in the labour market, and green energy replacing hydrocarbons. Technology remains our friend and indeed our saviour.

Given the extraordinary rate of technological progress over the last four decades, it is hard to ascribe the blame for stagnant wages and low growth in the UK and US on anything other than poor economic and social policies. It is hard to see the financial crisis of 2007/08 as other than the product of poorly functioning financial markets. It is hard to see how anyone seriously believed in 'trickle-down' economics. It was not a 'courage to act' to have uncontrolled monetary growth, but a bizarre refutation of both monetarist and Keynesian economics. On the social policy side, as well as the economics, it is hard to see why – 50 years after the Equal Pay Act – we still have such disparities across demographic groups and such a lack of social and economic mobility.

Economists seem to still believe that we've been remarkably astute in policy, but have suffered from shocks – financial shocks and real shocks (such as the pandemic). Rather like the bad actor who is pelted with fruits and vegetables on stage but observes how brilliantly he was performing but for the interruptions.

The unlucky generation

Thornton Wilder (1967: 17) describes the perspective facing a previous generation born in a new millennium: 'He had no doubt that the coming century would be too direful to contemplate – that is to say, like all the other centuries.'

Generation Z has faced one challenge after another. If these things were random, as the 'shock-based' economists would have it, this could already be categorized as 'the unlucky generation'. Whether it's the state of the economy, their inability to rent and plan to buy flats and houses, to obtain a first-rate university education without incurring large debt, to find fulfilling jobs and not be flung into the gig economy, and to avoid addictions to opioids and exposure to pandemics, or – in the UK – to be able to be part of the European community they never wanted to leave. In the US, to not have a Supreme Court that finds more and more bizarre and illogical bases for taking away democratic rights in the attempt to create an 'originalist' view of the Constitution which was no doubt perfect despite its acceptance of slavery.

In this book, we will focus upon Generation Z in the UK and the US. The methodology of economics is not conducted in the laboratory with photons and electrons. Even when we use the 'laboratory' for 'experimental economics', we tend to use our own students as the subjects. We develop theories (which are really carefully constructed logical stories or 'models') and do imperfect empirical work where we look at a very noisy world and try to draw conclusions. My models and empirical work are based upon observations and data from those two countries. An economist trained in the same PhD programme with the same supervisor, but who is based in another part of the world, will be making different observations and probably using local data. I would need to tread on their territory extremely cautiously to avoid making a basic error in understanding culture and institutions, which matter to economic outcomes.

Before we turn to the events that have characterized the lives of Generation Z in the UK and US, we should run a parallel thread of optimism. This is not just due to technology, which has already given us the tools to set ourselves on a survivable and sustainable pathway, but the apparent resilience of this generation. The Office for National Statistics in the UK reports that (contrary to press coverage) the rate of suicide has been going down or remained relatively stable since the 1980s. Indeed, the suicide rate is twice as high for mid–life males and females (45–64) as for young males and females (10–24). The percentage of young people (16–24) not in education, employment or training has been falling consistently from 2012 (16.2%) to 2021 (10.2%). Despite the challenges, Zoomers are hanging in there. But there are warning signs. There is a potentially concerning growth in suicide among young females more recently, from 1.6 per 100,000 in 2012 to 3.6 per 100,000 in 2021. The effects of the pandemic on the physical and mental health of this generation, as well as on their education, remain to be seen.

Political economy challenges

While we wish to view these as 'events' rather than 'shocks', since it seems unwise to put such major occurrences as outside the causal analysis of political economy, it remains the case that Generation Z has faced a bumpy road to date. There is no end in sight to the stormy weather.

Generation Z came in just as the dot-com bubble was bursting in 2000. The FTSE 500 stock market index fell by almost half from the beginning of the new century to 2003. Unrealistic valuations of technology companies came to an end. Fortunately, it was only the stock market that crashed – dire predictions that aeroplanes would fall from the sky due to the 'millennium bug' causing computer systems to shut down proved unfounded, perhaps because large expenditures on upgraded systems anticipated and resolved the potential disaster. On the geopolitical side, Al-Qaeda destroyed the World Trade Center on 11 September 2001, and we entered into 'regime change' wars in Afghanistan and Iraq. There were massive public demonstrations against the Iraq War with millions of people taking to the streets to no avail.

Just seven years later, the economy entered the Great Recession and 'Financial Crisis' of 2007/08. The FTSE 500 had recovered by June 2007 from its millennial falls and was once again at 1999 levels, but this euphoria also soon passed, and by 2009 the FTSE 500 had again fallen in half. In contrast to the bursting of the dot-com bubble, which had little impact upon the real economy, this time unemployment rose sharply from 4.7% to 8.5%. The Occupy movement arose in response to the bailouts for bankers. It began in Wall Street and spread to St Paul's in London, but faded away with little reform of the financial ordering of the economy.

Monetary and fiscal policy was extremely expansive and unemployment fell back to 3.8% towards the end of the next decade, by which time the FTSE 500 had again recovered to 1999 levels and a bit beyond. This calm was disrupted by the COVID pandemic of 2019. Unemployment was reported to have risen to 5.1% but the furlough and other programmes meant that any measure was misleading – people were not actually working, but were not counted for the statistical measures as unemployed. By the end of restrictions, measured unemployment was 3.5%, full employment by any reasonable definition. After a substantial, but short-lived fall in the FTSE 500 at the worst of the pandemic, it recovered by 2022 to its pre-pandemic levels. On the geopolitical side, the Russians invaded Ukraine and the risk of nuclear war became real. Baby boomers recalled how they were given (what they recognized to be) pointless drills in school on how to hide from radiation under their desk.

More generally, what was seen as an inexorable move towards democracy became forestalled over these two decades. The Arab Spring had been largely reversed, democratic moves in Russia were stifled as Putin became more and more autocratic. 'Strong men' took over in China, India, Hungary and Poland, among other places where hopes for movement towards democracy had been growing. The 'me too' movement revealed the 'open secret' of the extent to which sexual harassment and discrimination persisted in the workplace and in society. In 2016, Donald Trump was elected the populist president in the US and the UK referendum voted in favour of Brexit. 'Black Lives Matter' responded to the killing of George Floyd in 2020.

Meanwhile, the climate change clock moved on. The 2021 intergovernmental panel assessment report (IPCC, 2021), as seen clearly from the US National Oceanic and Atmospheric Administration website (NOAA, 2024) showed that global surface temperature has been inexorably rising since 1980. It is measured as 0.8 degrees above the 20th-century average. If net zero carbon is reached by 2050, the perceived existential limit of 1.5 degrees will just avoid being breached. More recent calculations and observed weather patterns, as well as melting glaciers and ice caps, have hastened the day of reckoning.

It may well be that Generation Z is just particularly unlucky. Or it may be that they are being penalized by policies that have been adopted by earlier generations that, by intention or by unconcern or by poor planning, have come at their expense.

But, even more so, the climate crisis has changed the nature of the discussion. It is no longer just a question of whether the next generation will spend most of their lives in rented accommodation paying off their student loans while holding poorly paid and insecure jobs, but of whether or not they will face constant dangers from climate change. Are we moving – for lack of action – into a biblical series of plagues, from floods and fires to pandemics, mass migrations and starvation? Will we continue to face narcissistic demagogues threatening peace in the world, and the unleashing of threats and maybe the actuality of nuclear nightmares?

Intergenerational equity

This book was proposed before the pandemic and the Russian invasion of Ukraine. I had been teaching a course on intergenerational equity, and was becoming more and more interested in this as a research topic. It has subsequently become even more clear that the world inherited by the younger generations – just as the world inherited by other generations – is far from the Utopia that technological advances suggested should be around the corner.

David Willets (2010), began to raise the issue of intergenerational equity as a conflict between boomers and millennials. Subsequent observers have constructed lists of inequities that have grown over time since the publication date. University fees rose to £9,000 in 2012, housing has become more and more unaffordable, and defined-benefit pension schemes have largely become a thing of the past. The gig economy replaced the idea of 'jobs for life'.

Jenny Bristow (2019), argues that framing the questions about the future as ones of generational conflict can be unhelpful. To take an example following her line of reasoning, the full state pension in the UK is just over £9,000 per annum, roughly equivalent to the maintenance loan available to university students living away from home outside London. Neither amount represents an adequate living allowance. Instead, issues such as social class and within-generation wealth and income disparities can be important. Elliot Major and Machin (2018) document the continuing lack of social mobility, also emphasized by Friedman and Laurison (2020).

Joseph Sternberg (2019) extends the generational questions to monetary and fiscal policy. In response to each of the crises above, the government and the central banks have run large deficits and printed money to keep interest rates low. The housing market has regularly been bailed out. It has been argued that the central banks have as well targeted rising (or at least not collapsing) stock prices as an important objective. All this can be viewed as protecting and enriching the older generations at the expense of millennials, Generation Z and generations to come.

But it is past time to talk about intergenerational equity and about sustainability. The pace of climate change necessitates a shift to issues of extinction. Discussion of the environment has changed from worries about unhealthy but reversible pollution to concerns that we are facing an existential climate emergency. The philosopher William MacAskill (2022), stakes out the logical issues of how actions taken today can be decisive in locking in a bad equilibrium for the future or how some (nuclear war or engineered pandemics, for example) can end humanity before its time. While I disagree with some of his arguments (notably the focus upon AI as a threat beyond that expressed by HAL in *2001: A Space Odyssey* in an isolated circumstance) and his conclusions (that population growth can be a good thing), the shift in thinking is an accurate reflection of where we are today.

While not directly related to the issue of generational equity, Edward Chancellor (2022) emphasizes that the zero interest rate policy adopted by central banks has had profound effects on the economy. In general, unless there is very good reason, setting a disequilibrium interest rate (in this case, substantially below historical rates of interest) is suboptimal and creates distortions. The inflation after the pandemic was an accident waiting to happen. As Stephen D. King (2023) observes in the title of his book, 'We need to talk about inflation'.

Economic welfare measures such as employment, earnings and debt disguise the full experience of being born in the 1990s and 2000s and growing up in the new millennium, in the same way as describing an income below the poverty line fails to incorporate the profound, devastating impact on the humans involved. It matters that people born in the 1990s quickly hit the dot-com bubble and perhaps saw their parents or relatives lose their job. When things had recovered, the financial crisis hit, and perhaps a neighbour lost their house and had to move out. Then they faced the pandemic and observed people – perhaps now their closest family members – becoming extremely ill, while they themselves had their education or early career disrupted. All this takes a psychological and social, as well as economic, toll.

And that is even before we consider the sword of Damocles represented by dictators with nuclear capability and a world facing climate extinction.

'Works as planned' or 'poorly planned'

Most observers find Generation Z to be perfectly amiable. They are our sons and daughters, our nephews and nieces, and our cousins. They are neighbours and citizens. It is therefore unlikely that conscious decisions have been made to impoverish this generation. Rather, an inequitable or unsustainable or extinction equilibrium persists because the participants in our society, individually or in groups or organizations, have not yet found it optimal to break it apart. We might not have deliberately constructed this equilibrium – except for the very wealthy, things don't seem that great for anyone – but we are finding it hard to come together politically to find something better. Since economics is an impressive theoretical and empirical construct, it seems implausible that we couldn't come up with policies that effectively address our problems. So far, we just haven't had sufficient imperative to overcome the political obstacles and we persist with ineffective or even counter-productive policies, sometimes at great expense.

Oluo (2020) observes that the persistence of discrimination is not an accident but is because the system 'works as planned'. This does not mean that mediocre white males regularly get together (although they do) to find ways to extract surplus from the rest of society, but that fundamental reform is blocked and that even well-meaning policies are flawed by a lack of careful analysis – the 'unintended consequences' from adopting a policy. As an example, 'implicit bias training' has been readily adopted in companies and other organizations. It's a soft measure that doesn't call anybody out about their behaviour. The problem is that it just doesn't work; research shows that it can actually increase discrimination by reminding people about their differences from other people and the stereotypes sometimes held about the characteristics of other demographic groups.

Another example of well-intended but flawed policy lies in university funding. With Norman Gowar and Michael Naef, I wrote about this in our book *English Universities in Crisis* (Frank et al, 2019). English university tuition fees went up in 2012 from £3,000 to £9,000. The rationale was not to penalize the current generation of students, but primarily to allow the expansion of university education to a broader and more diverse intake. Income to universities per student would go up by about 50%, and this could be used to strengthen the educational offering. Students of diverse backgrounds, in particular, might benefit from individual tutoring in their first year, something that has been shown to be very effective. Rather than commuting into the university on teaching days, students of less well-off backgrounds could be given subsidized campus accommodation to encourage their full participation in academic and social life. Indeed, universities were required to spend a significant amount of funding on 'widening participation'.

Further, the government set up an income-contingent student loan system that allowed students to borrow for fees and maintenance costs (rent and other living expenses). This protected students who ended up in low-paying employment and would not be able to repay their student loans. The ONS calculated that nearly half of student loan amounts would be written off and the government was required to allow for these expected losses in its current accounting. The taxpayer was covering half of the fee and maintenance costs, getting the other half back in due course when loans were repaid.

The problem is that the scheme encouraged much of the additional income to universities to be spent on marketing and 'student satisfaction' rather than what we traditionally might view as education (lecturing and administrative support staff, and buildings such as lecture theatres and seminar rooms). The government itself has complained about the resulting bureaucracy and lowering of standards through devices such as grade inflation, and the poor economic returns to some degrees. Yet, despite the Augar Report in 2019, very little has changed.

The rise and rise in the price of housing is partially due to interest rate policy, but also to schemes intended to help out first-time buyers. The house price to earnings ratio in England is 9.1, a level that is historically unprecedented. Yet the government persists in offering one scheme after another. 'Help to buy' was a £29 billion scheme to provide equity loans to first-time buyers of new-build homes – this loan was interest free for the first five years and represented up to 40% of the house price in London (Hammond, 2022). Stamp duty (the tax on house transfers) holidays were introduced during the pandemic to support house prices. The 'Help to Buy ISA' allowed first-time buyers to save and have the government top up their savings by 25% up to £3,000. And on and on. Again, a poorly designed set of policies, since they end up increasing demand for housing rather than supply, further driving up prices.

When the pandemic arrived, we had policies ranging from the ludicrous 'eat out to help out' (£850 million) that seems actually to have encouraged disease spread, to the ludicrously expensive furlough programme (£60 billion) and the largely ineffective 'track and trace' (£37 billion). On the other hand, the vaccination programme (£12 billion) has been judged by the National Audit Office to be good value for money. As a general observation, we do best in policy when we explicitly encourage and harness technology, rather than rely on vague economic ideologies such as 'markets' or – for monetary policy – to 'do whatever it takes'.

In each case of poorly targeted policies, there are major beneficiaries. Oluo's 'mediocre white men' are holding senior posts they could never achieve on merit. Vice chancellors (VCs) of universities have been able to regularly don hard hats (something that they seem to find remarkably fulfilling) and have their picture taken breaking ground for another student centre. Existing owners of homes are sitting on large and increasing capital gains which they could in principle cash in by downsizing or through 'equity release'. Even if these groups were not wishing to harm Generation Z, they don't have a personal imperative (except where an actual son or daughter is involved) to take action to achieve greater generational equity. Even when we get to the existential issue of climate change, the well-off may feel that inherited benefits (education, nepotism and actual financial support) will shield their offspring and their offspring's offspring from the effects. While the advantages of birth are politely under-emphasized in discussions, they remain immense. But as the tides rise in Sandbanks in Dorset, millionaire's row may also become submerged.

No label economics

I pay a premium, for most of my clothes, in order to avoid labels. This makes perfect economic sense – if Ralph Lauren cannot put a polo player on my shirt and gain free advertising, I should have to pay a bit more. In the same way, although trained as a Keynesian and believing that I remain very much a Keynesian, I propose that we conduct 'no label economics' in this book. The reason is that current policy flies in the face of traditional Keynesian and monetarist analysis, as well as the general equilibrium theory of efficient economies.

Economics comprises a powerful set of tools and models for understanding the world and developing policies for addressing the profound issues facing us today. We just need to get away from the groupthink that has led to 'trickle-down' economics, a hugely bloated financial sector, insane prices for housing, zero interest rates, the atrophying of unions, excessive benefits in place of well-paid work, destruction of pensions, continued racial, gender and other discrimination, and – most of all – the wrecking of the environment. The label I gave the current mix of economic policies, in my earlier book, was 'ecstasy economics' – it's all good. Except it's not.

The policy mix over the last four decades is not traditional Keynesianism. Keynes observed that he was proposing a generalization of macroeconomics to allow for the role of aggregate demand. In particular, when there was high unemployment due to an insufficiency of demand, the government and the central bank should step in with judicious fiscal and monetary policy to increase demand. At full employment, typically taken to be about 4% in the US, the classical (monetarist) model would apply. Given that we've largely been at or above full employment for most of the last two decades, the US money supply should not have expanded by a factor of eight since 2000. Keynesian theory would predict a rise in inflation, whether or not there was a pandemic and whether or not Putin invaded Ukraine.

Ben Bernanke, ostensibly a monetarist, presided over much of this expansion in the money supply as Chair of the Federal Reserve Board. Yet the main tenet of monetarism (as described by Milton Friedman) was to maintain a fixed (modest) growth rate in money over time. Monetarist theory would predict a rise in inflation, whether or not there was a pandemic and whether or not Putin invaded Ukraine.

There are broader political and policy beliefs often associated with the two main schools of macroeconomics, although logically they are independent. Friedman had some ideas that were viewed as extreme in the 1970s – such as free trade and fully flexible exchange rates – that have subsequently been largely adopted. He also had some sensible ideas such as the 'negative income tax' – now commonly called 'universal benefit' – which would have paid every citizen a fixed amount, rather than relying on a cumbersome and expensive (as well as leading to negative incentives on behaviour) welfare and benefits system. He also argued for the legalization of drugs, not because addiction to drugs is good, but because the crime associated with a 'war on drugs' arguably destroys more lives than the actual drugs themselves. Arguably, the debacle in Afghanistan and the restoration of Taliban rule with all its implications for women and others living under that regime, followed from the profitability of the illicit opium trade.

Keynesians typically have a greater concern for the distribution of income and for equality and diversity. It is therefore not a surprise that, while Clinton, Blair and even Obama followed similar economic policies to Reagan, Thatcher and the two Bushes, they displayed some social accomplishments. Blair introduced the minimum wage in 1999 and Brown the Equality Act 2010. Obama finally brought national health insurance to the US in the form of the Affordable Care Act 2010. But this record was disappointing to their supporters, and Clinton's 1994 crime bill has been blamed for the rise in mass incarceration in the US and his 1996 'welfare to work' bill may have undermined even the limited safety net in the US.

Because of our 'no label' pledge, we can resist the temptation to use the pejorative term 'neoliberal' to describe the policy mix of the last 40 years. That monetary policy passed from Greenspan to Bernanke to Yellen (perhaps the leading Keynesian of her generation) with little change might only reinforce the views of those who see both leading parties in both countries as just variants of neoliberals. But it might alternatively, and perhaps more helpfully, be seen as the carrying out of the mandate of the over-sized and over-powerful baby boomer generation. As described by Twenge (2023: 126), the boomers went from being hippies to being yuppies and conservatives. There was nothing perhaps preordained in that shift, but it certainly was to the financial benefit of the generation as a whole, and to the disbenefit of first the millennials and then, even more so, Generation Z.

Sustainability of policy

Even if Generation Z and their predecessors, the millennials, were to passively accept their current fate in the generation game, the equilibrium of the last four decades is over. It is simply unsustainable. This is abundantly clear in the case of the environment, which we have classified as a situation not so much of sustainability but of survival. But it is more broadly clear for almost every aspect of the current equilibrium.

Part of this is political. Polling on whether the US is on the right track or the wrong track by NBC at the end of June 2023 showed that only 20% were content with the direction of travel. This either reflects or feeds into the divisiveness in the electorate, not just on religious and political views, but based upon geography, demographic characteristics and, importantly, on whether or not the individual attended university. In the same way, England has suffered from severe regional disparities that in large part explain the collapse of the 'red wall' of Labour seats in the North in 2019 and the earlier vote in favour of Brexit.

'Levelling up' could have occurred without Brexit, and seems not to be occurring once Brexit has led to lower growth and higher inflation in the UK, but Brexit no doubt could not have occurred without the need for levelling up.

On the economic side, US CPI (consumer price inflation) topped 8% for the year 2022, and UK CPI inflation topped 8.8%. Although there is no clear theoretical or empirical imperative, policy makers have adopted 2% inflation as their target, and this is the explicit policy of the Bank of England. The Bank, in its monetary policy report of May 2023, expects inflation to return to target by late 2024 and forecasts bank rate (their channel for interest rates) to go down to 3.7% in 2025. That is, the Bank seems to plan on a return to the low or zero interest rate monetary equilibrium that prevailed for the first two decades of the millennium, and not a return to the 5–15% bank rate of the previous two decades.

Despite their belief in shocks when convenient (to explain things going wrong), policy makers nonetheless have faith that there has been a structural shift in the economy and a structural shift in the abilities of policy makers (to explain things going right). In this somewhat asymmetric evaluation of their own performance, the current high inflation is due to shocks but the previously prevailing low inflation was due to their astute policies, such as explicit inflation targeting and forward guidance, along with the concept of a 'global savings glut', primarily due to the integration of China into the world trade framework.

Most macroeconomists would agree that the Bank can achieve a target inflation of 2% in 2025, but they differ on the extent to which a significant recession is necessary to achieve that aim. Judging by the stock markets in the US and UK (at or approaching record highs), the financial sector is not predicting a serious recession. Whether that means that they are expecting the central banks to allow for much higher inflation than the 2% target remains to be seen.

Insofar as analysts justify the idea of an ongoing shift to a more favourable economic environment since the millennium, it involves globalization (notably the role played by China on both the manufacturing and savings sides). But the US in particular has adopted an industrial strategy to bring manufacturing back onshore, with the CHIPS and Science Act 2022 funding this effort. Sanctions (based on claimed security issues with, for example, Huawei) are replacing open doors for Chinese imports. Further, because of this attempt to increase home manufacturing, the drive to build green projects for the environment and because the level of decay of the infrastructure has come to a critical point, there is likely to be a massive increase in investment in the US and UK. The US 2021 Infrastructure Investment and Jobs Act tops $1.2 trillion, and is likely to be just a starting point. It is hard to see how a 'global savings glut' persists into the future.

Meanwhile, government and other debt rose dramatically over the last two decades. In the US, gross domestic product (GDP) in the first quarter of 2023 is $26.53 trillion. Federal government debt is $27.15 trillion. Households and non-profits have debt of $19.16 trillion and non-financial business has debt of $19.97 trillion. At the millennium, the federal government had debt of $4.31 trillion, households/non-profits had $6.85 trillion and non-financial business $6.22 trillion. For a comparison, GDP was $10 trillion in 2000. As a percentage of GDP, government debt has gone from 43% to 102%. As with the mysteriously determined 2% target for inflation, there is an equally precise (if, we might think, equally arbitrary) rule of thumb that government debt to GDP should not exceed 100%.

It is difficult to provide a convincing rationale for the 100% rule. It compares a stock (the debt) with a flow (GDP). The closest equivalent on a household level is your mortgage, which traditionally might comfortably be three times your income. Just as a household can prudently pay back a 3 to 1 mortgage, so a government can take on more than 100% debt – indeed, at the end of the Second World War, the UK had a debt to GDP ratio of 250%. Many well-intentioned people argued for even more debt on the basis that borrowing costs have been low. In 2020, the US Treasury calculated the equivalent of a new 30-year government bond as carrying an interest rate of about 2%.

It's important to note that the US Government (and the UK Government, for the same reasons) has not locked in these low interest rates on all the debt. In the US, as part of its quantitative easing policy, the Federal Reserve bought about $6 trillion of government bonds, paying for this with electronic money that is being held by financial institutions in deposits with the Fed. The interest paid by the Fed on these deposits is not fixed but variable, set by the Fed as part of its efforts to control monetary policy. The Fed is currently (July 2023) paying 5.15% on these reserve balances. At that interest rate – or an even higher rate if necessary to control inflation – it is no longer clear that those well-intentioned people should continue to argue for running up the government debt.

These reserves enter into 'base money' which rose from $600 billion in 2000 to over $6.1 trillion in 2022. The simple quantity theory of money argues that this ten-fold increase in the monetary base might be expected to lead (after 'long and variable lags') to a ten-fold increase in the price level. For a simple monetarist then, the rise in US inflation to 8.7% at one point in 2022 should not be a surprise. It was an accident waiting to happen and the problem will continue even if we recover supply from the pandemic (somehow getting people back into the workforce and thence to the office) and resolve the war in Ukraine. Recalling that, at full employment, Keynesian analysis returns to the classical model, the accumulated high growth in the money supply represents a potential issue for Keynesians as well. While the Fed and the Bank of England can keep this 'money' dammed up in reserves by raising the interest rate, that does mean that they may have limited control on interest rates in the medium term, and the market – rather than the central bank – may dictate a higher rate.

There is a different approach to understanding inflation that might guide policy choices – inflation can be seen as the economy's way of dealing with severe imbalances. The biggest imbalance is between asset prices – which have exploded over the last four decades – and wages and goods/services prices – which have not. This has been seen most clearly in the house price to incomes ratio of 9 to 1 in the UK. While the monetary and fiscal authorities can try to maintain this favouring of assets over (for example) workers, there are alternative routes forward. The idea that we can achieve a soft landing, without a recession, but with inflation returning to 2%, seems unlikely but – even if achievable – seems to be suboptimal. Experience suggests we will have either stop-go policies as in the 1970s, or we will have a significant recession.

We will argue that a controlled inflation in goods and services, and wages, represents a more realistic and in any case better policy. Interest rates need to be set to cap nominal asset prices at roughly where they are now (or perhaps a 20% fall that is common in mild downturns). Traditionally, this would be a few percentage points above current inflation – that is, at the moment of writing this, rates should be about 7–8% in both the US and the UK. Forward guidance should put that figure into the Federal Reserve and Bank of England forecasts, with expected inflation remaining at 5% for the medium term. The government, for its part, should not be seeking to hold wage settlements down, but in fact should be encouraging them to run modestly above current inflation – that is, at about 8%. If this path was followed, in five years' time we would have cut the house price to income ratio from its current nine times to a sustainable four or five times, have restored stock market and other asset values to realistic levels, and have set the stage for a realistic moderately bumpy landing.

The challenge for Generation Z

The *Time Magazine* man of the year for 1966 was an entire generation, people under 25. As now, there was a far away war where the US was involved by proxy which eventually led to large numbers of troops on the ground. There was a threat of nuclear war, with school children being trained pointlessly in how to hide under their desk. Some people built nuclear shelters in their back gardens. Inflation arose in the decade, with hesitant monetary policy coming into play and then being withdrawn again, a cycle that was repeated several times until inflation was completely out of control.

But 1967 also marked the 'summer of love' with hippie culture spreading. Woodstock occurred in 1969 in the US and Glastonbury in 1970 in the UK, perhaps marking not just the chronological but the ideological end of the 'swinging sixties'.

On the political side, the Civil Rights Act of 1964 in the US was followed by the Voting Rights Act of 1965 and the Fair Housing Act of 1968. The Environmental Protection Agency was established in 1970 to enforce the new Clean Air Act. In the UK, the Equal Pay Act was legislated in 1970, following the US version of 1963. Man landed on the moon in 1969.

In 1968, dreams were shattered when Martin Luther King and Robert Kennedy were assassinated.

Progress does not occur in a straight line and Generation Z cannot link back to the world as it was in 1968 and ask for a 're-do'. But, if older generations are to have a positive message for the newer ones, it must be to rebel. To value the future over the present, to value the common good over individual acquisition. To treat nature with respect. To put the humanities and the arts over pecuniary acquisition.

If the period from 1945 to 1980 was the period of labour, the welfare state and growth, and 1980 to 2020 was the period of wealth and financial assets, what will the next four-decade cycle involve? Even with the challenges inherited from the poor policies of the recent past – tempered by remarkable technological progress – there is an opportunity not just for survival, but for developing the better world dreamed of by the 'baby boomers' in the 1960s but relinquished in the quest for material goods and financial wealth.

The plan of the book

Following this introduction, the book continues as follows.

Chapter 2: Doing and Undoing Economics

In a way, it is the remarkable consensus in views among economists that is indicative that we are in an unsustainable equilibrium. A healthy academic and policy equilibrium thrives on different viewpoints. Some economists could call out for bans on firms purchasing their own shares, while others could claim it was productive. We could have a debate on VAT charging for private school fees. Working tax credits, which – depending upon viewpoint – either help people off benefits and into work, or alternatively, subsidize bad jobs with low pay, could be debated. We could take different views on allowing or banning second homes, or taxing them at high levels. We could ask why credit cards have interest rates of 25% in a zero interest rate economy. Some monetary economists could call for a restoration of traditional 4–5% interest rates, while others extol the virtues of zero rates. And some could even – heresies of heresies – argue against free trade, particularly if it involves countries that are burning coal, polluting and accelerating climate change.

Chapter 2 is about how economics is really about storytelling, about how a good piece of economics presents one view of the world with as much argumentation as can be provided, with both logical and empirical support. During the last four decades – and particularly the last two – the world and the world economy have gone down dangerous paths, but a groupthink in economics led to remarkably little divergence in viewpoints.

Chapter 3: The Long and Short of It

When economic theory wants to consider a representative agent on their own, without anyone to trade with ('autarky'), we traditionally describe the Robinson Crusoe economy. Even on his own, and with a fixed supply of resources, Robinson Crusoe may decide on an 'extinction strategy'. He could simply decide to live well for a number of years and deplete the environment. Alternatively, he may have what prove to be overly optimistic expectations of rescue and is surprised that his consumption path proves unsustainable. Having an heir with him may cause him to value the future more, or he may in fact sentence his progeny to starvation with less reluctance than when it was only his fate at risk. The harsh reality is that the extinction equilibrium we are currently facing need not be due to ignorance but may simply be the optimal choice of the current generation. Extinction is more likely to be chosen if Crusoe has a high discount rate or doesn't value his heir's well-being as highly as his own. If there are others in the future generation, an unequal distribution of wealth may lead a wealthy Crusoe to believe that his heirs can prosper even if the rest of society is impoverished.

Generation Z cannot rely upon the good intentions and benevolence of previous generations, but must enter the political fray. As the population size, both absolutely and proportionately, of the baby boomer generation declines, political power will shift towards new coalitions who need to determine their own fate.

Chapter 4: The Fed Did It

A zero interest rate that leads to a consumption boom advantages the current generation over the future. The Fed adopted this policy, during the financial crisis, in part because of a belief that the Depression-era Fed was too slow to act. The policy – extended and amplified during the pandemic – has caused an explosion of the money supply. By traditional monetary policy, this carried a large inflation risk. Central banks, and particularly the Federal Reserve in the US, were not worried. Inflation remained stubbornly below the 2% target throughout the four decades. Central banks ascribed this, at least in part, to the effectiveness of inflation targeting. Further, since they introduced paying interest on deposits at the central bank, they felt that they had an effective control should inflation start to rise. But the reliance on a slow growth in inflation as a canary in the coal mine was inconsistent with traditional models such as the Keynesian Phillips curve. Inflation can quickly accelerate out of nowhere and policy makers – as with the current experiences – can learn that what they expected to be transient proves instead to embed itself in the economy.

Chapter 5: The Everything Bubble

An overlooked but fundamental feature of the monetary policy of the 1980s through to 2020s was not just that interest rates were low, but that they were consistently decreasing. This meant that the interest rate risk was one-sided – investors were convinced by observing the central banks that there was little risk that rates would ever go up. Because of the supposed 'world savings glut', the Fed in particular could always find a reason to lower rates. The flip side of decreasing interest rates is rising asset values, with stocks, housing and bonds all moving sharply and consistently upwards. This naturally benefits the holders of assets (the better-off in the current generation) at the expense of those without assets (the less well-off in the current generation and the bulk of members of future generations). But, when interest rates hit the zero rate floor, this equilibrium necessarily came to an end. This is the case even if we don't account for the need for substantial investment in the infrastructure and in manufacturing, as well as in education and new technologies, that will necessarily raise the demand for funds in the future.

The Fed and other central banks will have to find a new policy, irrespective of whether inflation proves to be transitory or sustained, whether or not their steps against inflation lead to a recession, and whether or not they care about future generations. But the nature of the equilibrium will differ, depending on whether we continue to run the economy for the older and the well-off, or for the broader population.

Chapter 6: Smart Motorways

Guardrails keep drivers or policy makers from diverging too much from a central route away from the edges of the road. Yet mainstream economic policy has argued against those guardrails as limiting policy and the ability to respond to 'shocks'. Those arguments might be more valid if every driver and every policy maker was remarkably capable, was devoted to remaining well away from the margins of the road, and had the interests of everyone in mind. The gold standard, abandoned in 1971, arguably provided too harsh a constraint on policy. But fixed exchange rates were also abandoned and mainstream economists even argued against the euro on the grounds that each European country needed to use its own monetary policy to address its own unique 'shocks'. Monetary economists in general moved to the Taylor rule which sought to anchor interest rates around a normal rate, varying the rate up and down to smooth adjustments if inflation or unemployment was high or low. But in the mid-2010s, policy diverged sharply even from the Taylor rule in an expansionary direction. The pandemic then provided a rationale for jettisoning even modest moves towards monetary policy normalcy.

Chapter 7: The Future of Work

A large part of the argument for the continued expansionary monetary policy in the 2010s was that it was necessary to raise wages. The economy would be 'run hot' for a period of time in order to tighten labour markets and boost wages. This was with a backdrop of essentially stagnant real wages over a period of decades. The stagnation in real wages is likely caused, at least in part, by the decline in trade unions, particularly in the private sector, as well as the decline in manufacturing and other high-wage blue collar jobs.

However, a high-wage economy goes hand-in-hand with a high-productivity economy, and strong long-term employment relationships are more efficient than the gig workforce. It is hard to see that monetary policy – rather than apprenticeships and investment in capital and infrastructure – is the route to rebalancing wages and profits.

Governments have become focused upon the most vulnerable rather than the traditional working class. Rather than having complicated benefit systems, there is much to be said for a universal benefit and making jobs attractive, rather than having an inefficient benefit system that then tries to induce or force people into bad jobs.

Chapter 8: People and Robots

Articles in the financial press often refer to the 'demographic crisis'. Remarkably, given the climate emergency and the near-doubling of the world population in the last four decades to 8 billion, the complaint is that fertility has – in most of the world – been going down. The expressed concern is that the next generation will not be large enough (will not have grown enough compared to past generations) to pay the pensions of the previous generations. But this ignores the fact that there is a diminishing marginal product to population growth since the increased population is being applied to the same – or in fact, with climate change – diminished natural resource base.

Ironically, while demanding more humans to take up jobs, the same mainstream economics worries about whether AI and the growth of robot use means that there won't be enough jobs. A consistent view throughout this book is that technology has been our saviour and will continue to be our potential saviour. Replacing population growth with robots and AI is good for both the well-being of workers, and their wages, as well as for the planet.

Chapter 9: Universities

Prior to the last four decades, it was understood that a 'mixed economy' of public and private provision was relatively efficient and best met the needs of the population. In the future, particularly as we adopt more and more technology (as we have consistently done over the last two or three centuries), there is a need for more and more education.

In Chapter 9, we look at universities because of the vital role they will play in the next few decades, and because the high and increasing cost of university to students represents a significant equity issue for Generation Z.

In 2012, students in the UK were subjected to a tripling of fees to £9,000 with a view to raising needed funds for universities and for expansion in participation, without having an undue additional burden on the taxpayer. An income-contingent repayment loan scheme was simultaneously established so that no potential student need be deterred by an inability to pay the fees and living costs. While this shift was clearly a generational redistribution against Generation Z, it need not of itself have been a negative change in terms of the quality of education and in the overall return to society from its expenditure on universities.

But this is a case study on how the specific design of systems matters. An inefficient market structure was established that gave universities the wrong incentives – a 'market for students' was about 'student satisfaction' rather than educational value. An effectively organized independent sector with significant public input, at arms-length from the government, was replaced by an inefficient 'market'.

Chapter 10: Housing

Nowhere has the generational divide been clearer than on housing. At the current price to income ratio of nine times, owning your own house is largely inaccessible to Generation Z, for the foreseeable future. Already high rents rose further in the pandemic. The monetary policy of the last four decades – low and declining interest rates – has driven house prices higher and higher, with little risk of price falls. Even in the sub-prime mortgage crisis of 2007/08, house prices only temporarily fell as the monetary and fiscal authorities re-ignited the demand for these assets. Given that any building programme will be small relative to the existing stock of houses, the policy emphasis on increasing the supply side (even building on the green belt) will have less impact than even a modest rethinking of the zero interest rate policies of the past two decades.

This case study, however, shows the nature of the political divide. Baby boomers, Generation X and even some older millennials are sitting on massive capital gains, just from being born at the right time in the right place. To date, those capital gains have been protected by monetary policy. If, as is likely, interest rates need to reset in the medium term to the levels that prevailed in previous epochs, this raises the risk of severe house price falls. Further, as houses are no longer one-way bets, people will downsize, will sell their second homes and buy-to-lets.

Politically, however, this is unlikely to happen, based upon experience of the last few decades. In the UK, with most mortgages being fixed at most for a handful of years (and not the 30 years standard in the US), the political cost imposed on homeowners – who will not only be paying more on their mortgage but seeing the capital value decline – is probably unsustainable for any political party. It is for this reason that we will argue for a controlled inflation over the medium term so that real values of houses (compared to wages) fall but nominal values are relatively secured.

Chapter 11: Let the Good Times Roll

For virtually every policy choice, there is an inefficient stopgap measure that kicks the can down the road, and a more efficient alternative that benefits future generations. Most recently, in the energy price cost of living crisis, the government is proposing to borrow from the future to pay gas bills of individuals today. As at least a partial alternative, there could have been a massive campaign to insulate housing and replace boilers and – where possible – install heat pumps.

A windfall tax could have been redistributed as a lump sum to individuals to meet the 'cost of living crisis', or as a reduction in the basic rate of tax or in VAT. Even if the government felt that they needed to tie government hand-outs directly as discounts to the energy bills that were skyrocketing, there could have been a two-part tariff. Only the basic energy consumption could have been subsidized, with the marginal usage still at the very high price caused by shortages arising from the Russian invasion of Ukraine. This is all basic economics that would have been the bread-and-butter of an economics textbook since Marshall wrote his *Principles of Economics* in 1890, but somehow doesn't seem to be guiding current policy.

As people awoke from the nightmare of the pandemic, there were thoughts of constructing a better society. There was talk of having 'universal benefit' where everyone was entitled to a basic income. One of the most effective policies of the pandemic was getting the homeless off the streets and putting them into vacant hotels. It is hard to understand why this commitment wasn't maintained when the pandemic abated. Students had had their education disrupted, and the National Health Service (NHS) had been stressed to nearly the point of breaking. A new focus on education and health could have been put in place.

If the basic thesis of this book is correct – that we have had unprecedented technological progress, but remarkably bad policy – the efficiency gains from better policy will be more than sufficient to address the truly bad inheritance we are otherwise leaving to Generation Z. There is no reason to think that the technological gains – in medicine, in computing and AI, and in energy-efficient living and travel – are slowing down. All we have to do is improve policy. A good place to start is to find an economics textbook from the turn of the century – the 20th century.

2

Doing and Undoing Economics

In Chapter 1, we observed that we should expect to pay a premium for a 'no logo' shirt, since Ralph Lauren implicitly pays me an advertising fee for having a polo player embroidered on my shirt. Now, in Chapter 2, we will instead observe that I should pay less for a 'no logo' shirt since I don't get the status value of observers noting that I had the popular and expensive Polo shirt. Indeed, the economist Thorsten Veblen observed in the Veblen effect that demand might actually go up as the price of the Polo shirt increases.

This is how economics works. There is no one right answer. Instead, we each – drawing upon our experience and judgement – tell our stories, our descriptions of the world. The exercise is an art, a craft. Something has gone wrong if we all tell the same story (not least, because we would then need a lot fewer economists). In the other direction, something has gone wrong if our stories are disconnected from the history of economic lore, and we start telling stories that would previously have been viewed as bizarre. I would argue that nothing in the past of economic thought would have argued for an extended period of zero interest rate monetary policy – particularly in full employment labour markets – sustained by a ten-fold increase in the monetary base. The worst situation is when virtually all of economists are telling the same, implausible story.

Economics is about using our endowments (natural resources, technology, physical and human capital) to produce outputs to meet our preferences. In the days of an isolated family farm, the organization of this exercise was straightforward. It suffered from the autarky of having to do everything oneself, without the benefits of social enterprises and regular trade. Now, the world is interconnected, and we can gain efficiencies of production and distribution as well as the social development of products and technologies. However, potential inefficiencies from poor organization and social decision-making can lessen or even eliminate the available gains.

News stories regularly appear of how two sides of a family fight in the law courts (or, following a methodology we will regularly use in this book, refer to the Dickens' novel *Bleak House*) and destroy the fortune that is the subject of the case. First-rate chief executives build a firm (or a university, as in our book *English Universities in Crisis* (Frank et al, 2019)) up, and mediocre successors let it wither and sometimes die. We can develop a vaccine for COVID in a remarkably short period of time, but we find it harder to get people to take it.

The last sentence reflects this economist's frustration at where we are today, and indeed the role of economists in getting us to the unfortunate starting point for the topics in this book. With arguably the best technological inheritance of any generation in history, we are leaving a world facing an existential climate emergency. Our institutions are so poor that the well-off are almost literally burning money (for example, the ludicrous prices paid for inherently worthless crypto currencies and non-fungible tokens) and a substantial proportion of the UK and US population is surviving by going to food banks. University education is impossibly expensive and continually declining in quality as students watch 'lecture-captured' videos on-line rather than attending live lectures on campus. If we have not blown our inheritance as far as our own consumption goes (reflected in the fact that many of us do not have remotely adequate pension provisions), we have certainly blown much of the value of what we propose to bequeath the next generation.

However, the big problems we face now are readily solvable and we know how. The issues are coordination and political, not technological. Further, we are now in such an inefficient equilibrium that it may be that the costs of addressing even our most pressing problems – other than the hard political work – may be negligible. As an example, insulating British houses to cut fossil fuel use (and household bills) is so obvious, yet isn't happening at the time of writing. Instead, the government subsidized the use of fossil fuels by paying part of people's utility bills through the 'energy price guarantee (EPG)', thereby discouraging the price mechanism's rationing of a scarce commodity, and subsidizing use of a commodity that is destroying the environment. *The Guardian* reported on 4 January 2023 that the EPG was forecasted to cost the government £37 billion.

At the gym

Doing economics as described above cannot be done in isolation. We advise first-year students to read the *Financial Times* and keep up with world events. But this is also what an economist does in deriving their world view, topics to research and approaches to take. A good economist is always inquisitive, and an everyday experience can lead to a publication in a good journal (already described as the measure of our productivity).

Consider the no logo versus labelled shirts example. Some economists claim that we can empirically determine whether a theory is right or wrong, and even estimate the coefficients defining the magnitude of a response to (for example) an increase in the minimum wage. But in fact, empirical work can only be suggestive, in the same way as observing the world, reading the literature and other inputs into our thinking are not definitive. How exactly do we compare a shirt with a logo and one without a logo? Ralph Lauren does not normally make its shirts in the two variants, so we would be comparing two different products. Particularly with the shift in production to China, the margin between the cost of production and the retail selling price of designer shirts is immense. Not surprisingly, sales of 50% or more off occur, at predictable periods of the calendar year. Shirts can go to outlet stores throughout the year, while other designers actually destroy a large part of their unsold stock rather than discounting. How do we compare a purple shirt with a blue one? Experience tells us that, in the sales, purple shirts are extremely cheap.

A lot of the understanding that enters into our stories comes about just by talking to people. Economics does not (yet?) have a methodology for conducting focus groups and structured interviews, as do our sociologist colleagues, but perhaps we should. In the interim, we talk to everyone. Why does Polo produce the purple shirts, knowing that they will enter into the sales each year and be sold at a large discount? In our models, this could be price discrimination – Polo can effectively sell purple shirts cheaply to people who want the polo player emblem but are unwilling to pay full price, while maintaining the blue ones consistently over the year at a higher price. But conversation led to a different answer – the whole range of colours is needed to provide the best display on the countertop.

Here's another example of the benefits of talking to people. It is a commonplace remark in the gym, when someone comes in and their clothes are in the neighbouring locker, to say 'it's always the way'. But maybe it's not a random event at all.

I was using my usual locker number 90, chosen because it was in the middle of the long row so there was plenty of changing room and because it was the only number ending in 0 in that row. The zero at the end makes the number easier to remember and – if forgotten – I only have to remember I've chosen the number ending in zero since there's only one in the row.

Someone came in to use locker number 89, and we exchanged the usual commonplace 'it's always the way'. He explained that 1989 was his birth year. It suddenly dawned on me why the lockers near mine were always in use – early 30s is a major demographic of a gym, being the period when people discover that, after 30, beer and pizza necessarily result in body fat that can only be remedied by joining a gym.

Statistics of the sort we do in economics would only have identified that these lockers were used more than a normal distribution might suggest. Something else is needed to guide our analysis and policy recommendations. Traditionally in economics, it was theory – that is, thinking about the problem. In sociology and other social sciences, it can be 'interviews' or 'focus groups' – that is, talking to people. If I was extremely clever, I might have guessed why the lockers in the vicinity of number 90 were in such high demand. But it might be more efficacious to get into conversation with my neighbours.

If we've decided that we need to talk to people to understand phenomena, and we are thinking about contemporary phenomena in another location, there's an easy (if sometimes expensive) solution – get on the train or plane and take in the atmosphere and engage. I'd recommend – if you're an economist wondering why Japan entered a low growth phase in the lost decades starting in the 1990s (a not particularly positive experience arguably copied, for no obvious rational reason, by Western developed economies in the last two decades) – you go to visit Japan. Observe, for example, a month's supply of taxis waiting for passengers at the Kyoto train station. It's the same thing an author would do to write a novel or historical work set in another location.

Just looking at statistics doesn't give you the feel to develop theories to guide your empirical analysis and policy prescriptions. Find a way to connect not just with the present, but with the past. We have museums with artefacts, we have books, we have films. It might seem a slightly bizarre methodology, in trying to understand economic phenomena today, to tell you to go see a film or read a novel, but what is the alternative? Discussing novels and films from the (relatively recent, given the invention of cinema just over a century ago) past is a methodology we are going to quickly introduce in this chapter, and that probably should have a greater role in social sciences.

This is one of many reasons why current proposals to cut the humanities in our universities – on the grounds that employment opportunities are higher in economics, medicine and STEM subjects – are potentially misguided. Arguably, studying literature or films will give a student a better grasp of business management than a 'marketing' or 'strategic management' textbook. The 1954 film *Executive Suite* describes the difficulties in trying to run a business with a quality line and with a downmarket line, coming down firmly on the side of quality, long-lasting furniture. At the same time, the film's 'hero' is firmly wedded to introducing modern technology.

Who to talk to, who not to talk to

But, in connecting with the 'real world', choose your interactions carefully. A new general manager is advised to spend their first months talking to everyone – the doorperson, the serving person in the canteen, assembly line workers – to really try to understand the mood and the reality of the business. Senior managers will have an agenda (which generally involves not letting on about the problems that may have led to the departure of the previous general manager, and which involve their own possible under-performance). After learning the reality of the shop floor, the general manager can assess the strategies of the managers.

But whom not to talk to – indeed people that one might sensibly be prohibited from talking to – is perhaps more important in politics and governance. Consider the following unspoken equilibrium. You have been elected senator or president, or been appointed to be the chair of the Federal Reserve, or you are Treasury secretary. You observe your predecessor going around the world talking to financial sector firms, being paid an annual salary in a night. You observe that your predecessor kept interest rates near zero and bailed out the banks. It doesn't take a huge leap of imagination to guess that, were your policy to be equally benign to the financial sector, you might also find your way on the Concorde-class speaking circuit.

Whatever you call that equilibrium, it's hard to call it economically efficient.

The inheritance

We will return to questions of approach and methodology, but first we need to define our overall discussion frame. Most discussions of intergenerational equity are a snapshot in time, of generations at different stages in the life cycle. Traditionally, but perhaps very unwisely, university students might own an old (in my day) Mini, which was clearly unsafe to drive, while their parents might drive a newer and larger Mercedes. A strong argument could be made that it makes more sense – even in terms of 'economic efficiency' – to allocate safer cars to those more likely to end up in a collision. In the same way, the housing ladder assumes that one starts in London with a studio flat over a chip shop and progresses over time to a larger flat or a small house, and then downsizes again when family size declines. A student loan that cumulates to £60,000 at a repayment rate of 9% of income might be more about tax rates on different individuals in 20 years' time (the graduate might be paying a tax rate significantly higher than a non-graduate of the same income), than about generational differences, if the average tax rate has gone down in the interim.

To talk about intergenerational inequity, therefore, we must make assumptions about the state of the world and the state of policy in a few decades. As a first step, we can consider the actual inheritance – the endowment – given to the population of the UK at a point in time. Imagine a modern-day *Domesday Book*, a 'great survey' of all the valuables – both tangible and intangible – extant within a country. This would include the land, the physical buildings and machines, and the human capital – the education – of the inhabitants. It might also include the ownership of these assets, and the contracts that govern their use.

There is nothing sacrosanct, however, about ownership or contracts. In a parliamentary system, the legislature has more or less complete power except insofar as it has bound its hands by, for example, committing to accepting the jurisdiction of the European Court on Human Rights. An ongoing theme of this book is that guardrails are good, and current proposals (at the time of writing) to move powers to a UK Bill of Rights and UK courts (including the Supreme Court) should cause an immediate raising of eyebrows. In the United States, the Supreme Court has been the ultimate arbiter on ownership and contracts. Indeed, it took a constitutional amendment in 1913 to allow the government to levy an income tax, a power confirmed by the Supreme Court in 1916.

That long inventory of assets for the future represents a maximum that might be distributed between different people of different ages and other characteristics. But in general, it needs to go through production processes. A pound of tin ore in a Welsh mine needs to be mined and processed, then transported. Land can be used for agriculture, or it can be transformed into houses. The houses can be second, vacation homes for the well-off, or starter homes for the grown-up children of local residents.

That process is the task facing the institutions and people of the country. Once you get beyond simple self-sufficient small farms, there will be significant waste. Modern economies have found that a judicious mix of private enterprise, regulation and public provision achieves the least waste. A desirable distribution of wealth and income can be achieved either organically by the design of the system, or by redistribution after the system churns out economic outcomes. We will discuss all these issues shortly. But it should be noted that, if a system is inefficient (as all systems are, to one degree or another), tweaks and modifications can potentially make it both fairer and less wasteful. There is no clear efficiency versus equity trade-off, as claimed at the beginning of first-year economics textbooks. To take an example, oligarchs draining the economy of their country to buy trophy houses in London and yachts are associated with inequity and inefficiency. This is before those billionaires distort the political system through donations, creating further inefficiencies and inequalities.

The inheritance of a new generation is that inventory of real assets. Within a fairly broad set of institutional frameworks, the efficiency at which those assets are utilized will not be widely different. Life in the relatively equal and homogeneous society of Finland differs from that in the unequal and contentious society of the United States. Most developed countries have universal health care, which is by most measures more efficient than the largely private system in the United States. Similarly, within a reasonable set of private and public sector allocations, including tax and benefit systems, the distribution of income and wealth will not be widely different. Deviating from those sensible policies in the middle, there are likely to be severe inefficiencies. Distorting – as the right wing would have us – to favour the well-off leads to both economic inefficiency and huge disparities in income and wealth. Distorting – as the left wing would have us – to a state-charity type system of high benefits for those not engaged in the economic system, and to government ownership and over-regulation for the sake of it, leads to economic inefficiency as well, with remarkably little redistribution from the wealthy to others.

No one can credibly claim (to this author) that the Reagan/Thatcherite revolution of free market economics led to a blossoming of economic efficiency. The data simply do not support that conclusion. Similarly, no one can credibly claim (to this author) that Jeremy Corbyn would – if he had become prime minister – have left the country in notably better economic circumstances than even the hapless Boris Johnson. In the spirit of Willie Whitelaw's famous observation of the Labour prime minister of the time that the latter was 'going around the country stirring up apathy', this book is firmly in the middle ground. Boringly, perhaps, the economic and political agenda has to be about restoring a degree of sanity and balance to public policy.

The real inheritance at this point in time is poor. Infrastructure has decayed, manufacturing plants are unused and rotting away, and – while university numbers are up – apprenticeships are down. The 'marketization' of higher education in England has led – in the view of many – to poorer education at higher cost. Underpaying school teachers, particularly in parts of the US, has led to poor education for students, even before the challenges of the pandemic.

Social capital

But if the real, measurable inheritance to be handed to the next generation (which they will share with the preceding generations that continue to have living members, and with the future generations that will overlap in time, while also expecting their own inheritance) is poor (except for science and technology), the institutional and social capital is in many ways worse. This is part of the inheritance as well, whether it is the written Constitution of the US or the unwritten Constitution of the UK.

A defining feature of the moment is the high level of conflict in thought and action in the political sphere. As we've already observed, nothing that has occurred has been unpredictable or indeed unpredicted (the 2006 film *Idiocracy* might be viewed as a fictional anticipation of the Trump presidency). The 6 January 2021 storming of the US Capitol, and the 8 January 2023 reflection in Brasilia, might have been disturbing but could not be viewed as completely unanticipated.

This break-down in the norms of political discourse and action has been developing over time. The Republicans in the Senate refused to consider the

2016 Obama nomination of Merrick Garland to the Supreme Court, despite the norm being to generally accept the right of the president to appoint justices (subject to a very strong reason, in the personal case, against the candidate). But all this is not unprecedented. Politically, in the US, Senator McCarthy led demagoguery in the Republican Party as senator from 1947 to 1957 and blacklisting became rampant in the US, notably in Hollywood. Remarkably, in 1954, a Democratic senator – in this febrile atmosphere – committed suicide in his office following his son's conviction for homosexual activity. Along with the Army Hearings held by Senator McCarthy that year, enough was enough and the senator was censured by the Senate in a vote of 67 to 22.

One of the methodologies we use in this book is to go back into the past by looking at films and novels. Historians will have their own stories to tell – just like economists – and give very different perspectives. Films and novels take us to the past rather more directly and can bring a focus to issues from the perspective of contemporaries to the events.

For example, the 1959 novel *Advise and Consent* by Allen Drury is about, not a Supreme Court confirmation process, but the fictional nomination of a secretary of state. The nominee favoured a more engaged approach between the US and the Soviet Union, to seek to find peace rather than nuclear war. It gives us a good picture of the thought process at the time, which is one where we find parallels with today:

> A universal guilt enshrouded the middle years of the twentieth century in America; and it attached to all who participated in those times. It attached to the fatuous, empty-headed liberals who had made it so easy for the Russians by yielding them so much; it attached to the embittered conservatives who had closed the doors on human love and frozen out all possibility of communications between people. (Drury, 1959: 36)

In effect, as now, the parties have split away from the centre. Perhaps related to this, the social norms on product quality had declined:

> This was the time when the job on the car was always half finished, the suit came back from the cleaners half dirty, the yardwork was overpriced and underdone, the bright new gadget broke down a week after you got it home, the prices climbed higher and higher as the quality got less and less, and the old-fashioned rule of a fair bargain for a fair price was indeed old-fashioned, for it never applied to anything. (Drury, 1959: 483)

And:

> The great Age of the Shoddy came upon America after the war, and Everybody Wants His became the guiding principle for far too many.

With it came the Age of the Shrug, the time when it was too hard and too difficult and too bothersome to worry about tomorrow. (Drury, 1959: 483)

In any business or social grouping, there is a prevailing culture and set of social norms. In a business, as we've already suggested, growth and improvement changes even current production as there is enthusiasm for making better products and providing better service. We will argue that, for the economy and society as a whole, a drive towards combatting climate change can be exciting and enthuse the country to do everything better.

Another post-war source that shows parallels with the post-pandemic economy of 2022 and the post-war economy is the novel *The Boiling Point* written by Richard Brooks in 1948:

'You got any idea what's happening in this country?'

'Employment going down! Why? No jobs? Like hell. Every company in this state's begging for workers. Folks say the veteran's got too much money in his pocket. Since when's an American refused to earn money just 'cause he's got some? Jesus, man, what's happening to the good old American way of thrift and progress and good common horse sense? Wages are up and efficiency down. Costs are up and production's down. How come?' (Brooks, 1948: 103)

Perhaps it was luck (particularly if you believe in the 'great person' approach to history), perhaps it was a natural development of having a large young generation at a time of technological progress and expansion of education, but the tedium of the 1950s and its 'rebel without a cause' youth culture led to the 'Camelot' of the Kennedy election. We have already described how *Time Magazine* extolled the new generation as 'man of the year'.

When 'Camelot' ended in heartbreak on 22 November 1963, the sheer hard pragmatism of the Johnson years resulted in significant legislation in areas from civil rights (the Civil Rights Act of 1964 and the Voting Rights Act of 1965) to the environment (the Clean Air Act of 1963), as well as the establishment of Medicare (a government health insurance programme for people over 65). The 'swinging sixties' and the 'summer of love' followed, albeit to end in sadness with the assassination of Martin Luther King and Robert Kennedy in 1968 and the expanding war in Vietnam. But much of the progress was absorbed. The treatment of Black people and minority ethnic people, women, and LGBTQI+ people did not return to where it had been. There was a trend – at least for some decades – towards democracy and civil liberties throughout the world.

The climate emergency has upped the stakes. As in the 1950s, we have other people's nuclear missiles aimed at us, and our nuclear missiles aimed at other people, and are reminded that one individual can at least credibly threaten to bring an early end to the human project on Earth. But now the default – if that momentary gross irrationality can be avoided – is a nonetheless calamitous, albeit potentially long-drawn-out destruction of the world through climate change. We now require active intelligence, rather than an avoidance of gross stupidity, to avoid disaster.

Among the misinterpretations of Keynesian economics that come up, many are associated with the quote 'in the long run, we are all dead'. This is not an invitation to ignore the future (with the climate emergency, in the absence of action, we and our children and their children will all be dead in an untimely way, certainly before their 'long run'). Rather, it is saying that the adjustment processes that might naturally occur in an economic or other dynamic system are slow, and – even if they eventually take us to the right place – can cause a lot of unnecessary pain along the way.

And in reality, dynamic developments might not be so sanguine. Left to the current structures, climate change might lead to greater use of ameliorating actions (such as air conditioning) that lead to greater use of fossil fuels that exacerbate the climate change. Fears of white nationalists about 'replacement theory' and 'critical race theory' might lead to voter suppression that allows for greater racial inequality that in turn generates greater intolerance between communities. The concentration of wealth can lead to greater expenditure by those beneficiaries on political influence, leading in turn to policies that increase the disparity of income and wealth. The poor may take to the streets, in peaceful demonstration (although a state response can be to make demonstrations illegal, generating violence) or violent actions (it is often forgotten that Nelson Mandela was, in fact, part of the armed movement of the African National Congress). This can lead to greater repression.

In a superficially contradictory way, restoration of the centre and constructive discourse is usually the way for the most rapid progress. That centre may appear soft to some, yet it preserves the ability to make change. It is in the genius of the British legal system, for example, that the people who threw the statue of slave-owning Edward Colston into the water were acquitted in court. Yet the centre has no difficulty in distinguishing between those demonstrators and the insurrectionists at the Capitol on 6 January 2021, who have been prosecuted and often thrown into jail. At the time of writing, the right-wing parties of the US and the UK have abandoned the centre. Their response to the Edward Colston event, or strikes in the public services, is to pass rapid and ill-thought-out laws banning the activity. The point, however, is that protest is one of the most important guardrails in political economy. When Thatcher hit the guardrails for the final time with the 'poll tax', the ability to protest brought things to an end.

The political impasse

Obama offered the US 'change we can believe in'. Macron elbowed aside the traditional parties with rather ill-defined slogans of 'Le république en marche' and was re-elected with the slogan 'Nous tous'. Unlike these centrist reform approaches, radical reform was offered by Trump in the US and Johnson in the UK, along with Brexit's 'Take back control'. But 'change' – when offered at the ballot box – has been remarkably successful. Given the stagnation in growth and wages and the decline in the public provision of goods from education to transport, this is hardly surprising. When offered the continuation of globalization and finance-centred economies, as from Hillary Clinton, for example, the voter said no. Even the hapless Jeremy Corbyn did surprisingly well in the 2017 election, with his anti-establishment left-wing rhetoric, only to be smothered by the more convincingly anti-establishment right-wing candidate in 2019. But what hasn't been delivered by any of these is the actual, desired change.

The voting system has been remarkably resilient in the face of challenges. In the UK, campaign expenses are tightly limited (for example, Boris Johnson reported expenditures of £11,636.07 in the 2019 election) and constituency boundaries are set by Commission and not designed to entrench incumbents by gerrymandering. Nonetheless, there are regular reports of large personal gifts and external employment allowed for ordinary members of parliament, although government ministers cannot have outside employment.

In the US, continued efforts at voter suppression have tinges of Jim Crow laws and campaign contributions have reached extraordinary levels. The case of Citizens United decided by the Supreme Court in 2010 gave corporations the 'right of free speech' and therefore the right to independently spend large sums on political issues. The system overall has ended up generating large donations, with both Biden and Trump spending well over $1 billion for their 2020 campaigns. The taxpayer Federal Election Fund isn't drawn upon, since it would have given each about $100 million but limited expenditures to that amount.

But in many ways the problem isn't donations and voter suppression, if these don't get out of hand. Requiring voter ID might be intended to cut participation by the less well-off who are less likely to carry a driving licence or have a passport. Longer lines at urban voting locations can similarly deter voters. But, unless these get totally out of hand, they are more an unfortunate social error on the part of those perpetrating them than a huge distortion in the voting outcome. Part of the centrist approach to politics is the time-honoured statement that one wants everyone to vote, whether or not they will vote for your party. These forms of bringing people together in a common goal are important in a well-functioning political economy.

The problem is more fundamental. 'One person, one vote' voting systems, no matter how fair, don't reflect the intensity of preferences. If everyone in the household slightly prefers peanuts to popcorn as a snack, but one person is allergic to peanuts, then in any rational system, the choice is popcorn. If 40% of the population thinks that abortion is murder, and the other 60% are fairly indifferent, then the US Supreme Court was right to overturn *Roe v Wade*. The US Constitution is designed to protect minority rights and – in that sense – it is working as planned if it reflects the extremely strongly held views (although the Constitution also casts doubt on the propriety of weighting religious views in a secular system) of a large minority of the country. The anti-abortion groups show their strength of feeling by harassing people at abortion clinics and in other aggressive ways.

If the anti-abortionists have 'won' by these aggressive tactics, why exactly is it wrong for others – with equally strong feelings – to ruin Justice Kavanaugh's dinner every time he tries to eat out in Washington, DC?

If 60% of the population would like cheap petrol, and 40% of the population feel strongly that they should be allowed to live out their natural lives without climate extinction, why exactly is it wrong for this sometimes younger and sometimes older group of futurists to block traffic?

From an economic efficiency perspective, then, voting is a start (and winning elections gives either *ex ante* or *ex post* legitimacy to changes that are first driven by non-electoral political activities) but not a full answer. The intensity of preferences needs to be measured. In some contexts, donations represent a further measure, but not when the well-off and corporations (particularly from abroad) put a very heavy thumb on the scale. Direct action provides a direct measure – being prepared to go to prison, whether it is to stand up to Putin in Moscow or to Bull Connor in Alabama or to Shell Oil – of intensity of preferences.

Winning the argument or winning the outcome

US polls consistently show that – by a margin of 60% to 40% – Americans did not support the overturning of *Roe v Wade*. Gallup (McCarthy, 2022) reported that polling for same-sex marriage in the US showed support rising from 27% in 1996 to 60% in 2015 just before the *Obergefell v Hodges* Supreme Court decision, to over 70% today. Yet, while this 'winning the argument' might well have supported the Supreme Court decision, few people are confident that the current Supreme Court won't overturn *Obergefell v Hodges*, even if public opinion does not change its views to align better with those held by Justice Thomas. YouGov polls (Sanders, 2021) reported that while there was a 66% negative rating of Martin Luther King in 1966, at the very time when civil rights legislation was cementing his place in history, he has an approval rating of 89% today, when the Supreme Court and Republican legislatures are undoing some of his legacy.

The science of pandemics early on made it clear that mask wearing (rather obviously) limited the spread of the virus, and – except in very limited cases – it's hard to understand why any rational person would decline vaccination. Even without any social responsibility at all, almost all individuals gained a private benefit from vaccination (particularly at the relatively low rates of vaccination – and therefore high rates of disease – in some US states). While it is true that the economic system did not fully penalize those individuals (for example, by letting them have their medical insurance lapse and making them pay – if they wanted to – for their own personal treatment for COVID), the needless potential for suffering a debilitating disease is hard to understand. The callous lack of concern for those with vulnerabilities, or children who could not get vaccinated, is remarkable.

The point is that, as we will discuss towards the end, even for the middle of the road approach of this book, the arsenal of political tools needs to be broad and matched to the intensity of the need for change, while balancing this with the fundamental principles of decency and integrity, as well as good humour. An environmental demonstration that shuts down a bridge in central London, but brings in plants and trees, provides music and free food, is better than a demonstration with vicious expressions and chants.

Equilibrium does not have to be 'sustainable'

The word 'sustainable' has become the well-dressed face of the environmental movement. City firms are advertising sustainability as an investment credo, and major institutions such as universities are adopting it for their endowments. ESG (environmental, social and governance) standards become a sales weapon. There is certainly nothing wrong with that, and it stands in contrast to the old capitalist maxim that 'the sole objective of managers is to maximize shareholder value'.

Yet sustainable is both too strong and too weak a term when we face issues of survival. Let's begin with an individual. Under UK law, while they are under 16, their associated adult(s) are largely in control, although 'Gillick competency' gives the young person some powers over, for example, medical treatment. At 16, they can in practice move out of the parental home although the parents retain 'responsibility'. At 18, they are adults. They choose their education and may incur large student debts that are likely to follow them for much of their life. Parents may be more or less intrusive, but parents no longer bear a legal obligation for the results of poor advice they may give to the now adult progeny. The individual starts on a career and – particularly if they follow the stereotype of Generation Z – moves jobs within a year. They struggle with rent and particularly with buying a place of their own, given that the house price to income ratio now exceeds nine times workplace income. They might get a 'decriminalized' but not actually 'legal' abortion in the UK – in the US, the Supreme Court has removed that right on a national level – and similarly have since 1967 been able to engage in same-sex activities and, since 2014, marriage.

During the 'prime of life', the individual is focused upon the labour market, hopefully building a pension (UK law now generally requires a modest pension contribution from the employer) and otherwise building their social and personal connections. The Equality Act 2010 seeks to protect them from discrimination, but has weak enforcement mechanisms. The NHS provides them with good, free at the point of service care and low-cost prescriptions, although dental treatment is rather less forthcoming. There is a safety net from Universal Credit, albeit at the far from generous rate of about £300 a month.

About half of you will be married, although 100,000 of you will be divorced each year. Half of the opposite-sex married couples have children in the household, the other half do not. Nearly two million lone parent households exist. In the US, you will on average have 12 jobs during your prime years.

Hopefully, you will have saved in your pension and eventually have bought a house. In any case, the standard state pension in the UK is about £200 a week and – even with a free bus pass and an energy credit payment annually – you would probably find this difficult to sustain your life. It may be tempting to remain in work, but recall the old adage about not leaving the field too late. One can then retire and, in due course, leave this 'mortal coil' with hopefully as much dignity as possible to the eulogy that one 'has had a good innings'.

'Life is change.' So, insofar as 'sustainable' means 'stationary', it makes no sense for an individual. Rather, we have in mind that someone, as they proceed in life, has made provisions such that they don't intentionally suffer a dramatic fall in their ability to sustain their lifestyle. They might downsize their house in order to fund other expenses, and there is nothing that would be viewed as particularly culpable in that plan. They might (before Brexit made it more difficult) have in mind to move to Spain for their retirement to save on fuel costs, and to substitute 'free' sun for market-bought commodities. In the same way, it's hard to argue that a particular generation has been irresponsible if they've planned for a managed decline. On an even more extreme level, the smoker that deliberately chooses (or deliberately chooses to avoid or disbelieve the scientific evidence) to keep smoking, with a high risk of cancer and other diseases, can be viewed as following a planned path, and indeed their planned path is perfectly sustainable.

'Sustainable' in that sense of stationarity also makes no sense for a society or for the planet. Technological progress – particularly at the unprecedented rate of the last century – means that things should constantly get better. If they haven't, it's not due to 'shocks' – there haven't been asteroids crashing into the Earth's surface, as likely caused the unfortunate fate of the dinosaurs.

It's due to selfish or poor policy making leading to economic and social inefficiencies. But this trajectory has proven to be 'sustainable' in the sense of 'resilient' – commentators have pointed out that the current policy trajectory is leading to a future where our children are either currently worse off than we were at their age, will eventually be worse off, or – for either our children or their children – may even face the fate of the dinosaurs without us having the excuse of an asteroid.

The current generation has decided – either intentionally or by ignoring the scientific evidence – on a pathway that leads to continued climate change and therefore a worsened inheritance for their children. Further, any cognizant being can see that there is a risk on the current (sustainable) path that climate change will lead to an uninhabitable Earth and therefore human species extinction. The plan to drive at accelerating speed off a cliff is a 'sustainable' trajectory in the sense that nothing automatically stops it, and we know that people, from time to time, do exactly that.

Guardrails limit both intentional and unintentional accidents, and we will argue strongly in their favour.

Standing on the shoulders of giants – Marshall and storytelling

It used to be said that, in order to understand economics, one just had to read Alfred Marshall's *Principles of Economics* (1890). Indeed, the title of the book lives on in first-year economics courses in many universities if – sadly – much of the nuanced economic analysis has been lost over the last century. In fact, a novice who had recently discovered that book, and read and absorbed it, would probably be better placed to advise governments on economic policy than a current graduate. This is not because we haven't – as a profession – learned important things about information imperfections, the role of implicit and explicit contracts in working around inefficiencies, in the arbitrage nature of financial markets, in econometric techniques – but because these insights haven't been sufficiently integrated into our policy discourse. Meanwhile, we have carelessly adopted incautious views about the effects of cutting taxes and about zero interest rate extreme monetary policy that violently conflict with established economics.

The reader may already be bemused that we are proceeding to understand economics by telling stories, referring to novels and by constructing anecdotes and even parables. But this is precisely the nature of traditional economics methodology. Marshall is most evocative when he describes family firms, a part of economics that he found particularly interesting:

> It would therefore at first sight seem likely that business men should constitute a sort of caste; dividing out among their sons the chief posts

of command, and founding hereditary dynasties, which should rule certain branches of trade for many generations together. But the actual state of things is very different. For when a man has got together a great business, his descendants often fail, in spite of their great advantages, to develop the high abilities and the special turn of mind and temperament required for carrying it on with equal success. (Marshall, 1890: 361)

This is almost indistinguishable from some of the quotations from novels that we have and will use in this book. But this is how good economists understand the world. It is why my understanding of events may differ from that of another economist, why we may have different predictions of the future (or, even more annoyingly to the non-economist, why I will say that this may occur, or that may occur, and may even if pressed put a probability distribution on those contradictory outcomes), and may give different policy recommendations. This is why the groupthink of the last few decades is particularly worrisome. The profession thrives on debate. Academic economics seminars, where one academic presents their latest research, are lively events with frequent interruptions and challenges. In other subjects, the audience is silent while the presenter may literally read their paper out. But the nature of economics – because it needs to sustain lively debate – is perhaps less personally contentious than other subjects. I argue about your model (though I accept that you have the right, and should utilize the right, to present a different viewpoint from the one I present). But – and this is further strengthened by the fact that you are typically presenting your model as a series of algebraic equations – the argument should be dispassionate.

Marshall then explains how the firm needs to shift from the entrepreneur's progeny to a more managerial style:

For a time indeed all may go well. His sons find a firmly established trade connection, and what is perhaps even more important, a well-chosen staff of subordinates with a generous interest in the business. By mere assiduity and caution, availing themselves of the traditions of the firm, they may hold together for a long time. But when a full generation has passed, when the old traditions are no longer a safe guide, and when the bonds that held together the old staff have been dissolved, then the business almost invariably falls to pieces unless it is practically handed over to the management of new men who have meanwhile risen to partnership in the firm. (Marshall, 1890: 362)

In this storytelling, Marshall gives his view of the development of firms, how they rise and how they fail. Note the importance of what we are calling 'guardrails' and Marshall describes as 'a safe guide'.

Given the availability of cheap, large-scale computing power, we might now be inclined to get a very large dataset with entrepreneur-run firms, family firms and stock market listed firms, and see how they perform. Just don't expect our econometric analysis to be definitive. For the vast bulk of issues that we want to explore, there is little equivalent to the experimental method in science. We don't normally have the advantage of the gold standard, 'randomized double-blind controlled trial' that is used in assessing pharmaceuticals. Of course, much of medical treatment is also based upon experience and judgement rather than these gold standard studies. That is why we might prefer to be treated by an eminent researcher or consultant than a newly trained medical student or junior doctor, even if the latter may have more up-to-date knowledge of the scientific literature at large.

David Card and Alan Krueger (1994) are noted for their contribution to methodology in their exploration of the effect of minimum wages in the fast-food sector. Economic theory – as is its custom and habit – predicts that a rise in minimum wages may cause employment to fall (if employers economize on labour) or to rise (if large employers were keeping employment down to avoid paying higher wages). Card and Krueger used 'difference-in-difference' methods in a 'natural experiment'. Minimum wages were raised in one location and not raised in a nearby location. The authors could then look at how employment changes in the two locations, adjusting for other variables that changed over time.

The reason that this work was so noteworthy (and led to a Nobel Prize for Card) is that natural experiments (or, more generally, good situations for 'identifying' the impact of a variable) are rare in the economy. More commonly, as with zero interest rate monetary policies, the relevant policies (in this case, determined by central banks) moved together. In a way, they had to – once most countries lowered interest rates, an outlier would see their currency shoot up in value, leading to a collapse in their exports. In fact, the US is so dominant in the international monetary framework that, once it has chosen an ultra-expansionary monetary policy that would lead to a significant decline in the value of the dollar, other countries largely have to follow.

This then leads to something of a contradiction in policies. The lack of a clear and decisive view of the world, and the necessary reliance upon judgement and experience, means that we can go wildly astray. We will argue that that is what has happened in the last few decades. On the other hand, however, we cannot shy away from hard measures even when there is a fair degree of uncertainty. We may not know the exact effects of various methods of cutting carbon in the atmosphere, but – given the life-or-death implications – we need to act and worry about the exact nuances from a perspective of decades away, once we have saved the planet. Perhaps the giveaway, the resolution of the apparent contradiction, is that we need to apply the utmost caution for 'easy' policies, and not be as worried about 'hard' policies. The Federal Reserve Chairman, William McChesney Martin, is regularly quoted as saying that the Fed needed 'to take away the punch bowl just as the party gets going'. Given that this hard decision – to raise interest rates and create a recession – is not going to be immediately popular, we can likely trust that the policy was truly needed whenever it is seen in practice. In the same way, a government that raises taxes or removes subsidies to fund increased expenditures on, for example, the NHS can be viewed with less scepticism than one that cuts taxes and still increases expenditure, seeking to borrow the gap from future generations.

The role of mathematics

Marshall is also often quoted (for example by Coase (1975): 25–31) on mathematics:

> But I know I had a growing feeling in the later years of my work at the subject that a good mathematical theorem dealing with economic hypotheses was very unlikely to be good economics: and I went more and more on the rules --- (1) Use mathematics as a shorthand language, rather than as an engine of inquiry. (2) Keep to them till you have done. (3) Translate into English. (4) Then illustrate by examples that are important in real life. (5) Burn the mathematics. (6) If you can't succeed in (4), burn (3). This last I did often.

There was a debate in economics about whether or not it should be so mathematical – to the chagrin of many of our students, mathematics won. Writing things in mathematics (to be translated into language and illustrated by examples) has one unique advantage – it is absolutely clear precisely what one is assuming. The 'model' can be checked for internal consistency.

Naturally, our explicitly stated assumptions (the beginning of our story) cannot be 'true' as a general description of the world, in the same way as a particular novel is about particular characters. 'Jack had brown hair.' 'Jill carried a red umbrella.' I recently published an article about the gender pay gap among professors in English universities. I quickly made assumptions such as 'for a professor of given underlying ability, the probability of publishing in a good journal each year is independently drawn from a probability distribution'. Consider a football player – if I know their underlying ability, knowing whether or not they scored a goal in their last match conveys no additional information about the likelihood of scoring a goal in the current match. If you believe in 'hot streaks', then you will not accept that my assumption is fully accurate. Alternatively, you might think the player got tired out after scoring the goal, and was less likely to score in the next match.

The point, however, is that you know exactly what I've assumed, and (if you look up the paper) you'll have the mathematical statements of my assumptions and the mathematical equations and derivations that followed. If you don't like my assumption, then you can think about how the analysis would differ if you made a different assumption (what you cannot do is analysis without making an assumption to replace mine, since you won't be able to 'solve' the problem – your story will be incomplete and any conclusions will be unfounded, even in your little story world). You could look at the data on football players and see if they are suggestive (as we've already indicated, without a 'natural experiment', you won't be able to reach a conclusive answer, and perhaps not even then) that my assumption is wrong and should be replaced by a better one. Of course, scoring by a player could be bunched because of the reactions of other players on their team (they send the ball to the given player more often) or on the opposing team (they err on the side of caution in avoiding penalties). That is one reason why empirical observations – which are necessarily incomplete – can only be suggestive.

As we go along in this book, you may not like the models presented – which by the very nature of 'stories' are incomplete as descriptions of reality – but at least, if I've done my job, you will see what I am presenting without ambiguity. There is one further, but major advantage of the mathematical framework and underpinning to economics. Even when talking 'in English', having followed Marshall's advice of translating back from the mathematics, the economist has the mathematical equations running through their head. Put simply, there are no emotions in mathematics. Policies may be misguided but they are dispassionate, which does not mean that they cannot be partisan.

Economist as barrister

As a middle-brow theorist, I take pride in my ability to construct a mathematical model to fit any observations from empirical data. The methodology is not to have a model in advance and to test it and hypotheses against the data, but to look at the data in an informed way, and then construct a story or stories surrounding the results from the data. This is analogous to the way a natural scientist might proceed. There is an unexplained or even paradoxical observation, and the scientist seeks to construct a model that fits.

In economics, however, the aim is not just to describe more effectively, but to come up with policy recommendations. Should the central bank raise interest rates? Should the minimum wage be raised to £15 an hour? Of course, these questions do not have a purely technical answer, since there are winners and losers from any policy. But we can – like barristers – argue the case.

Will Brexit over time engage the British economy to new innovative growth and regional and social balance? I can model a world where exactly that happens – cut off from European labour and markets, British industry restores apprenticeships and rebuilds the industrial heartlands of the country, using the most modern technology. Or I can model a world where Britain loses the advantages of trade efficiencies (we specialize in finance and trade financial services for manufacturing from elsewhere) and labour market mobility (acquiring skilled building trades workers and service workers from elsewhere in Europe).

Depending upon the forum (whether I'm writing for an academic journal or a blog, seeking to engage in public debate), I will write this in a different way, but in each case, I am selling to you my view, hopefully with appropriate caveats. The resurgence of Britain after Brexit might – in my discussion – depend upon building a modern, high-speed rail network between Manchester and Leeds, and between the 'Northern powerhouses' and the South.

As long as I stick with current empirical and theoretical techniques, and present my work in an honest way, there is nothing objectionable in this. You can judge my case, because you will have the reasoning in front of you. A barrister in court who just says, 'My client is innocent', or tries to justify the case deviating from legal norms (when the barrister risks rebuke from the judge), will – more often than not – find the client behind bars.

There are few legal cases where no plausible argument can be made – if that rare exception is the case, then the barrister should advise the client simply to plead guilty, or settle a civil case, and indeed the barrister is required to give best advice. Unfortunately, there is no such requirement upon a practising economist, who could be an expert witness (either in court or in public debate) stretching theories and data to try to support the improbable.

As with the legal system, none of this is dealing in certainties. We are working with 'on the balance of probabilities' or on 'beyond reasonable doubt'. This is more than just the uncertainty about coefficients that arises from econometric work. When you run an econometric regression with your data, the output shows coefficients – the impact effect of changing the underlying variable magnitude – with measures of standard errors. For example, the regression may include the minimum wage as an explanatory variable. The coefficient will show that raising the minimum wage by £1 has an average impact of maybe 5% job losses as a result, but with a range of true impact values – maybe the range goes from 1% to 10%. But, as we've already discussed, you had a model in mind when you did the empirical work. You might have included the concentration of jobs across firms within a region. If one firm dominates the local or regional labour market, and can use this power to keep wages down, then your underlying model of what happens is totally different than if there are lots of small firms competing for workers. In that model, a statutory wage may actually induce more workers to show up, either from home or from neighbouring localities. Running the regression on this model might show an impact of raising the minimum wage of increasing (rather than decreasing) employment by 5 to 10%.

If your opponent across the court room – or the lecture theatre – has a different model in mind, that does not make them stupid or unethical, or even necessarily wrong. With the climate emergency, up until a certain point one could hold the view (what we call a 'model') that the observed changes were a natural progression, just as ice ages had occurred in the past before humankind took to impacting upon the world. The believers in that model would look for evidence to support their case. In the academic world, they are not allowed to cheat with the data, but there is a broad range of allowable leeway in handling the data, which can only be interpreted in the context of a model. As in the courtroom, if I disagree with someone's presentation – in the form of a peer-reviewed academic paper – I can work on the data myself, or different data, and come to my conclusions.

Of course, there comes a point when the data – no matter how interpreted – settle the argument among reasonable people. It is hard to see someone who now resists the observation 'climate change is man-made and due to excessive use of carbon fuels' as being anything other than an ideologue and an extremely dangerous one at that. However, they can still take the position that 'climate change is man-made' and 'climate change will lead to extinction', but care more about having cheap petrol for their car.

But for other issues, divergences of modelling and therefore policy proposals can persist. At one point, 'earned income tax credits' were a popular approach to providing financial support to the less well-off. The argument was that this additional government support – payable even if the individual earned less than tax thresholds – would encourage the unemployed and those not in the labour force to take up jobs. They would gain self-respect and the other advantages of contributing through employment.

As it happens, I share the belief that people are in general better off if they are working than if they are lazing about on the sofa watching TV, and that young people are even more advantaged by taking even a low-status job than becoming involved in drug trafficking and gangs. But – along with a fair number of others – I don't favour in effect subsidizing low-wage jobs in this way. If you subsidize low-wage jobs, you'll get a lot of them.

Far better, in my model, to have living wage laws that require jobs to pay decent wages and have decent working conditions. Rather than subsidizing the 'gig economy', we should eliminate it. If this requires the government to subsidize investment in human and physical capital, that's fine.

That you and I may have these different views – which are a combination of our underlying beliefs and the data, as we see them through the lens of our underlying views – doesn't however mean that we cannot compromise and come up with policies. On the most important divergence, climate change, one is reminded of the old argument on believing in God. If you don't believe in God (man-made climate change), and he turns out to exist, you are in serious trouble.

It may be, however, that one of us has a view rooted in ideology and impervious to any degree of scientific evidence and argument. As a useful exercise, ask yourself on each belief you hold what is the probability that you are wrong. If you say that you are 100% right, it will be almost impossible to talk to you on that subject. That does not mean, however, that we cannot talk about subjects in the round. You may believe absolutely that abortion at any stage is murder, and you may believe that capital punishment is a vital response for the crime of murder. (How those two statements interact is perhaps a wonder to behold, and avoided by the Catholic Church since it opposes both abortion and capital punishment.) But your political budget may not encompass sufficient resources to achieve both, and you will still have to prioritize and negotiate. Alternatively, you may compromise elsewhere – for example, on climate change. We come back to all this in the final chapter.

The methodology of macroeconomics

The area of economics where there has probably been the greatest overall convergence in views has been macroeconomics and monetary economics. The problem is that the consensus view of the last two decades is completely at variance with the consensus view preceding it. The very high UK inflation of the 1970s and late 1980s is associated with the 'Barber Boom' and the 'Lawson Boom' as recognition that expansionary policies got out of control. In the same way, the US sought to maintain non-military public spending at the same time as funding the Vietnam War, all without raising taxes. The lesson was that Keynesian aggregate demand management (through monetary and fiscal policy) could be used to smooth fluctuations in the economy, but could not be used prudently to turbocharge the economy on an indefinite basis, or to prevent rather than mitigate recessions, without causing high inflation.

But subsequently – enticed by the popularity of low and decreasing interest rates, and corresponding high and increasing capital values, most notably in housing – as a profession we largely jettisoned even the basic planks of our common models. Ben Bernanke referred to the 'global savings glut' and Larry Summers revived the 'secular stagnation' theory. In either case, interest rates and fiscal policy could justifiably be expansionary by previous standards. We have already argued that, given the extraordinary rate of technological progress, it is hard to see that the world has shifted against productive investment. Along with the poor state of both physical and human (education and health) infrastructure, there is more plausibly a 'glut of investment opportunities'.

Paul Romer, a leading macroeconomist, wrote a devastating critique in which he stated, 'I have observed more than three decades of intellectual regress' (Romer, 2016: 1). As we've observed, related arguments are raised by Edward Chancellor (2022) about the effects of persistently low interest rates.

Romer observes: 'Macroeconomists got comfortable with the idea that fluctuations in macroeconomic aggregates are caused by imaginary shocks, instead of actions that people take' (2016: 4). He proposes: 'The best indicator of monetary policy is the real Federal Funds rate – the nominal rate minus the inflation rate' (p 1).

By this measure, rates have gone down and down over the last four decades. In the post-pandemic period of high inflation, the Bank of England spent considerable time raising bank rate to 5.25% when inflation climbed over 10%. CPI inflation was 4% for 2023. The US Federal Funds rate has reached a target of 5.5% with US CPI of 3.4% for the year. These are normal real rates of interest, but nonetheless there is a groundswell of demand for lowering rates (into negative real rates) immediately.

But this book generalizes the issue – if there is an easy answer ('lower taxes' or 'lower interest rates') with a pretend explanation ('this will pay for itself in productivity' or 'there is a worldwide savings glut'), the last few decades have seen policy makers rush for it. It is easy to build jails, particularly if one can hire private companies to run them, but it is hard to run intensive youth programmes to support people growing up in less idyllic communities, with less successful schools. The methodology of economics allows for this. Powerful people, and less powerful academic economists, can weave the stories they like. The piper will be paid – if these stories are wrong – but Generation Z will get the bill.

Congratulating ourselves

Central bankers and economists congratulated themselves for avoiding the Great Recession turning into a second Great Depression. Ben Bernanke, the Chair of the Fed Reserve at the time, received the Nobel Prize in 2022 for his 1980s research on bank crises and the Great Depression. Similarly, policy makers have congratulated themselves for navigating the pandemic without a depression. But in fact, the policies adopted in the UK during the pandemic were extraordinarily wasteful. What is even more surprising is that there weren't contingency plans in place.

The easiest policy to ridicule was 'Eat Out to Help Out'. On Mondays, Tuesdays and Wednesdays between 3 and 31 August 2020, people who dined within an establishment (it didn't apply to takeaway food) got a 50% discount up to £10. This cost the taxpayer, according to the House of Commons Library, £849 million. Thiemo Fetzer (2022) found that the scheme may have driven up COVID infections by about 8–17% in August and early September.

This expenditure was dwarfed by that of the furlough scheme. The House of Commons Library estimated the cost of £70 billion with nearly 12 million jobs on furlough. Despite the scheme, however, the number of unemployed rose from two million to six million. While the government was paying up to £2,500 a month to 'furloughed' employees, Universal Credit paid to the unemployed went up by only £20 a week. Even that derisory sum was withdrawn during the autumn of 2021.

John Kenneth Galbraith wrote *The Affluent Society* in 1958. This book is best known for popularizing the term 'conventional wisdom' in economics as a disparaging expression. But he also made concrete proposals along the way. One is that, during a time of high unemployment (when it is hard to find a job), unemployment insurance payments should go up. The argument for limiting them, in normal times, to a below comfortable level is that policy makers worry about diminishing the incentive to go and find work. But during a severe recession, or during a pandemic, there may be no work to find (or that should be found for the clinically vulnerable). Therefore, there is no disincentive effect to limit a significant rise in Universal Credit rates during a pandemic.

But why would one give those on furlough a multiple of the amount given to those on Universal Credit? The furlough scheme was capped at £2,500 a month. Universal credit runs to a few hundred pounds per month for a single individual. As we will encounter frequently throughout this book, this is not – from the economist's point of view – a fairness issue. Governments encourage and benefit from running lotteries that leave some citizens millionaires while others remain in relative poverty. It is a question of economic efficiency and the sensible use of taxpayers' money.

In the furlough scheme, companies could offer their workers the option of going on furlough rather than making them redundant. The worker could not work for the firm while on furlough (though they could work for other firms). Until the end of June 2021, the government would pay 80% of the salary. The company could choose to top this up to 100%, but was under no obligation to do so. It did, however, have to pay national insurance and pension contributions. From July 2021, the scheme was phased down in that companies had to pay 10% and then 20% of the wages. Where was the economic efficiency gain in having these unemployed (in the sense of not doing any work for the employer) workers notionally on 'furlough' rather than being made redundant and classified as being 'unemployed', particularly since the furloughed workers could work somewhere else?

The government also set up various guaranteed loan schemes for business, which have totalled £77.1 billion, according to the Department for Business, Energy and Industrial Strategy. While some of the schemes had an 80% guarantee to the lender, the Bounce Back Loan Scheme had a 100% guarantee and the government paid the interest for the first year. The Office for Budget Responsibility estimated the loss rate across the schemes to be about 27%, for a total loss of about £20 billion.

Importantly, the guarantee is over the whole amount lost and not a back-up guarantee after the lender has taken the first tranche of losses. That is, if there is a £1 million loan and the loss (after personal guarantees, some repayments, and so on) is £500,000, then the bank (with an 80% guarantee) suffers a loss of £100,000. In the case of 100% guarantees, but even with these partial guarantees, banks do not have the full incentive to be careful in their lending. In contrast, if the scheme had required banks to absorb the first 20% of the losses, they would have been much more careful.

There may have been all sorts of political reasons for the government to offer these schemes, but it is hard to see either efficiency or equity reasons.

The cost of living crisis

After the Second World War, economists were expecting a recession. Demand would collapse as the munitions factories shut down. The returning soldiers would lead to significant unemployment. In the event, there was a boom. US veterans went to university under the GI bill, women who had entered the workforce for reasons of national necessity were no longer needed and were sent home, to be replaced by men. Savings amassed during the war were put to use buying consumer goods.

Like a war, the pandemic (and the policy responses to the pandemic) have had great impacts upon the 'animal spirits' of the populations. We have seen the 'great retirement' where people simply do not want to go back to work. Others do not want to go back to the actual workplace, seeking to extend 'working from home'. Some firms observe at least a temporary opportunity to save on travel budgets and on renting office space.

Developments of technology (notably high-speed broadband) made it possible for much of the economy to continue during the pandemic. But it was 'black-and-white' rather than in colour. Given the choice, the experience of live theatre and concerts dominates recorded or live-streamed events. Universities had already moved towards 'lecture capture' where students could watch lectures and seminars from their bed (being careful to turn off the camera), because students found it more convenient. The disguise of 'this allows students to watch the lecture several times in revision' fooled no one.

The experience of wars suggests that we should hardly be surprised that inflation was an accident waiting to happen, and it arose – along with low unemployment – after the pandemic. Further, one does not have to be a monetarist to anticipate that a ten-fold increase in the monetary base would ultimately be inflationary.

This is a book about economics, and we will, in the last chapter, come back to how to deal with the economic issues we face. Commentators and the public often misunderstand economics, and think that it is all about 'Homo economicus', some dreadful creature (hopefully only encountered in literature and not in real life) who is entirely self-interested and particularly upon money. Economics is about incentives and about how they guide individual action and how individual actions come together in organizations, markets, polities and communities. Economics done well can advise a firm on how to maximize the welfare of its workers and its consumers, rather than on how to maximize what might be a highly inaccurate financial market valuation. For those of us who work in universities, we can use our tools to encourage students to show up to lectures, whether by required attendance and monitoring technologies, by offering better lectures (requiring the institution as well to determine a pay and promotions system that rewards productivity), or by improving the ability to make and meet their friends.

Some of the limitations of economics have, however, been exacerbated by the pandemic, and by the enforced social isolation of that period, and by a difficult restoration of normal social interaction. Those of us who work in universities are all too aware of the scarring of the generation of students who worked from home and took disrupted examinations. While it would be a good thing to more formally develop interdisciplinary approaches to studying problems, in the interim economists have to use their storytelling abilities to the maximum, to incorporate as best they can those social and political elements into the story, without jettisoning the logical rigour of our methodology.

My stories

This book contains my stories, drawn upon my experiences of the US and UK economies over the last four decades. The point of going into economics methodology in depth is to make clear that these stories rise or fall depending upon how convincing they are. If these stories are well-directed, we are in a time of remarkable challenge and remarkable opportunity. The decline in birth rates and populations is to be celebrated, as is the rise of robots and AI. By investment, we will substitute infrastructure, machines and robots (it seems polite not to lump them in with machines, particularly as AI develops) for human labour, at a large benefit to the environment.

The next 20 years can be an exciting time, or they can be mired in grievance and retribution. I choose to tell optimistic stories.

3

The Long and Short of It

This book is about the equilibria we are currently facing as a society. There are wildfires and floods, pandemics, wars, insurrection at the US Capitol, autocratic demagogues and fanatical religious leaders in countries throughout the world. It is not hyperbole, but reality, that humans on Earth are facing an existential crisis.

Economics is about the decisions and actions taken by individuals and the coordination of these actions into an equilibrium. This sometimes is mediated through a market, sometimes through government or international agencies, sometimes through units such as families and neighbourhoods, most often through a combination of all of the above in a 'mixed economy'. This means that we cannot blame 'shocks' anytime something goes wrong. Since our building block is the individual, it also means that each of us bears a degree of personal responsibility.

For grown-ups and economists, it is not good enough to say that we are where we are due to shocks. It would be like a very bad insurance company that seeks to get out of every claim on the basis that the problem was 'an act of God', not an insured event. Instead, we need to figure out how we have collectively chosen to be where we are. Even if we had planned reasonably and did suffer from bad luck, we collectively have the choice to respond positively to the situation. We don't need to continue to have climate change, to have wars, to have poverty and poor education, and to have polluted rivers and skies. Either our individual decisions are poor, or the coordination mechanism is poor. Keynesian economics, for example, is about how individuals might in a recession not want to be laid off and how individuals might want to go out and buy the new washing machines that would keep the workers employed, but somehow the coordination mechanisms in the economy have failed to bring these demand and supply factors together.

Economics begins with individuals, their endowments and their preferences. This chapter is about how individuals, mediated through markets and organizations, can land themselves or their progeny in a bad situation.

This can be through sins of commission – deliberately choosing the bad pathways – or omission – not summoning the will to change equilibrium. We continue to distinguish between a stationary bad situation, an unsustainable pathway in either of the two senses we have described – planned decline or pursuing a trajectory that will (to the surprise of participants) reach an unexpected dead end, and finally a failure in planning so bad (at least from the perspective of future generations and those that care about the existence of mankind) that it can lead to extinction.

Following economics methodology, we will tell some stories. We begin with the old story of Robinson Crusoe alone on an island, so any decisions – good or bad – are his alone. Crusoe, given his endowments, might in fact choose different paths of consumption over time, and might even choose extinction. While 'luck' can play a role – will he be rescued? – his choices determine the extent of the role of 'luck'. If he has chosen to consume his food stock over ten years in anticipation of rescue during that time frame, and he isn't rescued, he is unlucky but he chose to put himself at that risk. One can be both unlucky and imprudent, a situation we will argue is the correct characterization of the current policy predicament.

To look at coordination issues, we then add other inhabitants. Property rights are fundamental, as is Crusoe's relationship with the newcomers to his island. Issues of mediating preferences and coordinating actions become pertinent. We also explore the role of discord and revolution. Not surprisingly, if Crusoe might contemplate choosing his own extinction (or to take needlessly risky choices that may lead to his own extinction), he may well be more likely to choose extinction for unrelated acquaintances, including future generations.

Trouble in Tahiti

The Intergovernmental Panel on Climate Change was invited to prepare a report on the effects of a 1.5 degree rise in global temperature (www.ipcc.ch/sr15/). This level of global warming is expected to occur, in the absence of action, between 2030 and 2052, and would have significant deleterious effects. Going beyond 1.5 degrees raises the prospect of severe costs or indeed even extinction.

Economics as a discipline is non-judgemental about preferences. MacAskill (2022) gives us a philosophical framework for accounting for future generations, but nothing prevents decision-makers in the current dominant generation from simply not caring (as sported on the coat worn by Melania Trump on a trip to Texas in June 2018).

To abstract at first away from coordination issues, we follow the approach in economics that considers a single inhabitant in the 'Robinson Crusoe' economy. Charles Boyle wrote in *The Guardian* on 19 April 2019: 'Robinson

Crusoe at 300: why it's time to get rid of this colonial fairytale.' That the book describing Crusoe's adventures is now a relic of empire and colonialism perhaps makes even clearer that as economists we accept preferences (and indeed prejudices) as given. When Crusoe was shipwrecked, he was on a mission of slave-trading. Sadly, it is unlikely that the author intended the shipwrecking as punishment for this endeavour.

In our re-imagining of the tale, Crusoe lands on a deserted island and finds food supplies in a cabin. The tins of baked beans can be augmented by the coconuts growing freely in the trees. What is his optimal strategy for consuming the food? The good news is that he will be able to live on the coconuts indefinitely. He doesn't know if and when he'll be rescued, so his planning is under uncertainty. If he is too conservative in protecting his future bean supply, he may feel a degree of regret if he is rescued at an early date (although this is likely to be compensated by the joy of being rescued). Crusoe balances out his impatience (his 'discount rate'), his utility gain from eating beans in a small or a large portion, and his attitudes and calculations of risk, and comes up with a consumption pattern. In the absence of new information, there will be no reason to deviate from his plan going forward.

In fact, the most important eventuality – being rescued – should already be incorporated in the plan. Crusoe may start out quite optimistically but his plan recognizes that, if he is still there after a decade, his initial optimism wasn't validated. In that case, his optimal plan is likely to involve decreasing consumption over time, even if Crusoe is not otherwise gluttonous or imprudent, but only unduly optimistic.

This is an important point, since arguments for discretionary policy by central banks (or in general) – rather than following rules – are often misguided. In my early days as a lecturer, I would go to exam boards that determined students' final degree classifications. The rules mapped course unit grades into a class of first, upper second, and so on. Rules might be simple averages, or they might be preponderance in nature (to gain a first, one needed a majority of grades at first class, plus perhaps no grade below a lower second). The rules would typically weight the three years of the degree differently, with the final year getting a higher weighting.

The board would still have the right to use its discretion (typically in the upwards direction). Arguments would include that, if a student did particularly well on their independent dissertation, they might be pushed over the borderline. But note that this could have been included in the rule – the dissertation could have been over-weighted when taking the average or preponderance. Another common argument was that the student had improved and their final year results were better than previous ones. But a senior econometrician pointed out that the rule already allowed for higher weighting for the final year, so why were we arguing for higher, higher weighting? We will later use a similar argument to query why student loans have a contingent repayment different from the progressive structure already built into the tax code.

Note that the rule already takes account of contingencies – it doesn't say that student X will get an upper second based on their arrival qualifications, but upon their measured performance along the way. There are some contingencies that are more complex to assess, such as extenuating circumstances. It is hard to put into a rule how being in hospital for surgery for a month during the second year should be accounted for in the overall degree outcome. Instead of trying to have a mechanical formula, one could wait until the end, see where the student's overall grades lay, and then see the gap that needed to be filled by the extenuating circumstances. It's not that one couldn't construct a full set of rules in advance, but that it is uneconomic or impractical to do so. Rather than consider all possible eventualities in advance, it is easier to wait until the actual set of circumstances is known and then act upon it.

Of course, if we do so, and we have the sympathies of normal people, we are likely to be overly generous when push comes to shove. We will leave the exam board feeling just that bit better about the world when we give the student the benefit of the doubt, even if in some sense this is unfair to students who didn't claim extenuating circumstances to which they might have been entitled. An employer may rely on our slight upgrading of the individual and hire them in place of someone who is actually more qualified. If middle-class students are better at writing and documenting extenuating circumstances, our generosity may play a small part in supporting class advantages. But at the end of the day, a modest change upwards in one student's degree class will have little negative impact on the world, unless we construct unlikely hypotheticals that the student may take the place in medical research of an alternative, better student who would have invented the cure for cancer. As we have said already, much of how we analyse things depends upon 'continuity' – a small change in inputs makes a small change in outputs. The potentially big difference in the one student's future prospects will normally mean an unobservable small impact upon society as a whole.

Unfortunately, if a central bank similarly hasn't bound itself to a rule, their generosity (and their being able to bask in the approval of financial markets and governments and mortgagees who can borrow at low rates) may lead to significant longer-term problems that we discuss later. But the major problem is not so much the failure to follow a rule, but the degree of generosity that has been shown in recent years, as well as the large impact on the economy and society as a whole.

If we return to Crusoe, living alone on his island, his planning only has impact on himself. He can plan his consumption pattern for beans. In the terms we have used, it may be declining over time – this incorporates his discounting of the future (his impatience to consume) and the rising likelihood that, if he hasn't been rescued in the first year or two, he is unlikely to be rescued in the next year or two, and greater saving of resources may be called for. A somewhat more complicated issue is how much he appreciates having a full tin of beans one day (and none the next), versus having half a tin each day. Economics generally assumes (for reasons that have to do with continuity) 'convexity'. This means that having half a tin each day is better than having a full tin every two days. This is by no means obvious, and – in the fuller story we have constructed – the daily dish could be beans and coconut, so there is variety that might be greater than beans one day and coconuts the next. But these are assumptions and we reiterate that the economist makes their assumptions because it is the story they choose to tell. Another economist could make different assumptions and tell a different story, with different policy conclusions.

Crusoe is in some sense relaxed because we have set him in the tropical equivalent of a modern affluent economy. Although his endowment of tins of beans is limited, he envisages the coconut trees will supply food forever. Things can only get better in the consumption sense if he discovers animals to augment his diet, as in fact he does in the novel. In the modern UK and the US, there is much more than ample fundamental supplies of food, energy, housing for everyone, if we choose to set up a system that distributes these necessities in that way. Different economists and politicians can make different arguments as to whether a more equal distribution would be more or less economically efficient – would the pie grow as fast (or even faster) if more equally distributed, or do we need unequal outcomes to provide incentives for individuals to work harder? But it seems daft to argue that we cannot house, feed, educate and provide medical and social care for everyone at a reasonable standard, given our technology and other resources. Throughout the book, we will keep coming back to the point – we can do these things, why are we choosing not to? In our no label economics, of course, that doesn't necessarily mean doing this by universal benefits and hand-outs; it can mean returning to workhouses and other unpleasantries we can read about in Dickens.

But, back to Crusoe. He has the coconut trees, he will discover and in fact raise livestock for food, so he perceives no risk of starvation – there is no extinction equilibrium. But it may not be optimal for him to choose a stationary consumption level where each day he consumes the same number of beans and coconuts. He may well choose a diminishing consumption because of impatience or because he expects to be rescued imminently so defers sacrifice until it becomes clear that it isn't going to happen. And one day he may simply deplete his supply of tinned beans. No doubt an inconvenience, and one measure of unsustainability, but not a disaster.

The arrival of Adam Smith

In a simple world where Robinson Crusoe lives on his own, he will necessarily bear the consequences of his own decisions. There is no coordination problem with other people, Crusoe – subject to his endowment of beans and the natural coconut productivity of the island – makes his own decisions. He may later regret them, if he runs out of beans and grows tired of coconuts before he is rescued, but he has no one else to blame.

After some years of loneliness, another individual – let's call him Adam Smith – is shipwrecked on the same island. At that point, Crusoe has already taken possession of the tins of beans. This was not because of any special effort or merit on his part – indeed, the fact that he was shipwrecked first may be a negative indicator of his value as a sailor – but simply because he got there first. In the same way, the Boston Brahmins (known, coincidentally, for the quality of their baked beans) and other aristocracies may have rather less to do with effort or ability, and rather more to do with simply being the first (once the native Americans were pushed aside).

The choice of the name 'Adam Smith' is of course not accidental. Adam Smith might – in the logic of his namesake the Scottish economist – want to engage in trading or creating 'markets', although the latter is a bit ambitious in a two-person economy. Since Crusoe is in possession of the tins of beans, but the coconuts have remained in the commons, Smith might propose to trade his labour – collecting coconuts – for tins of beans.

Smith might set up a market stall and put a price tag on the coconuts. If he has paper and pen, he might put a high price on the coconuts, demanding several tins of beans for each coconut. Crusoe has a choice of how many coconuts to buy, either doing without or climbing the trees himself to harvest coconuts to eat. In practice, the two occupants of the island are likely to bargain over the price. Economic models of bargaining often suggest that the surplus from the trade is divided fairly evenly – the utility that Smith gets from the beans less the disutility of his labour roughly equals the utility that Crusoe gets from no longer having to collect coconuts himself. This by no means equalizes the well-being of the two inhabitants of the island, Crusoe still gains mightily from having ownership of the stock of beans. Assuming they are both in similar physical shape, both have the same opportunities for harvesting coconuts, but Crusoe has his endowment of beans in addition to that labour productivity.

While this might be an economic equilibrium, it might not be the outcome in reality. Smith might fail to see the legitimacy of the arrangement, and use force to take over the tins of beans. Even the threat of force is potent. In bargaining over the price of coconuts, Crusoe realizes that – were he to harvest coconuts for himself – he would have to leave his tins of beans untended. Property rights come with fairly high security costs. Alternatively (and this is the second reason for choosing the name of the second arrival), Adam Smith might call upon the 'impartial spectator' from his namesake's book *The Theory of Moral Sentiments* (1761) to inform Crusoe that the existing arrangements are unreasonable, and Crusoe might voluntarily agree to a more equal distribution of beans.

Even if one believed in markets, the initial endowments are important. When people talk about equality of opportunity, they are not usually proposing that we take half the tins of beans away from Crusoe and redistribute them to Smith to provide a level starting point for the two. In the recent terminology of Generation Z, the 'nepo babies' may be putting in hard work to become actors, but the high proportion of success for the offspring of famous and wealthy parents is unlikely to be ascribable to effort alone.

How on balance does Crusoe feel about the arrival of Smith? If the impact is human company and conversation, and the ability to trade tins of beans for the coconuts harvested by Smith, Crusoe gains from the arrival. But if Crusoe has to worry about Smith claiming half the endowment of beans, or indeed Smith deciding to 'steal' all the tins, the fear and worry may impact negatively on Crusoe's life.

Crusoe's son Junior

Now let us suppose that Crusoe was shipwrecked with his son, Junior. Further, let us assume (as an example of how economists are allowed to make any assumptions, so long as they are explicit) the rather unlikely situation that Junior and Crusoe are the same age, have the same health characteristics and consequently the same life expectancy. Further, they have the same preferences in regards, for example, to how impatient they are in deciding whether to consume today or conserve for the future.

The reader will be reassured that – unlike much of the economics literature – we will shortly drop these clearly impossible assumptions. The art of doing Economics relies upon making assumptions that are not the whole story, but this is a case where the assumptions are not just incomplete or stretched, but clearly biologically impossible. Having said that, it would be possible that Junior had unhealthy habits and therefore had the same expected remaining lifespan as his father, and we could have made that assumption without quite stretching the credulity of the reader as much.

If Crusoe is in charge but cares about Junior, and weights Junior's well-being the same as his own, they share equal amounts of the beans together. To conserve the supply while awaiting rescue, the consumption per person is not as high as if Crusoe was on his own. In optimism of early rescue, they may consume at a relatively comfortable rate at first, and then become more and more cautious in consumption as the anticipated rescue fails to arrive.

We now drop the assumption of equal anticipated lifespans. Junior is likely to well out-last his father. First suppose that Crusoe and Junior were separated on arrival and each located an equal cache of tinned beans. Assuming they have the same discount rate for the future (but will be applying this to different lifespans) and the same expectations of the likelihood of being rescued, then Crusoe plans a higher daily consumption of beans than does Junior. Junior plans for a longer period of being on the island, given his longer expected remaining lifespan, and hence spreads his endowment over a longer period.

Crusoe and Junior are delighted to discover they have both survived and arrived, and that each has a stock of beans. If Crusoe and Junior are both altruistic within the family, and each values the other's utility as much as their own, and further they both have the same discount rate as already specified and the same expectations about being rescued, they can easily reach agreement on a consumption plan. Assuming, as economists typically do, that there is decreasing marginal utility (each additional spoonful of beans is less enjoyable than the previous one), a natural outcome is that each shares the same meal (which, for reasons discussed already, is likely to entail smaller bean portions over time). The portion size each day is somewhere between Crusoe's high consumption if he was on his own and Junior's low consumption if he was on his own.

If the rescue doesn't eventuate, Junior's consumption after Crusoe's demise either remains the same as just before, or increases/decreases depending upon whether or not Crusoe passed away at the expected time. As with our examination board example, Junior could have planned this in advance – if his father dies in the seventh year, he will increase his consumption; but if his father dies in the twelfth year, he will decrease his consumption. Both of these are relative to the declining pattern of consumption over time that they shared together waiting for the rescue that never arrived.

As seen from this case where there is no coordination problem, there is still unsustainability in the sense that – along the optimal consumption path – fewer beans are consumed each day. This can be because Crusoe and Junior are impatient, and want to consume the beans now rather than conserve them for the future. Alternatively, it can be because the failure of a rescue to arrive causes them to keep downgrading the likelihood of imminent rescue and, consequently, to keep adopting a more conservative and prudent approach.

In itself, this means that Junior's average consumption of beans – each day over his lifetime – is less than for Crusoe. In contrast, in the affluent country where we reside, the pace of technological progress has meant that we can easily have an increasing consumption. We don't have a fixed supply of beans; instead, our ever-improving technology means that we can produce more beans with fewer inputs each year. Younger generations will be better off than earlier generations. If that's not the case – for example, due to climate change or over-population or under-investment in developing or implementing new technologies – that is a choice that we have made. We didn't need to adopt and retain inefficient fuel technologies and we didn't need to expand the world's population.

Population growth

With the appearance of either Adam Smith or Crusoe's son Junior in our story, the population on the island has doubled. In either case, in the story so far, Crusoe is potentially delighted with the new arrival. Adam Smith is harvesting coconuts for him, in a free trade, so Crusoe has benefitted. If Crusoe didn't like the price, he could go harvest coconuts for himself, as he did before Smith showed up. There is a fear that Smith will rebel and liberate the tins of beans, but – other than that – the company is welcome.

Even though Crusoe needs to share the island's stock of tinned beans with his son, we have assumed that he values his son's well-being the same as his own – giving his son one of the scarce tins of beans gives him a derived utility just as if he had partaken of the contents himself. With the usual grace of family discussions, Junior will no doubt volunteer to do the coconut harvesting, saving Crusoe from that chore.

Adam Smith, on the other hand, would have preferred to have been the first arrival and gained the stock of tinned beans for himself. He might even resort to force if suasion about moral imperatives on sharing does not work, and therefore be a threat rather than a benefit in Crusoe's mind. With respect to his son, given that utilities are added together, Crusoe is better off with the arrival. He has less direct utility (since he has to share his bean supply), but the sum of his direct utility and that of his son may well be greater than his sole utility before. That is, the total utility of two people having a modest meal together may be greater than that of one person bingeing out alone.

In any case, GDP in total has most likely gone up, since more coconuts are being harvested. There are all sorts of issues in measuring GDP (are the tins of beans consumed counted if they are not traded, or is it like housework that doesn't enter into GDP), but let's measure GDP by consumption. There is still the weighting to be put on coconuts and beans, a non-trivial problem, but let's use the weighting given by the price paid to Adam Smith as Crusoe buys coconuts with tins of beans. That doesn't really work in the case where Crusoe gives Junior beans out of altruism so chooses how many to give him in a 'gift exchange' for whatever coconuts Junior chooses to harvest. But nonetheless, in the absence of some other factor, unless Smith or Junior are remarkably adept at harvesting coconuts, consumption per head has gone down. The fixed stock of beans has to be spread over a greater population.

Generally, in our world, when population increases, the Crusoes of the world – who hold the endowments – benefit, while those without significant endowments lose out. This is all the clearer if two John Smiths (it is a common name) arrive at the same time, and bid each other down on the rate of trade between their harvested coconuts and Crusoe's endowment of beans.

Of course, with two John Smiths, Crusoe will lie awake at night in ever greater fear of a revolution that redistributes his stock of tinned beans. In a democracy, the two John Smiths will simply out-vote the single Robinson Crusoe and introduce a 'wealth tax'. The advantage to Crusoe is that he need not spend sleepless nights worried about protecting his property rights. The politics of the last few decades (post Reagan and Thatcher) show, however, that those with high endowments will engage in robust efforts to maintain their wealth and pass it on to their children. Milton Friedman (1962) sought to have us believe that capitalism and freedom went together. But recent events – such as the capitulation of Apple and Google to Russian despotism (see Troianovski and Satariano, 2021) to the storming of the Capitol on 6 January 2021 – show the extent to which the well-off will seek to protect their endowments.

The fall of the coconuts

Due to investment in human and physical capital, and a remarkable rate of technological progress (perhaps, as Mazucatto [2013] argues, largely ascribable to the impact of governments and not so much to capitalism), the post-Second World War US and UK economies are ones of affluence. There is more than enough to go around such that no one need face poverty – it is a political choice. In the example we have given, Crusoe and his compatriots can always harvest coconuts and survive. Some other countries in the world are not so fortunate – whether this is due to lingering impacts of colonialism that have never been rooted out, to unrelated poor governance and corruption, or to excessive population growth, is beyond our remit. The climate crisis entails that even well-off countries may find themselves no longer reliably affluent, while less well-off countries (particularly if they are at sea level) may find themselves no longer in existence.

Consider how Crusoe's world might inform a modern-day climate crisis. Either because they were never there, or there was a blight, or Crusoe in a mood of optimism turned the palms into a hut and furniture, or burnt the wood over time to try to attract the attention of a passing ship, like the signal fire in *The Lord of the Flies* (Golding, 1954), we shift assumptions to an island where there are no coconuts. It doesn't matter which of the reasons given were the case, since bygones are bygones. But Crusoe now accepts that his life depends upon the tins of beans as the only source of food.

It may be that the supply is sufficient such that, even if he is never rescued and lives a long natural life on the island, there will be enough tins to see him through. This may require some degree of restraint, or it may be that he can consume to satiation. But even in this relatively benign state of affairs, Crusoe may end up in an 'extinction equilibrium', where he doesn't show sufficient prudence to ward off eventual starvation: 'Having perceived that my bread had been low a great while, I now took a survey of it, and reduced myself to one biscuit-cake a day, which made my heart very heavy' (Defoe, 1938: 120).

The main factors in whether or not that outcome eventuates are Crusoe's discount rate, satiation levels, risk-aversion and optimism. If Crusoe discounts the future a lot, he indulges himself today and faces the problem of an empty cupboard in a future year. If he is by nature abstemious, that is less likely to occur. Crusoe calculates the likelihood of rescue and, even if he is reasonably confident of being rescued within a decade, he has to decide how to allow for risk. Finally, Crusoe has little objective basis for determining the probability of being rescued in a given year. It is therefore not irrational for him to have almost any initial estimate, no matter how optimistic.

If he was risk-averse, it would however be natural for him to adopt a 'max-min' approach to his decision-making, trying in effect to minimize the chance of starvation. We have seen this in various national responses to the pandemic. New Zealand adopted the aggressive approach of seeking to go for zero COVID, which China persisted with until it became impossible, while the UK at an early stage sought to find ways of living with the virus. For different reasons, both the extremes of the UK and China were risky. The UK opened up and decided to 'live with the virus' before it was known the potential effects (and indeed, a more virulent strain still cannot be ruled out). China failed to prepare for its late exit from zero COVID by effective vaccination.

The overall point is that there is nothing irrational in Crusoe having a happy life despite the risk he will at some point die of starvation, in the same way as a smoker might continue to smoke or a drug addict continue on that pathway. There is no obvious reason why we should feel that we know better than Crusoe about his preferences, or impose our moral and ethical judgements upon him, as long as he is living in isolation, at least while we have our economics textbooks open in front of us. If Crusoe consumes at a rate that depends at some point on rescue to avoid eventual likely starvation, then his consumption path is unsustainable and risks extinction, but it is his choice.

In fact, Crusoe did quite the opposite – expecting to remain on the island until his passing:

> I carefully saved the ears of this corn, you may be sure, in their season, which was about the end of June; and, laying up every corn, I resolved to sow them all again; hoping, in time, to have some quantity sufficient to supply me with bread. But it was not till the fourth year that I could allow myself the least grain of corn to eat, and even then but sparingly. (Defoe, 1938: 115)

Extinction equilibrium

But Crusoe is not living alone, and decisions made about the consumption of the tinned beans impact on the others. The most interesting cases, for our purposes, involve generations, either Junior or perhaps Junior and another younger person, who is of no relation.

Return to the multi-generational family where Crusoe and Junior are living together and contemplate their survival (or otherwise) strategy. There are now a lot of possible outcomes where Crusoe and Junior have a life of plentiful consumption, but at some time well into the future, Junior dies of starvation. If both are altruistic – so the sum of their discounted lifetime utilities determines the best choice – then a sufficiently high discount rate may mandate that outcome. That was a possibility when Crusoe was on his own, his younger self had a pleasant life at the expense of his elder self, in the same way that individuals today may fail to save sufficiently for a decent standard of living in retirement. But here the cost is eventually borne by the younger generation.

As within-family altruism fades, the chances that Crusoe and Junior will agree on a consumption strategy decline. Crusoe will more and more weight his own lifetime consumption utility in coming to a view, while Junior will similarly weight the discounted utility to be gained over his longer horizon. If the older generation has control of the bean supply, there will be – from Junior's point of view – over-consumption and eventual extinction.

At an Extinction Rebellion event, the demographics are disproportionately older boomers and younger zoomers, with less apparent participation by those in the middle Generation X. This may be because the latter are in full-time work so cannot easily take the day off, and they may also have a greater potential loss due to being arrested. Another innocuous possibility is the general observation in any extended family gathering that grandparents and grandchildren bond, having a high degree of mutual care but not constrained by the parent–child roles.

But a different explanation for the preponderance of grandparents and grandchildren at the demonstration is that their positions on the life cycle may cause a convergence in views on what is optimal. Given their limited remaining life, so that current consumption of beans (across all the generations) is unlikely to dent stocks to the point of extinction, members of the older generation may be more focused upon the future of humanity. For the young, given their reliance upon the future for lifetime happiness, they similarly project decades out.

Family values and extinction

One might expect Extinction Rebellion events to be widely populated by believers in family values. Civil rights marches in the US in the 1960s relied upon churches and 'people of faith'. Part of why non-violence was an effective tactic was that it allowed ministers of all faiths to participate in the struggle, and to call upon other religious leaders and followers. While 'family values' is not synonymous with religion, those extolling the concept often are associated with organized religions. Why aren't these people in the forefront of the fight for the future?

Parents who put their children's future above their own (going even beyond the altruism level discussed so far) should be demonstrating, or indeed as their anger rises, rioting, not over the loss by their preferred candidate for president, but against the major oil companies and others contributing to global warming. But the mystery is solved by taking the term 'family values' as meaning precisely what it says. It is not saying that it values the well-being of the children, but of the 'family'.

As described by Seth Dowland (2009: 629), 'opposition to abortion, feminism, and gay rights constituted the heart of family values'. To see the difference clearly, under a child first approach, Crusoe would go hungry to ensure that Junior had tins of beans long after Crusoe's own demise. Under 'family values', it is the family dinner that takes precedence so Junior's survival in the future gains no weight at all.

Even more extreme examples are found in some other cultures, including the Orwellian doublespeak terminology of 'honour killings' of family members. A child is murdered simply because the child found love outside the family's preferred circle.

Another explanation for why there is, to date, less rebellion over potential extinction lies in the idea that Crusoe can protect Junior even as others of Junior's generation starve. Suppose that Crusoe shares the island with Junior and another young person of Junior's generation, whom we might call 'Spare'. Crusoe may have complete altruism with respect to Junior, weighting his well-being the same as his own. Further, Crusoe is not without human feelings in general, and in the early years (when he still hopes for rescue) willingly invites Spare to the family dinner on an equal basis. But over time, as the tins become depleted and Crusoe can see that Junior's future is being imperilled, Spare may find that his portions grow smaller and smaller.

Identity

If we had arrived on the island with Crusoe, and he was optimistic about rescue and we were pessimistic, only time would tell in validating one view or the other. Even then, he could have been right about the underlying probability of rescue but still we might be waiting on the island a decade later, because we were unlucky. In any case, if we each had our own supply of beans, Crusoe would be consuming away while we displayed prudence.

There has now become a mantra of 'follow the science' which ironically gets quoted on both sides of an issue. Usually, as in the example just given, the 'facts' are not totally clear. We will never know if Crusoe's optimism or our pessimism was right. In economics, one equilibrium or another can be sustained just because the initial beliefs – here, the probability of rescue – can never be proven or disproven.

Sometimes, however, the science seems clear and rational individuals can only come to a common conclusion, based upon the science. Vaccinations for COVID, at the time of writing (and it is in the nature of scientific analysis that it can change as new data are observed), have for most individuals (with the exception of younger people) a clear balance – based only upon their individual self-interest – in favour. The possibility of getting severe COVID, being hospitalized and potentially dying, falls so dramatically with individual vaccination that it is hard to see how anyone could rationally decline the offer. Having said that, preferences can be anything, so it is legitimate in economic analysis for someone to say, "I know the vaccine works, I know there are limited side effects, I know that on a calculation of health I would be a damn fool not to get vaccinated, but I have an aesthetic distaste of vaccination, so I'm not getting jabbed".

Those same people are often demanding access to expensive and supply-constrained experimental anti-viral treatments when they fall seriously ill with the disease. Their aesthetic objection to the vaccine (as new, rushed and therefore not fully tested with regard to long-term effects) is therefore not a general one to new, rushed and therefore not fully tested medical treatments. Indeed, as seen in the fads for ivermectin and the earlier push to hydroxychloroquine, individuals who identify with some groups are happy to prefer clearly unsupported alternatives to vaccination.

An economist would observe that, in part, the suboptimal behaviour arises because the pricing structure encourages 'moral hazard' – those who chose not to get vaccinated (at a cost of about £20) and instead be treated (at a cost in the thousands) if they get a serious manifestation of COVID are not bearing the costs of their decision. Someone who becomes hospitalized is generally covered in the US by their medical insurance (and, in the UK, by the NHS). This led Delta Airlines, for example, to impose a $200 monthly health insurance surcharge on unvaccinated staff, require such staff to be tested weekly, remove their pandemic pay insurance, and set up a large vaccination site. United Airlines, rather more directly, simply required employees to be vaccinated. In the last chapter, we will come back to which sort of policies make the most sense.

Even with moral hazard of the sort described, it's hard to see why a rational individual would not get the vaccine. This suggests that some form of 'identity' motivation is in play (see Akerlof and Kranton, 2010). The irony of left-wing and right-wing anti-vaxxers coming together (see Higgins, 2021) could be viewed as a repetition of the old adage that politics is really a circle, and left-wingers and right-wingers have more in common than either does with centrist viewpoints. But once something becomes part of an identity (either hipsters in Shoreditch or Trump supporters in Florida) it is hard to argue against, as in Berman's 2020 book *Anti-Vaxxers.*

Everything is scripted

There is one sense in which we could have some sympathy for the consistency of some anti-vaxxers. Let us suppose counter-factually that science had shown that in general vaccinations were a bad thing, causing more side effects than potential benefits. A new vaccine then comes along, and – without doing intensive study – anti-vaxxers simply applied their general beliefs to the new vaccine. This is of course what those of us who favour vaccination as the solution to epidemics do, in reverse.

This could be explained as Bayesian statistics, which begin with someone's prior belief and then propose a rule for updating as new evidence accrues. In the case of the island, Crusoe, Junior, Adam Smith and even Thomas Bayes, were he to join this motley crew, have very little basis for a belief on the likelihood of rescue. There may be anecdotal evidence – Crusoe had spent considerable time on board ship, and had some basis for judging whether or not rescues were common or rare. As we have described above, at a certain point, Crusoe recalibrated and cut his consumption of his scarce initial supplies.

Unfortunately, Google search was not available on the island, and neither Crusoe nor (under our usual stereotypes) the more computer-savvy Junior would be able to look up the number of shipwrecked individuals and the rate of rescue. Even if he could, the starting point on determining how seriously to conserve the endowment (whether it is tins of beans or the Amazon rainforest) becomes largely a matter of conjecture.

Generally, political parties, groups and individuals follow scripts. Quite simply, life would be extremely complicated if we had to consider everything we do and optimize (particularly if we optimize taking account of all the long-term implications). Instead, we revert on most occasions to a script. "How are you?" "I'm great, thanks." We only deviate from the script when it's important to do so. There are rules to guide us on almost everything – the 'rule of 85' for age of retirement, or the '4% rule' for how much of your pension to withdraw and spend each year. The 'rule of 110' tells you how much of your pension fund to put in stocks.

Getting people off the script is hard to do. Civil rights demonstrations served the role of challenging people. Saying that you were fine with Black people getting jobs, just not at your place of employment, or living in nice houses, just not in your neighbourhood, was part of the script until it was aggressively (if, by and large, peacefully) challenged over time. 'State's rights' were a 'rule' that allowed segregation to persist in the US. Saying that you didn't care about whether someone was homosexual, but why did they have to shove their sexuality in your face, was part of the script until it was aggressively (if, by and large, peacefully) challenged over time. Currently, trans people are challenging traditional feminists who want to define gender in birth biological terms.

There has been a vogue for promoting 'nudge' – rather than brute force government policies or aggressive (if, by and large, peaceful) protesting – as a way of dealing with problems we face as a society and in the world at large. It is interesting to see that, when push comes to shove, even one of the originators of 'nudge', Richard Thaler (2021), stresses the limitations on something with as high a level of externalities (if you don't get vaccinated, I am more likely to get COVID) and public health implications as vaccination.

But in a world where decision-making is concentrated, where there is a high discount rate and over-consumption of scarce resources (notably the environment), extinction equilibrium has to be challenged aggressively.

The roles of science and policy in preventing extinction equilibrium

Prior beliefs can be almost anything. People can look up and see that the Sun is revolving around the Earth. Phlogiston can explain numerous properties observed of combustion. Vaccination causes autism. The role of science (including economics) is to be clear in shooting down extreme theories – whether they be 'trickle-down' tax cuts for the rich, unfettered free trade or zero interest monetary policies, or the economic 'need' for population growth – that have instead somehow become the conventional wisdom of our time.

Crusoe – if he lived on an island that could, with prudence, provide for his needs for his lifetime – only faced extinction before his time if he was unduly optimistic about rescue, unduly unlucky, or had a high time discount rate such that he was prepared to die of starvation in return for a comfortable interim period (if he was unlucky enough not to be rescued in time). Science would only have a role in the first, providing realistic estimates to Crusoe of his objective probabilities of being rescued.

If Crusoe was living on his own, and his actions had no implications for others, it is hard to see why policy interventions (if somehow a government could intervene) would be desirable. Our concept of individual liberty by and large allows Crusoe to make poor life choices, provided that others do not have to pick up the pieces.

Once we introduce others onto the island – particularly if they are of different generations – the problem changes dramatically. Economics does not judge outcomes that meet the criterion of Pareto-efficiency. This technical term means that a given production and distribution allocation is 'efficient' if no one (no matter how poor) can be made better off without making someone else (no matter how rich) worse off. In effect, we put distributional issues to the political – rather than economic – sphere.

An outcome where Crusoe has property rights and uses them to maximize his utility while allowing the others to starve, either during or after his own natural passing, can be Pareto-efficient. If Crusoe cares about his children, but not those of others, and there is a mechanism by which he can protect them, it can be Pareto-efficient for other people's children to starve in the future.

Legacy admissions to US universities, the handing on of social class advantages to children in the UK (whether or not privately educated), helping your child with a deposit to buy a house and with childcare costs, are in one sense about a lack of social mobility and the unequal distribution of income. But insofar as they also mean that we are not all in this together, it means that we may fail to adopt policies vital to our well-being and even our survival.

I was taking the vaporetto from Marco Polo Airport to Venice City Centre, and got into chatting with a successful 'creative'. He was visiting his son, for whom he had arranged an internship in the arts through his connections. As he put it, he 'didn't want his son spending all summer on the sofa watching *Friends* episodes'. But who does?

This anecdote encompasses two of the ways in which the better-off can guide the future for their children. One is by pulling strings and finding opportunities. Another is making sure that their children take those opportunities. But we didn't talk – in our vaporetto ride – about a third, and important, safety net for children from better-off backgrounds. Provided it isn't too heinous a deed (and usually even then), parents seek to avoid their children getting a criminal record with its lifelong implications. Even the Trump administration enacted the *First Step Act*, which built upon the *Fair Sentencing Act*, to remove some of these class disparities in reducing the implications of bad decisions.

It is perhaps no surprise that the parents who are most influential in decision-making for our society think they can protect their children from the rising tides. It is no surprise that – whatever their explicit politics, on the left or right – they seek to do just that. Science and economics say that they are, in the current context, just wrong, they are holding first- and second-class tickets on the *Titanic*.

4

The Fed Did It

Zero interest rates

The (attempted) murder weapon was monetary policy. The culprit was the Fed. The location was everywhere.

We now turn to the role that monetary policy has played in creating the current generational dilemmas. Quite simply, the zero interest rate policy of the last decades created a consumption boom that borrowed from the future.

It's hard to overestimate the role low or zero interest rates have had on intergenerational welfare. The interest rate, as Chancellor (2022) points out right from the title of his book, is *The Price of Time*. It connects the world of future generations – who by definition live in a future time – with the current generation. As Sternberg (2019: 136) observes: 'Given the negative consequences of ultralow interest rates and quantitative easing for Millennials, the obvious solution would seem to be to return monetary policy to something closer to normal.' Since he wrote his book, we have had the pandemic and central banks have doubled down on lower interest rates. The post-pandemic inflation, rather than equity concerns both within and across generations, has led to some – at least temporary – reversal of the policy. For these reasons, it will be impossible to talk about generations without a couple of chapters on monetary policy, not always everyone's subject of choice. Should we follow Sternberg's advice and 'return … to normal'?

A thesis of this book is that, for all the talk of unique challenges and extraordinary responses, for all the credit given to innovations in macroeconomics and monetary policy, very little that happened from 1980 to the time of writing is inconsistent with the economics framework from the early 1980s. It's like a car with 160 mph on the speedometer – in a country with a speed limit of 70 mph, the full capabilities of the car (and the no doubt lesser capabilities of the driver) will never be observed. The zero interest rate world – and its supporting cast of quantitative easing, forward guidance and (in Japan) yield curve control – was always on the monetary map, it's just that sailors were too cautious to go there. The map was clearly marked, 'there be monsters there'. It just needed a whispered 'Weimar Republic' to stop a central bank in its tracks of monetary expansion.

What differed in the response to the 2007/08 financial crisis and the 2020–22 pandemic, compared to past episodes of monetary policy, was not an innovation in monetary theory but the removal of the guardrails that constrained central bank behaviour. It may be that institutional memory had faded – for example, the European Central Bank was not, as some had feared and others positively anticipated, a wider version of the very hawkish Bundesbank. Economists may have recovered their nerve from the traumas of the stagflation of the 1970s and early 1980s but may have moved from fear of action to fear of missing out. As in the title of Ben Bernanke's (2015c) book, central banks developed 'the courage to act'. Perhaps instead, one could update Ronald Reagan's joke about too much government interference in the economy, to take account of the impacts upon future generations: 'I'm from the Fed, and I'm here to help.'

Ben Bernanke's (2002) remarks to honour Milton Friedman end with: 'Regarding the Great Depression. You're right, we did it. We're very sorry. But thanks to you, we won't do it again.' It somehow became conventional wisdom that, as Friedman had claimed, the poor policy of the Fed led to the severity of the Great Depression, and the Fed's undue haste in withdrawing support led to the 1936 relapse. As we've observed, it's difficult in economics to be sure exactly what is happening today. It's even more difficult going back into history and coming to a definitive answer as to what happened. Looking just at interest rates, the 1930s' Fed was extraordinarily expansive – on that metric, it's hard to see what more the Fed could have done. Bernanke's own research in 1983 therefore concentrated upon 'Non-monetary effects of the financial crisis in the propagation of the Great Depression'. As has been observed, this research provided the intellectual framework for the policy responses (not just interest rates but bailing out the banks) to the Great Recession in 2007, when Bernanke was Chair of the Fed. Rarely has an academic work in economics had that level of 'impact' on the real economy, and it is not surprising that Bernanke received the Nobel Prize in 2022 for his 1980s' research.

The same data from the past (both in the 1920s and the 2000s) can be interpreted in opposite ways. A minority of economists (including this author) think that the Fed did likely cause the Great Depression, not because of its actions in 1929 and the 1930s, but by blowing up and blowing up the 1920s' bubble which finally burst. Those economists conclude that the modern Fed did exactly the same, showing a remarkable failure to learn from history that is worthy of a 'time travelling' *Twilight Zone* episode. Given the chance to go back in history and try to change the outcomes, President Lincoln is still nonetheless assassinated. The millennial Fed, just as the 1920s' Fed, kept feeding the boom and – as is the historical wont of bubbles – it burst. The Fed then blew up the bubble again and – with the pandemic – again. The current monetary problem is well beyond the post-pandemic inflation. It involves what interest rates to set for the medium term (and to convey to the markets through 'forward guidance'). Even today, the Fed 'plot diagram' shows rates peaking at about current levels of 5.5% and then falling back towards 2.5%.

Even if these low interest rates were sustainable over the medium term, they remain unfair to younger generations seeking to buy a house, build up a pension or survive a climate catastrophe. It may seem ironic, but lowered interest rates do not help the first-time buyer seeking a mortgage, since they drive up asset prices (which we discuss in the next chapter on the everything bubble) faster than the savings on a starter mortgage. Further, the beneficiaries of low interest rates are primarily those with the best credit situation (having, for example, a large percentage of the house price to put up in cash), the better-off members of older generations. Others are having to take out credit card debt at 20% or more, and for them the notional zero interest rate is irrelevant.

Later in this chapter, we will consider why central banks were not and are not unduly worried by the extreme monetary policy undertaken since the millennium. To give a couple of spoilers, they thought that inflation would be the canary in the coalmine and they would get plenty of warning if monetary policy needed to be tightened. But further, by introducing the payment of interest on bank deposits with the Fed and the Bank of England, they thought they had a quick, simple method of tightening policy should the need arise. And they did – they could raise rates in the economy to 10% or 15% in the blink of an eye. But what they failed to do was institute the monetary equivalent of an 'automatic braking system' as used on trains for well over a century. Not surprisingly, the central banks have found it easier to lower interest rates than to raise them.

What happened in responding to the financial crisis crossed ideological lines. In the Great Recession, while right-wingers did not like the high government deficits, and left-wingers did not like the bailouts to the wealthy, very few individuals or groups seemed to oppose the zero interest rate policies or the 'too big to fail' bailouts for large financial institutions. 'Occupy Wall Street' very quickly failed as a political movement, running for 59 days, shorter than most Broadway openings. Boomers wanted their asset values protected, and millennials didn't want to lose their jobs. Zoomers weren't at the table.

The discount rate, the interest rate and natural guardrails

The role of the interest rate in the economy is complex, and it is not necessarily the case that low interest rates benefit the current generation at the expense of the future. If the policies of the last four decades had focused upon creating an investment boom rather than a consumption boom, a low interest rate might indeed have been a boon for the future. Electric cars and a nationwide charging grid, free high-speed broadband for all, non-polluting manufacturing and electricity generation, high-speed rail, energy-efficient housing in ample supply in the desired locations, top quality education and health care for all could have left the country, and particularly future generations, in a great position now. That the governments of the day went for consumption-boosting tax cuts rather than infrastructure investment was a political choice. What is perhaps less clear is why firms, instead of boosting investment, gave back their high profits in the forms of share buybacks and buying other firms (with all the antitrust implications for pricing and supply). The zero interest monetary policy might have had very different effects in a different policy framework.

But back to the real world, ironically we can see what actually happened in our usual way, by telling a fictional story. Let's return to Robinson Crusoe and his problem in deciding how much to consume over time. We have already used the terminology 'discount rate' for Robinson Crusoe's weighting of the future against the present. A lower 'discount rate' means that Crusoe cares more about the future, relative to the present, than if the 'discount rate' was higher. But it's important to distinguish the 'discount rate' – how Crusoe views the future – from the 'interest rate' – the rate at which Crusoe would be able to borrow and lend if there was a bank on the island. The 'discount rate' is about Crusoe's philosophy, the 'interest rate' is about the marketplace. A low 'discount rate' encourages Crusoe to save for the future, a low 'interest rate' encourages him to borrow from the future.

To make the generational issues clear, suppose that Crusoe and his son Junior do not overlap in time. Crusoe has given up all hope of being rescued, expects with a fair degree of confidence to pass away from natural causes in 40 years, after which Junior will begin to live for 40 years. This is one of our regular reminders that everything in economics begins with the assumptions made by the particular economist in question and which are chosen to make the storytelling as clear as possible, rather than for their immediate plausibility.

There are two different reasons why Crusoe might 'discount' Junior's future. One is that Crusoe does not value Junior's well-being as much as his own. The other is just that Junior's life will be in the distant future, and Crusoe might lack the imagination to really envisage how his actions now impact on the future. The latter has much in common with people failing to save for their retirement, not because they want to be impoverished in old age, but because they simply lack the foresight to prepare sufficiently with ample pensions.

This book is in large part about – annoyingly, no doubt, to any currently conventional economists that stray into its ambit – the value of guardrails.

One guardrail in Crusoe's world is that only so many coconuts grow in a season. Crusoe can consume that amount (plus any he has saved from past years), but he cannot consume today coconuts that will only grow in 40 years' time. If there are 100 coconuts produced by the trees a year, that limits Crusoe's consumption. If that is the rate of production in 40 years, then Crusoe and Junior have the same consumption levels.

If Crusoe has a positive discount rate – meaning he discounts the future compared to today – then he is not overjoyed at this outcome. He would like to consume more coconuts now, at the expense of Junior's future consumption. But he has no physical way of doing so. In our world, the current generation can increase consumption by degrading the environment – cutting down the Amazon rainforest to rear cattle. To repeat, guardrails are good.

Now suppose that a trader lands on the island. Let's call him China. China arrives with a boat full of oranges and proposes to trade with Crusoe, oranges for coconuts, at a rate of exchange China determines. The 'free trade' argument invariably cited by economists is that – whatever rate of exchange (or price) quoted by China, Crusoe benefits by trade. This is because, at the quoted price, Crusoe can choose not to trade. If Crusoe chooses to trade, he must be better off than by not trading, which was his initial position. Consequently, the economist concludes, free trade must be good. In this particular case, China actually offered – following 'mercantilist' approaches – to provide its export goods at a very low price in order to expand its sales abroad. By conventional economics, this is even better for Crusoe!

Since free trade has involved the opium wars – forcing China to allow the British to import opium into China – slavery, dangerous child labour and massive pollution, there may be other arguments as to why it needs to be controlled ('guardrails', again). But your conventional economist is remarkably able to set those aside and extol the virtues of free trade. The 'free traders' of our time, as in past times, have an extraordinary agility on these issues not unlike those who argued against sporting boycotts (of, for example, apartheid South Africa) on the grounds that 'sport is above politics'.

In fact (or in our fictional story), China proposed a different deal to Crusoe. It proposed to give him more coconuts today than his island naturally produced, in return for his son's harvest of coconuts in the future. In the real world of the 20th century, Crusoe had already been producing electronics, household appliances, shoes and clothing, so the trade with China was not for new goods that Crusoe could not supply for himself. In the fictional world, Crusoe could either have more leisure – let his home supply of coconuts dry out unharvested – or just have more coconuts in total. This would work if Crusoe issued IOUs that his son would have to pay back in the future. In the real world, Crusoe could take more leisure or produce more service goods, shutting down his factories, and import manufactured goods from China. China would run a trade surplus and acquire real and financial assets in return.

According to the Office of the US Trade Representative, in 2020 the US exported $124.5 billion of goods to China and imported $434.7 billion, a goods trade deficit of $310.3 billion. The US exported services to China of $40.4 billion and imported services of $15.6 billion. Adding all this up, the US ran a deficit of $285.5 billion. This is financed by net borrowing from China (taking account of actual direct investment in both directions, where the US invested $310.3 billion and China invested $38 billion). The US Treasury reports that China holds $870 billion in US Treasury debt.

In Robinson Crusoe's world, China would tell him that he could have 100 coconuts a year from China, and that his son would have to repay the coconuts with accrued interest. The lower the interest rate, the more attractive this deal, assuming that Crusoe cares at all about his son's well-being. Assuming that the debt is written in terms of coconuts to be repaid, the story is pretty simple. A mercantilist China sets a very low interest rate to encourage Crusoe to buy coconuts today. Unfortunately, Crusoe has landed his son with a massive debt to repay and – in the worst case – actual extinction as all the coconuts are shipped away.

Who sets the interest rate?

In the modern world economy (simplified but perhaps not distorted in our Crusoe example), who is setting interest rates? Is it China? Or, as all the press coverage would indicate, the Federal Reserve? The Federal Reserve controls the reserve currency for the world, the US dollar. When the world went off the gold standard and fixed exchange rates in 1971, the Fed was essentially given control of world monetary policy. If other countries sought to set a different interest rate than that on the dollar, they could expect severe inflows and outflows from their currency due to the 'carry trade'. If they did not want their currency to sharply decline (Japan) or increase in value (Switzerland), they had to respect the views of the Fed. For this reason, our discussion for the time being will focus upon the US and the Federal Reserve.

According to Ben Bernanke (2015b), the Chair of the Fed during the financial crisis, it is however actually China that sets the interest rate:

> My conclusion was that a global excess of desired saving over desired investment, emanating in large part from China and other Asian emerging market economies and oil producers like Saudi Arabia, was a major reason for low global interest rates. I argued that the flow of global saving into the United States helped to explain the 'conundrum' (to use Alan Greenspan's term) of persistently low longer-term interest rates in the mid-2000's while the Fed was raising short-term rates.

As in our stylized Robinson Crusoe economy, China offers goods today to be repaid tomorrow at a very low interest rate, and the United States – certainly the US Fed – is unable to decline this offer. The US runs a trade deficit financed by bonds (and other investments) acquired by China. Bernanke is not perhaps suggesting that, were the Fed not to accept the offer, China would engage in the opium wars in reverse, and send gunboats to US and UK ports forcing us to accept their manufactured goods on credit. Instead, he seems to think that US monetary policy cannot offset this equilibrium of low long-term interest rates arising from China wanting to sell manufactured goods and save the proceeds – a 'global savings glut'.

In this conventional worldview, the Fed deserves a lot of credit for saving the world economy from the financial crisis. Suppose that due to the 'global savings glut' we are already at near zero interest rates. Now there is a negative shock due to the financial bubble bursting, notably in the housing market, or due to a pandemic. Aggregate demand falls, so the Fed would like to use monetary policy to offset this effect that might lead to another Great Depression. The conventional view is that the central banks did the near impossible by doing 'whatever it takes' through extreme monetary policy (lowering short-term interest rates to zero or below) and unconventional policies (purchase of unusual assets other than government bonds, forward guidance, and quantitative easing). They were aided by governments taking extremely expansionary fiscal policies.

The view in this book is that the equilibria we see are either consciously chosen, or consciously not unchosen, and that it is wrong to focus upon 'the slings and arrows of outrageous fortune'. An alternative equilibrium existed with higher interest rates, a lower government and trade deficit and slower monetary growth. If there was inadequate aggregate demand, fiscal policies to encourage needed investment in the green economy would have filled the gap. As every first-year economics student is taught, there is a 'balanced budget multiplier' where the government deficit can be cut in an expansionary way (by taxing those with high incomes and wealth, and consequently lower marginal propensities to consume). We will later discuss how restoration of the prohibition on companies buying back their own shares, and similar policies, would have redirected the economy towards greater investment.

Why was a low interest rate, low tax on the well-off and corporations, high asset price, gig economy, low investment and low productivity economy chosen in the US and the UK? The losers from the policy – working people who rented rather than owned their house, or owned a house in low-price areas of the country rather than expensive urban centres, as well as future generations – were simply not at the table when the decisions were made.

The exploding money supply

Despite a lot of new terminology (much of which may be renaming existing concepts), it's not clear that much has positively changed in our understanding of macroeconomics since the 1980s. For a detailed but hopefully accessible description of the state of monetary and macroeconomic theory in the 1980s, have a look at my book, *The New Keynesian Economics* (Frank, 1986). There were two keystone features of Keynesian economics that might perhaps be recalled at this point. One is the Keynesian view of money – it was not that 'money didn't matter', but that 'not only money mattered'. A balanced portfolio of monetary and fiscal policy worked best, not to have undue reliance (as might be argued has been the case for the last 40 years) on monetary policy alone and the 'resilience of the American consumer'. As we've just argued, the policies would have looked very different if supported by an investment-focused fiscal and financial policy. The other keystone view is that the purpose of policy is to facilitate and smooth adjustments, not prevent them. It was never intended by traditional Keynesians that the Federal Reserve or the Bank of England should avoid recessions by an ever-exploding money supply.

We've gotten slightly ahead of ourselves, since we're talking about money without actually having defined the term. For our purposes, let's look at the 'monetary base', alternatively called 'high-powered money'. This is composed of currency (the Federal Reserve determines how much to print) and bank reserves held at the Fed. The idea is that these are incredibly liquid assets in different ways. One is that I can, within five minutes, go to the local shops and spend the currency in my wallet. Banks can take their deposits with the Fed and immediately loan them out to waiting applicants, or the banks can use them to buy other financial assets. Think of this as a reservoir of water – it's just there and can easily flow (or flood) if the taps are opened (or if the dam bursts).

Since the millennium the money supply was growing at high rates, but it truly exploded during the financial crisis and again during the pandemic. Very little of this was drained off during the period between the two events.

The US monetary base in December 2023 was $5,827 billion, made up of currency at $2,333 billion and bank reserves of $3,491 billion (see Figure 4.1). This is compared to a US GDP of about $28 trillion, and is extreme by historical standards.

Traditional monetary theory, encompassed in the 'quantity theory of money', suggests that this sort of growth will flood the economy – albeit with 'long and variable lags' – driving up prices proportionately. The five-fold increase in monetary base after the financial crisis should – by the simplest version of the theory – lead to a five-fold increase in prices in the economy – a massive amount of inflation. In fact, the outcome could well be

Figure 4.1: US monetary base

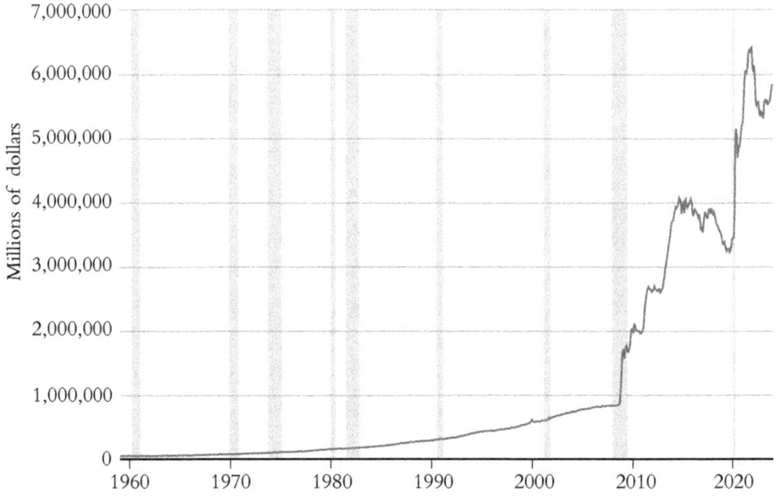

Source: Board of Governors of the Federal Reserve System (US), Monetary Base; Total [BOGMBASE]. Retrieved from FRED, Federal Reserve Bank of St Louis; https://fred.stlouis fed.org/series/BOGMBASE, 27 February 2024.

worse due to the growth in electronic money (instantaneous bank transfers by computer) over the decade. In the terminology of the quantity theory, the 'velocity of money' is expanded by the use of credit and debit cards, electronic wallets and on-line cash transfers. ATMs are everywhere (and, in the UK, usually free of charge for the withdrawal of cash), so there's a further reason not to hold currency – you can easily obtain more, 24 hours a day, seven days a week.

Keynesians emphasize the interrelationship of the money supply and interest rates. Going back to the velocity of money, this slows down if interest rates are very low (near zero). Given the opportunity cost (the interest rate gained by transferring funds to a savings account), there is no reason not to hold a lot of currency and for banks not to hold a lot of reserves with the central bank. If you deposited cash (perhaps you have several hundred pounds in your desk drawer) at the bank, you would gain essentially near zero interest – it's hardly worth going to the bank, and in any case the branches near to you have probably closed. In the same way, banks are holding large reserves at the Federal Reserve (or the Bank of England) since they would get minimal return from lending them out. Banks are further constrained by the capital and liquidity requirements arising from Basel II that encourage the holding of these safe assets.

But just as the near zero interest rates have helped keep all the money dammed up, a small hole in the dam – a modest rise in interest rates – starts to unravel everything. The velocity of money picks up since there is a gain to using it. In effect, the immense growth in the monetary base was an accident waiting to happen. The pandemic and the war in Ukraine are just the sparks that lit the fire.

As we will discuss, the central banks were not unduly worried since they think they have an ace up their sleeve by the ability to pay interest on reserves – they could keep the excess reserves held by banks dammed up. While this is true, it comes at a cost, as we will discuss. In practice, it kept the inflation from remaining at very high double-digit levels. Whether it will – at a peak interest rate of about 5.5% – bring inflation back down (to the 2% target beloved of central banks) remains to be seen.

Where did all this money come from?

There is general consensus on the source of all this money – the 'quantitative easing' engaged in by the central banks throughout the last few decades but greatly expanded during the financial crisis and the pandemic. Whether the magnitude of quantitative easing was forced upon an unwilling Fed by China or by shocks, or whether it was advisable, is a different question not answerable just by looking at the chart.

Quantitative easing is, in large part, the use of 'open market operations' wherein the central bank electronically prints money which it uses to buy government bonds (and, in recent times, other assets such as mortgages) in the market. A general rule of central banking is that they do not buy new bonds directly from the government since this would be seen as clearly funding the deficit, something central banks avoid doing too openly and always deny if questioned. It's hard to see why doing this indirectly makes much of a difference – if the government knows that the central bank will cover their back when they run deficits, they are more likely to run deficits since it won't lead to voter-alienating interest rate rises. For those who remember the short-lived experiment in Trussonomics, the government proposed to cut taxes and run substantially increased deficits, issuing bonds that the Bank of England declined to purchase, causing sharp increases in interest rates and the rapid fall of the prime minister.

The impact of open market operations is straightforward and seen in a simple supply and demand diagram for money (Figure 4.2). People economize less on money if interest rates go down.

In order to get people to hold more money, the opportunity cost of doing so – the interest rate on deposits – must go down. Put in reverse, if there are fewer bonds in the open market because the central bank has bought up a number of them, then the interest they need to pay to attract buyers goes down.

Figure 4.2: Money supply

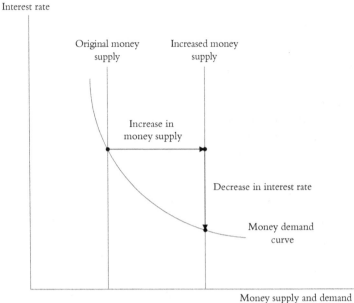

During the various stages of quantitative easing, the Bank of England bought up £895 billion of bonds (£875 billion government bonds and £20 billion corporate bonds). To put in context, total UK Government net debt was about £2.5 trillion in 2022. In a comparison that both the government and the bank would rather we didn't make, net public sector debt was £310 billion in 2002. A large proportion of the increase in debt, roughly 40%, was (coincidentally, of course) funded by the Bank of England in quantitative easing.

Why isn't the central bank afraid? Part 1, inflation targeting

An economist waking up in London or New York in 2023, having fallen asleep in 1985, would look aghast at the money supply figures – even if the economist had the foresight to consider the possibility of a 'financial crisis' (and, since they occur not infrequently, the economist would surely not be surprised by one) or even a 'pandemic' (also predictable and predicted). So why aren't the central banks quivering in their boots, while awaiting a flood of liquidity that will drown the economy in inflation?

There are two changes in the handling of monetary policy that the central banks believe – rightly or wrongly – make it different this time. One is inflation targeting. Single mandate central banks (which might be taken to include the Bank of England and the European Central Bank) have a primary responsibility to maintain price stability. Under a traditional monetary policy, this might be viewed as having an effective cap on inflation – 2% was viewed as the most inflation that could occur without frightening the horses. In that world, central banks would panic (in a good sense) if inflation topped 2%, and rush to chill down the economy.

Inflation targeting has taken that same 2% figure and viewed it as a good thing rather than a ceiling. In part, this is because of the New Keynesian economics espoused at MIT which (relying upon notions of wage rigidity that were more familiar to readers – if any still exist – of Arthur Pigou's 1933 *Theory of Unemployment* than to readers of Keynes' 1936 *General Theory* – also, if any still exist) saw inflation at moderate levels as a beneficial lubricant to the economy. The idea is that there is downward wage rigidity so the 2% inflation allows real wages to fall by all of 2% in a year. It's not clear why the economists at MIT think that a 2% wage change (which can be undone by changing benefits such as free coffee) will make a huge difference in employment at a firm, but that is their view to which – as we've pointed out many a time – there will be no empirical evidence to conclusively support or disprove. Perhaps not surprisingly, when inflation seemed to be heading above 2%, some economists saw clearly that 2% wasn't the right figure, and instead the natural target of ideal inflation was 3% or 4%. The Federal Reserve itself decided to use the personal consumption expenditures price index for this magical 2%, in preference to, for example, the CPI inflation, which tends to report a higher number, again giving a push to having modestly higher inflation. The Bank of England was given independence in 1997 and assigned a 2.5% inflation target on the Retail Price Index (RPI) which became 2% when the bank switched to the consumer price index in 2004. So apparently, it's 2% on the personal consumption expenditure (PCE) deflator that's magical in the US and the CPI in the UK.

Perhaps a stronger argument for the 2% symmetrical target – with a commitment to expansionary monetary policy below and contractionary monetary policy above – is that it serves to anchor expectations. We are unlikely to get deflation, perhaps, if everyone in the economy can be confident that the central bank will open the monetary taps in a slowdown; we are unlikely to get runaway inflation if everyone in the economy is confident that the central bank will clamp down. Since we argue in this book for guardrails, surely a commitment to achieving 2% inflation, come hell or high water, on whichever price index the national central bank has chosen, represents extremely strong guardrails?

There are two obvious problems that arise. One is whether or not the central bank can in fact attain that target, and the second is whether or not the central bank will in practice do what is necessary to attain that target. The central banks – notably the Bank of Japan – have emphasized the difficulties in reaching 2% from below. It will be ironic if they now discover the difficulties in reaching 2% from above.

The second difficulty is in whether or not the central bank, faced with inflation well above the target, will find 'the courage to act'. For the Bank of England, if inflation deviates from 2% by more than 1%, in either direction, the governor must write a letter to the chancellor of the exchequer. Strangely, the governor of the bank found this to be not an insurmountable challenge even when inflation went into double digits. In his letter of 15 December 2022, the governor observed: 'The Committee will continue to act as necessary to ensure that CPI inflation returns to the 2% target sustainably in the medium term.' As Keynes might have commented: 'In the medium term, we are all dead.'

When we discuss our proposals for money and inflation, balancing house prices and incomes for future generations, we are guided by history – in the 1960s and 1970s, central banks tightened money just enough to bring the inflation rate down a bit, but then eased when stock markets and economic conditions started to worsen. In this 'stop-go' cycle, they then tightened again once inflation rose, loosened again as soon as they could, and so on, until Paul Volcker stepped in and stopped inflation dead with extremely high interest rates.

There is no reason to think (despite all the new terminology) that the levers of monetary and fiscal policy have greatly changed in terms of the inflation and economic activity trade-offs, or that central banks and politicians have somehow become more inflation averse than in the period of bell-bottoms and long hair. It therefore seems to this author that the Fed, the Bank of England and the European Central Bank are unlikely to knock inflation dead at the first go. In the same way as film monsters need to be killed three times, and woefully appalling defeated American presidential candidates won't just go away, we are likely to see significant cumulative inflation over the next decade.

The Phillips curve

We've already presented one model of inflation, the quantity theory of money. In that model, albeit with 'long and variable lags', high-powered money eventually flows into the economy, leading to inflation. The 'long and variable lags', however, make that model somewhat less than useful for short- and even medium-term policy. The Phillips curve was used by Keynesian economists – at least until the stagflation of the 1970s – to fill the gap. Professor Phillips (1958) published evidence that low unemployment rates were associated with higher inflation rates in wages, that might reasonably be expected to feed through into prices. This is shown graphically in Figure 4.3.

Figure 4.3: The Phillips curve

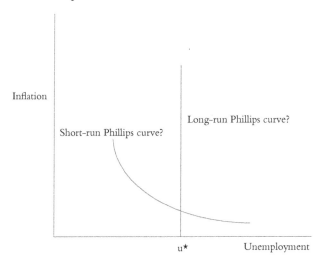

In the 1960s, traditional Keynesians viewed this as a policy trade-off. It was not inconsistent with the quantity theory in that it could be interpreted as providing the channel by which money operated. However, Milton Friedman and other monetarists argued that the 'natural rate of unemployment' u★ was the only sustainable level. In the short run, the monetary and fiscal authorities might lower unemployment, but at the cost of accelerating inflation and an eventual return to u★, albeit at a higher built-in inflation rate. That is, there was a short-run trade-off but in the long run, the Phillips curve was vertical. By the 'natural rate' model, at least as unemployment is concerned, it doesn't matter whether the Fed targets 0%, 2% or 10% inflation.

If the current relationship between the quantity theory and central bank monetary policy seems obscure, that with the Phillips curve seems absolutely clandestine. Janet Yellen, Fed Chair from 2014 to 2018, at the Brookings Institution on 3 October 2019 was more revealing than most: 'The Phillips curve has long served as the "workhorse" model of inflation and it's used by most economists, including Federal Reserve staff, to analyze and forecast inflation trends.' She argues that – perhaps because of anchored inflation expectations as we have discussed in the preceding section – the curve is now much flatter than in the past, and presents a viable and desirable trade-off where 'allowing the labor market to run hot could bring substantial benefits'. In effect, Yellen is expressing the traditional Keynesian view, only adding the suggestion that 'anchoring beliefs' has improved the trade-off from that in the 1960s and 1970s. Since Yellen was not renewed in the post of Fed Chair by Donald Trump, it is possible that her views were not fully shared by others who might be less inclined to 'run the economy hot' to benefit workers.

A worry about relying too much upon the Phillips curve is that a take-off of inflation may occur too rapidly to be an effective 'canary in the coal mine'. Experience from the 1960s and 1970s may suggest that, at a certain point when unemployment was pushed by policy to be 'too low', inflation would rapidly take off. For the US, this was typically thought to be below 4%. Hence, the 3.9% unemployment rate in December 2021 was already associated in time with inflation of 7%, well before the Russian invasion of Ukraine (February 2022).

A second worry is about the dynamics of inflation. Keynesian analysis in the 1970s had shifted from the static Phillips curve to dynamic Phillips loops (Figure 4.4).

The important point is that the return trip from high inflation back down to acceptable levels is on a less favourable road than the initial journey there. Inflation would be high during the recession period of rising unemployment – 'stagflation'.

The 'immaculate disinflation' of US inflation back down to about 3% (December 2023) without a rise in unemployment is an example of our general point that observation in itself doesn't answer questions. Inflation elsewhere – in the UK CPI inflation was at 4% in December 2023 and euro inflation was also about 3% – has shown a similar pattern. Since a significant

Figure 4.4: Phillips loops

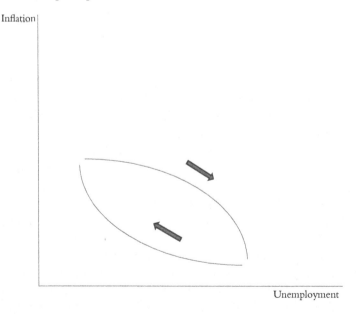

part of the inflation pattern was due to a significant rise and then reversal in oil prices (from $32 a barrel for Brent crude at the worst of the pandemic to $112 at the worst of the invasion effect back down to about $80 in the autumn of 2023), there is a large negative inflation component from oil even though – taking the period as a whole – oil has gone up significantly. Whether inflation goes up again, plateaus at 3 or 4%, or returns to the target of 2%, remains to be seen.

But the third reason is the one we have emphasized in this book. Even if the 2% inflation, zero interest rate combination was a sustainable one, is it a desirable one? Mohamed El-Erian (2023b) wrote in the *Financial Times*:

> We should do our utmost to moderate the pull of the comforting convergence narratives. Failure to do so would not only translate into a premature relaxation of the efforts needed to overcome remaining short-term challenges. It would also leave us in an even worse position to handle the secular and structural problems that face our generation and those of our children and grandchildren.

Why isn't the central bank afraid? Part 2, interest on reserves

We have described the explosive growth in the monetary base, first in response to the 2007/08 financial crisis, and again in response to the pandemic. In both events, governments adopted extremely expansionary fiscal policies. Even in between, there was a view (expressed notably by Janet Yellen) that the economy should be 'run hot' in order to benefit workers whose real wages have sharply fallen during the last few decades. Both traditional 1960s/70s monetarists, and their Keynesian contemporaries, might have worried about either the growth in money or the potentially dangerous points reached on the Phillips curve. Why weren't the central banks worried? One answer is that inflation targeting might have improved the trade-offs facing the economy. The other is that by paying interest on reserves, the central banks had a rapid and powerful tool to dam up money, raise interest rates and put the brakes on the economy.

The Federal Reserve Bank in 2006 gained the authority to start paying interest on the reserves deposited by commercial banks at the Fed. In 2008, the Fed began paying interest. The Bank of England began paying interest on reserves in 2006. This gives the central banks considerable direct control on interest rates, rather than the indirect routes through open market operations and other financial market interventions. In particular, they can easily and quickly raise interest rates to stop any unexpected inflation that goes above the 2% target.

UK banks are required to hold 12.5% reserves against short-term liabilities. The US Federal Reserve eliminated the reserve requirement in 2020. Banking regulation in both countries still requires capital and liquidity constraints to be met. Partially as a result, banks hold very large 'excess reserves'. British banks hold about £1 trillion of reserves at the Bank of England. US banks hold about $3 trillion of reserves at the Fed. These reserves are part of the 'high-powered money' or 'monetary base' in the two economies.

The Bank of England in December 2023 is paying 5.25% bank rate on reserves. The Federal Reserve is paying 5.4%. These are considerable sums of interest – the £1 trillion reserves at the Bank of England translate into payments to banks of £50 billion out of a total debt interest service for the UK Government estimated in 2022 to be £120 billion. These interest payments, while initially made by the central bank, are eventually covered by the Treasury. The Treasury either receives a cheque from the Bank of England, or pays a cheque to the Bank, to receive or pay the profits/loss of the Bank. During the period of quantitative easing, central banks made large profits – they held as an asset government bonds with significant interest rates, and held as a liability bank reserves with low interest rates. As interest rates in the economy have risen, the central bank's holdings of government bonds still pay roughly the same fixed interest rate, but the interest it pays on reserves has gone up substantially. Not surprisingly, there have been calls to stop this transfer from the taxpayer to the banks.

The central banks, in creating all that high-powered money through quantitative easing, did not have to worry – or so they thought – about the money flooding into the economy. The central bank could dam it up at any time by paying a high interest rate on the reserves. In effect, the central banks knew that – by paying suitable interest rates on reserves – they had a very effective brake on the economy. If inflation started to take off, interest rates could quickly jump to whatever level the bank thought desirable.

But having a very effective brake doesn't mean that it will be used. This is why inflation targeting did not really set guardrails at all – the central banks, although 'independent', are still part of the political process. As the rate of interest rises sharply, the Treasury will have to write large cheques to the Bank of England to cover the high interest rate on the reserves. Further, in the UK, with its tradition of variable or short-term fixed interest rate mortgages, a significant rise in the interest rate – double-digit inflation would suggest we could have interest rates at 10% or more – would impact homeowners in a dramatic way. Even the current rise in bank rate to about 5% is causing the monthly cost of mortgages for some individuals to double. The political impact of a 10% interest rate – and this happened in the 1980s and early 1990s – would be immense.

In the US, there is a presidential election in 2024. It would be a brave Chair of the Fed that raised interest rates further on the eve of the election.

Beer milkshakes

John Steinbeck (1945), in *Cannery Row*, develops a character who in turn develops a fixation on trying a 'beer milkshake'. But he knows that this would be viewed as weird by any bystanders and eventually goes out of town to order one. He explains: 'Doc knew wearily that he couldn't explain, couldn't tell the truth. "I've got a bladder complaint," he said. "Bipalychaetorsonechtomy the doctors call it. I'm supposed to drink a beer milkshake. Doctor's orders".' What with all the talk of 'worldwide savings glut', 'forward guidance', 'quantitative easing', 'anchoring inflation', 'secular stagnation', 'interest on reserves', and so on, perhaps we've just seen a lot of explanations for ordering a beer milkshake – or, in this case, zero interest rates.

If we go back to the 1980s, after Paul Volcker (Chair of the Fed, 1979–1987) had tamed roaring US inflation of over 14% by raising the Fed funds interest rate to over 20%, there was a fair degree of commonality in the understanding of macroeconomics and monetary policy. Indeed, Volcker played it by the book – traditionally, to drive inflation out of the system, you need to set real interest rates (the given rate of interest minus the inflation rate) at a positive level. It is therefore somewhat ironic, at the time of writing, to see debates on whether central banks have gone too far in raising interest rates – the Bank of England slowly raised rates to achieve a 5.25% bank rate in a time of near double-digit inflation. To our 1980s economist, this would not have been viewed as a serious attempt at addressing inflation.

But even this level has caused consternation on the basis that it might cause a recession. Traditional models of the Phillips curve dynamics suggest it is unlikely that inflation can be brought down significantly without a recession. There are legitimate arguments that central bank policies have so distorted borrowing levels that interest rate rises have greater leverage than before, so a serious dose of medicine is more likely to kill the patient than in the past. But a homeopathic dose of medicine is pointless. By putting rates up to 5.25%, the bank has really just restored normality to interest rates after an extraordinary 40 years of expansionary monetary and fiscal policy. Yet, as we've observed, the central banks in the US and UK publish projections that rates will return to the very low levels of the recent past, in a relatively short period of time.

Let's take at face value the idea that there was a 'global savings glut'. It is hard to see how this continues into the future given the assets accrued by China and – on the other side of the ledger – the high indebtedness of borrowing countries such as the US and UK. Further, all countries have signed up to massive investments in eliminating their dependency on carbon-based fuels. University education and housing are unaffordable for younger generations in the places where they want to live. If this is the case, it is hard to see what is served by the Fed and the Bank of England continuing to project a return to very low interest rates. It is unlikely to be achievable and – in any case – is clearly undesirable.

An alternative view is that there was nothing particularly novel in either the world economic environment or in the available policies. The extraordinary success of the Chinese economy (largely, we will later argue, supported by the one-child policy as well as the opening up of trade) mimics that of the US a century earlier. What can be viewed as a definite positive is that, unlike the first half of the 20th century, we avoided having two world wars. But, even on its own terms – financial stability – the low interest rate environment may not have been a great success. In the last 25 years, we have had the dot-com bubble, the financial crisis, and then the high inflation following the pandemic. It is hard to understand why central bankers would be congratulating themselves on their handling of monetary policy.

The 'conventional wisdom', to borrow the phrase from Galbraith's 1958 book *The Affluent Society*, gives governments and central banks immense power from the observation that they are not like households. The profession ridicules the misguided and century-long outdated analyst who worries about the budget deficit and the accumulated national debt. The government can spend at will and, in a time of zero nominal (and negative real) interest rates, only the most parsimonious would begrudge almost any expenditure or tax cut proposed. Similarly, the central bank can print money with the profits remitted to the government to spend.

Like any 'conventional wisdom', there is a hook of truth to anchor these beliefs, but they are in practice more wrong than right. Because of the power and leverage of governments and central banks – and particularly because there is not really a 'free lunch' – what they do is particularly important.

Governments give themselves two powers that households do not have. The government has the power to tax, and it (through a central bank that may be independent to various degrees) has the power to print money. Together, these powers allow the government to issue debt that is free of default risk. The government, if it does not wish to tax to repay the debt, can print money (or an independent central bank can do it for them). Further, it is good that the government – to an appropriate extent – runs a deficit and issues new bonds and money. Having a default risk-free asset is useful to an economy, and money serves an important role in facilitating exchange. After 'long and variable lags' and following a pattern predicted in the short and medium terms by the Phillips curve, imprudent policies will lead to inflation. Central banks are surely right that – with the payment of interest on reserves – they can stop an inflation. But, just as previously when the medicine was to stop printing money, the Phillips curve suggests that this will cause a recession that will, in turn, bring inflation down.

The government has regulatory powers on banks and financial institutions, particularly those that wish to issue 'near money' of some form. It typically delegates much of this to the central bank. The central bank can require banks to deposit reserves with it, on terms (such as interest rates) dictated by the bank. In effect then the banking, and more generally the financial sector of the economy, operates at the discretion and control of the government and central bank. If the central bank wishes the Bank of America to make profits, it can do so, or it can effectively regulate and 'tax' away those profits. The millionaires and billionaires on Wall Street are there at the nod and wink of the central bank, which became rather more explicit during the extraordinary support provided during the financial crisis. In the same way, instead of paying interest on reserves (to keep money from flooding into the economy), the Fed could restore required reserves at a high rate. The one policy gives the banks profits, the other takes profits away. If banks find themselves illiquid or insolvent, the central bank and the government can bail them out, or it can nationalize them, or do a combination as occurred during the financial crisis.

Governments throughout the world agreed at Bretton Woods in 1944 for the US dollar to be the reserve currency of the world. This led to highly profitable 'seigniorage' – in both government bonds and currency – for the US, not just in terms of the $100 bills used by drug dealers throughout the world. In some ways, it is surprising that other countries have not demanded that the euro and the yuan take over the role. Even more surprising is that the Federal Reserve and other central banks haven't as yet – with the exception of recent moves by China – stepped in to stop the non-governmental printing of money in the form of electronic currencies such as Bitcoin. This lethargy is all the more puzzling since Bitcoin generates huge real costs in its production, in the form of computer chips and energy needed to 'mine' the coins. One of the many ironies in our world today is that gamers might simultaneously support Extinction Rebellion and set up carbon-wasting factories to produce Bitcoin, or speculate in it. There is neither an efficiency nor an equity argument for allowing (non-governmental) electronic currency or the clearly bizarre trading in what must essentially be valueless non-fungible tokens. It is entirely sensible for the US Fed to finally be introducing an electronic currency, something that should be backed up – as with paper currency – with the prohibition of private money. The role of the US dollar in the world economy also means that the Fed largely determines monetary policy for the world.

It may seem natural that, given the power to print money, governments find it hard to raise taxation and offend at least some of their voters. This is one of the cases where residual historical memory has played a role. Particularly in the Bundesbank (whose role was largely superseded by the European Central Bank, perhaps not irrelevant in recent monetary policy determinations), a cultural memory existed of the hyper-inflation during the post-First World War Weimar Republic. It reinforced a central tenet of central banking, that one must never monetize the debt. This is mostly reflected in central bank governors regularly issuing statements that they are not monetizing the debt (when they are quite clearly doing precisely that), such as Bank of England Chair Andrew Bailey writing in the *Financial Times* on 5 April 2020 that the 'Bank of England is not doing "monetary financing"'.

Consider a game between the Fed and the government where the government moves first with, for example, the 2017 Trump 'Tax Cuts and Jobs Act'. This cut top corporation tax from 35% to 21% and most individual tax rates. Does the Fed compensate by tightening monetary policy or even keeping it the same, or does it facilitate the government action? We now have a clear example of what happens if the central bank doesn't play along. The new UK Chancellor Kwasi Kwarteng (as part of Prime Minister Liz Truss's new government) presented on 23 September 2022 a mini-budget that cut the basic rate of tax and eliminated the 45% top tax bracket, along with cancelling the planned corporation tax and national insurance rises. The Bank of England made it clear that it would not provide policy support for the mini-budget, the pound collapsed to $1.08 and seemed to be approaching parity. Liz Truss became the shortest serving prime minister in British history.

The politics of interest and inflation rates

Even if one accepts the concepts of 'global savings glut' and 'secular stagnation', there were other macroeconomic equilibria that could have been chosen, at least by the government and the central bank working together, if not necessarily by the central banks on their own. There could have been massive spending on the infrastructure rather than tax cutting. Instead of austerity in the UK, there could have been expenditure on public goods. Salaries for doctors, nurses, teachers and academics could have kept up with inflation. With recruitment difficulties alleviated, more staff could have been hired in the NHS and schools. Firms could have been induced to invest – particularly in carbon-neutral, climate-saving technologies – rather than engage in financial engineering. Between them, the government and the central bank have immense powers. We can divide these roughly between fiscal policy (taxation and spending), monetary policy (the control of interest rates) and regulatory policy. Even if the 'global savings glut' viewpoint was accurate, the impact of world zero interest rates upon the US or UK economies is mediated by the government through its fiscal and regulatory policies.

One of the examples we develop in this book concerns housing. We will argue that the zero interest rate policy, not a lack of house building, has been the cause of unaffordable housing for new entrants. The reason is that there is a huge stock of housing, built over centuries, and – even if construction of new houses was to multiply by a significant factor – new-build will have only a small percentage impact. The important policies are to utilize the existing housing stock effectively, rather than to devote much of the stock to the pursuit of capital gains. To see the difference, consider children's toys that come up for auction – if the child kept their rare Dinky toy in the box rather than playing with it, 60 years ago, it will be worth considerably more today. Most children do not consider bringing their childhood toys to a future 2060 version of *The Antiques Roadshow*, when they are deciding whether or not to play with their new birthday present, but owners of investment flats do consider these issues. Even if bought on a mortgage, monthly payments at a near zero interest rate do not require getting a tenant. If one is buying a new-build flat in central London for capital gains, or as a secure way of storing overseas money, why bother with the inconvenience of having tenants at what is to them a high rent, but is to you a modest net increase in income compared to your capital gains?

Heavy taxation of vacant properties, or even prohibitions on investment properties or second homes – that is, the use of fiscal and regulatory powers – can free up a huge amount of underutilized housing. Similarly, when we discuss the labour market, regulation – the encouragement of trade unions and the prohibition of zero-hours 'gig economy' contracts, for example – will raise wages without the need to 'run the economy hot' through monetary policy of low interest rates.

That the Fed and the Bank of England have been able to raise interest rates to 5% suggests, however, that a near zero interest rate equilibrium is not now (if it ever was) mandated by the 'global savings glut'. We are now at full employment coincident with the 5% interest rates, so the 'secular stagnation' model also seems, at best, rather over-stated.

In this book, we will argue for a medium-term policy of 'normalized' interest rates of about 5% during periods when inflation is running at 2–3%. The question is how we get there, and perhaps surprisingly, we will argue for a continued burst of controlled higher inflation. This is in order to address imbalances in the financial and real economy in a politically viable way. Cumulative post-pandemic inflation has added up to about 20%. The policies of the last four decades (monetary, fiscal and regulatory) have worked together to raise asset prices relative to the price of labour and goods. Governments have taken on immense debt, some of which is in the form of long-term treasuries and some of which is in the form of extremely liquid reserves held by financial institutions with the central bank. The cumulated inflation, just over the last few years, has effectively wiped out in real terms 20% of the debt and brought house prices relative to incomes 20% closer to a realistic level.

There is both a political and an economic argument for a controlled but significant inflation. Politically, even as power shifts towards the younger generations, the older generations – particularly homeowners with large capital gains embodied in their houses – have a strong incentive to fight anything that lowers the price of their house. Inflation largely preserves the nominal value, while allowing the ratio of house prices to incomes to fall significantly. The economic argument is that a large fall in asset values (the alternative way of rebalancing asset values, including the stock market, to incomes) will have a sharp effect on consumption and create, in the short run, a Keynesian aggregate demand recession.

More generally, inflation can be a less politically ambitious way of removing some of the imbalances in the fiscal structure of the economy. 'Fiscal drag' occurs when tax thresholds do not rise with inflation, so – for a given real income – the tax rate goes up. If the government needs to raise taxes, and is unwilling or unable to do so explicitly by raising rates, this is a relatively innocuous way of doing so. Another example we will discuss is home student university fees in the UK. These were tripled to £9,000 in 2012, raised modestly to £9,250 since then, but have essentially decreased in real terms to about £6,000 in 2012 pounds. Perhaps not coincidentally, this is back to the level generally recommended by the Browne Report as being reflective of the cost of education per student. Inflation here has removed the distortions created by setting fees well above the cost of education.

Inflation would also erode the real value of the debt overhang. Richard Koo has emphasized the 'balance sheet recession' in his books from 2003 to the present (see, for example, Koo, 2003). There is considerable debt overhang, not only in government borrowing, but in student loans, in heavily leveraged small and medium-size enterprises and even in local government borrowing. Just recently, the central government has issued an emergency bailout of local authorities with an additional £600 million. Inflation would eat away at the debt.

We propose a policy where the Bank of England targets (or 'predicts', if that is a more accurate term) 5% inflation for the next five years. It also predicts interest rates of 5–7% on an ongoing basis. Higher mortgage rates should keep a cap on the nominal values of houses, keeping them from rising further. Inflation of the amount indicated would – if household incomes rose at the rate of inflation – gradually lower the house price to household income ratio to more realistic levels.

But note that this requires the right kind of inflation – inflation in incomes and goods prices. Having had roughly four decades of asset price inflation – at the expense particularly of the wages of those who aren't university educated – we now need a combination of asset deflation and wage inflation to remedy the imbalance. The governor of the bank should not, as the *Financial Times* reports on 23 June 2023 advise: 'We will get inflation back to its target. To do that ... we cannot continue to have the current level of wage increases and we can't have companies seeking to rebuild profit margins.' That policy, exacerbated by the implicit incomes policies of the current Sunak government, is trying to recreate the last four decades rather than moving forward into an economy with high growth through green investment, a better distribution of income between wages and profits, and higher expenditure on public services.

5

The Everything Bubble

Steadily declining interest rates

An overlooked feature of monetary policy over the last four decades is that, while it involved very low interest rates towards the end of the period, it is characterized by consistently falling interest rates over 40 years (Figure 5.1).

As we will discuss in this chapter, this means that capital gains on all assets were virtually assured. Even if you (or your pension fund) had been fully invested in government treasuries at a low interest rate, the fact that the rate was falling meant that you would get capital gains to add onto your total return. Stocks and housing did even better, in part because of the perceived 'Greenspan put' – there was no risk, because Chairman (of the Fed) Alan Greenspan – called 'the maestro' – was believed to ensure that any falls in the stock market or slowdown in the economy would be countered by monetary expansion. Even the housing crisis of 2007/08, during 'helicopter' Ben Bernanke's period in charge, only temporarily dented house and stock prices.

A thesis of this book is that the policy makers know what they are doing in the sense that they are deliberately choosing their policies, wise or unwise. It is unlikely that the policy makers of the early 1980s sat down and drew up explicit plans to consistently lower interest rates over time. Instead, this pattern might be a natural development of their initial policy choices as reinforced by the policy makers' subsequent decisions. But, at the very least, the policy makers have had numerous opportunities to take a different path, and have chosen not to do so.

But, if declining interest rates – and the associated 'guaranteed' capital gains – must stop when they hit a zero interest floor, then the 40-year boom in asset values had to come to an end. It did not have to end in inflation, but could have ended with an implosion in asset values. When the post-war boom came to an end in the US, the Dow Jones Industrial Average peaked at 9,400 in 1966 and slowly but inexorably fell to 2,500 in 1982. The Japanese Nikkei average approached 40,000 in 1989 and fell to about 8,000 in 2003.

Figure 5.1: Market yield on US Treasury securities at 10-year constant maturity

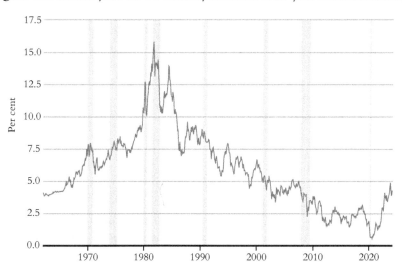

Source: Board of Governors of the Federal Reserve System (US), Market Yield on U.S. Treasury Securities at 10-Year Constant Maturity. Quoted on an investment basis [DGS10], retrieved from FRED, Federal Reserve Bank of St Louis; https://fred.stlouisfed.org/series/DGS10, 27 February 2024.

In the same way, while the rise in interest rates to about 5% over the last two years will allow for one more act in the story of four decades of lowering and lowering interest rates, the end of this strategy is at hand. The boom decades for assets – from long-term bonds to housing to the stock market – are over.

At the end of the preceding chapter, we argued that the Fed and the Bank of England should announce a 5% interest rate expectation for the indefinite future. This was partially to do with the reality of investment needs and the prospect of inflation. But it was also particularly to do with the desirability of a more historically normal policy mix. But any policy mix impacts on different individuals and different generations in different ways – we now need policies that, for example, make houses affordable to the younger generations, rather than policies that guarantee capital gains for older generations.

Asset prices

When one buys an asset (household durables such as a washing machine, a car, a house, stocks or bonds), one is buying a stream of either real or financial benefits over time. Once you own your washing machine, you don't have to put coins in the slot (as at the laundromat) each time you use it. There are, of course, costs of electricity and repair bills, and eventually the machine breaks down or is uneconomical and it is better to get a new, more energy-efficient model.

With a house, you get housing services. You don't pay this year's rent, but instead have fixed the price of your house on purchase, and pay the mortgage loan you have taken out, along with maintenance and insurance. At any point, you can sell the house and repay the mortgage, along with selling fees and any taxes.

With stocks, you get dividends but you are often primarily focused upon the idea of capital gains, you will be able to sell the stocks for more than you paid for them. There is risk in this, since the price of shares is typically volatile both for company-specific risk (the next model of car produced by Ford is not a market success) and for economy-wide risk (there is a recession and Ford and other automobile makers cannot easily sell their cars). One of finance theory's major insights is that – by diversification of your share portfolio – you can largely eliminate company-specific risk (by owning shares in all the car companies), and all that is left is economy-wide risk. As we've observed, Alan Greenspan's put sought to eliminate even that risk.

With bonds, you get the coupon value each year – the specified interest to be paid. How capital gains arise on long-term bonds when interest rates change is straightforward to understand. The fixed coupon interest can be readily compared to today's market rate. If you've bought a long-term, 30-year bond with a coupon rate of 5%, and current interest rates are 2%, you've got a valuable asset so its price goes up sharply. This has been the experience over the last 40 years. As investors have discovered over the last two years, however, this can work in reverse. If your bond has a coupon rate of 2%, and today's interest rates are 5%, your bond isn't that attractive to potential buyers, and the price must fall to be something like the market 2% rate.

The easiest way to see the relationship between current interest rates and asset prices is to look at a 'consol' or perpetual bond that need never be redeemed, but could be bought back at face value by the government. For example, the UK issued 4% consols in 1927 which are to be repaid in 2015 as reported in the *Financial Times* (Moore, 2014). Consider a £100 face value consol at 4%. This pays £4 a year (the coupon) to the holder. Let's suppose that current bonds are issued at 2% with a coupon, on a £100 bond, of £2 a year. Then it follows that people would be willing to pay £200 for the consol – the £4 coupon would be an interest rate of 2%. This is why the government was delighted to buy back the 4% 1927 consols and issue – for example – 1.5% gilts (government bonds) with a fixed maturity of 2047.

In general, governments issue long-term bonds without the option to buy them back (at face value) before maturity, since those would not be unduly attractive to potential buyers (having removed the opportunity for capital gains). But new debt issued by the government – certainly during the period

2010–2020 – could be sold at a much lower interest rate than the historical norm. Some economists argued that borrowing was essentially free, and the government should do more of it. But, as we've discussed in the preceding chapter, the low interest rate was sustained as the central banks engaged in quantitative easing, buying significant amounts of existing debt. Along with pension funds and other significant investors, they are now sitting on (unrealized, paper) losses on their purchases. Further, the central banks are having to pay interest on bank reserves at a higher rate than much of the bond portfolio they are carrying on the other side of their ledger.

Pension funds are also big investors in what was described as a 'safe' investment, and a number in fact leveraged their ownership of government bonds beyond face value through various forms of financial instruments. When the Truss budget came out, and interest rates went up, these pension funds ended up in a calamitous situation and the Bank of England had to intervene. In a similar way, the Silicon Valley Bank recently went under, since it also was a major investor in government bonds that suffered large capital losses when interest rates rose. Ironically, economists who go around saying 'fallacy of composition' to those economists who want to adopt prudent finances failed to understand their own 'fallacy of composition'. What might work for a small action (maybe another £100 million of government debt) may not work for a large action (trillions of government debt).

Returns and risk on bonds – interest rates and inflation

Virtually all long-term assets have 'interest rate risk' in the sense that a rise in the interest rate impacts negatively on their value. For government bonds in the US and the UK, given that the likelihood of actual default – the government not repaying the interest or principal on the debt is negligible, interest rate and inflation risks are the only notable risks. Actually, there is an asterisk since the chance of default was negligible until the Republicans in Congress in 2011, 2013, and now again, have made the debt ceiling authorization into a cause célèbre. Although we argue in favour of guardrails, trying to put them in place retrospectively when the car has already left the road is not a serious policy – at that point, as we will discuss in the final chapter, all you can do is call the tow truck and make a booking at the repair shop.

But, as we've discussed earlier, bonds have interest rate risk. Let's suppose you've bought long-duration treasuries (say, 30 years) at 3%, paying about the face value of £100. If interest rates now go up sharply, your bonds are competing with newly issued ones at perhaps 6%, and you will suffer a severe fall in the capital value of your bonds. If you've bought bonds of shorter duration, your interest rate risk is less. In the extreme, you can hold money, which doesn't have any interest rate risk at all in terms of your capital value.

If interest rates go up, that's great, since you will get the higher interest rates (on money market or savings accounts) which you can then lock in by buying (at the new, cheaper price) long-duration bonds.

The increase in interest rates may be associated with higher inflation – the central bank may raise interest rates to fight inflation. But first consider inflation risk in the absence of any interest rate change. If inflation goes up from say 1% to 6%, and interest rates are unchanged, your bonds won't fall in nominal value but – in real, inflation-adjusted terms, your bonds fall in value by 6% a year (as do the coupon payments).

You might hope to avoid the inflation risk by buying index-linked bonds, which were first issued in the UK in 1981. These make up the inflation losses on your principal sum by paying you the inflation as well as the coupon interest. Interestingly, the Thatcher government thought that these would constrain future governments away from inflating the economy as a way of writing off debt – an application of guardrails. The problem, as we'll argue, is that these guardrails are always further down the road and don't stop a government from pursuing imprudent policies in the short and even medium run. Index-linked gilts now make up about 25% of UK Government debt, but only about 8% of US Government debt.

Index-linked bonds would protect against inflation except that they suffer from interest rate risk, as do any long-term bonds. Further, interest rates and inflation tend to be correlated. When inflation rises, central banks typically raise interest rates to slow the economy and lessen inflationary pressures. So you might easily find that, as the economy enters an inflationary period, the interest rate effect dominates the inflation effect, and you've lost value in your index-linked bond portfolio as well as your traditional bond portfolio. During the 40-year period of declining interest rates, these fell not only in absolute terms but relative to inflation (see Figure 5.2).

Even as inflation has jumped up, real interest rates have gone negative. When inflation in the UK and US peaked in early 2023, inflation in the UK was 10.1% in January 2023 and bank rate was 4% (February 2023). In the US, inflation was 6% (February 2023) and the Federal Funds rate had a target of 4.5–4.75%. Since interest rates didn't rise commensurately with the increase in inflation, the holders of index-linked bonds gained.

To summarize, for traditional long-term government bonds, there is interest rate risk where the capital value falls if interest rates go up and there is inflation risk (even if interest rates are unchanged) that the real values will fall with inflation. Even with index-linked bonds, the investor cannot buy full insurance against inflation since interest rates are likely to rise when inflation is high. However, during the 40-year period of consistently declining interest rates, investors in bonds were largely guaranteed capital gains on both traditional and index-linked bonds. Both nominal and real (relative to inflation) interest rates fell and the capital value of the bonds went up.

Figure 5.2: Market yield on US Treasury securities at 10-year constant maturity: inflation-indexed

Source: Board of Governors of the Federal Reserve System (US), Market Yield on US Treasury Securities at 10-Year Constant Maturity. Quoted on an investment basis, inflation-indexed [DFII10], retrieved from FRED, Federal Reserve Bank of St Louis; https://fred.stlouisfed.org/series/DFII10, 27 February 2024.

But note what happens as interest rates actually approach zero – even with the most accommodating central bank in the world, the interest rate risk suddenly becomes a one-way bet in the opposite direction, that rates will rise. If interest rates are at zero, any changes can realistically only be positive and entail capital losses. The holder is almost guaranteed a negative return. As the 40-year run of declining interest rates took rates to very low levels, everyone kept expecting the 'bond vigilantes' to come over the hill and declare a bloody end to the monetary expansion – the bet against bonds became a guaranteed one-way loss. It may be that, but for Liz Truss, we'd still be waiting but – even then – not for much longer. As we've noted, the rise in Fed and Bank of England rates to about 5% can postpone the reckoning or – if rates are maintained at 5% as we advise – might even be sustainable for the medium term.

Returns and risk – stocks

Stocks are valued as the profits over time (sales value minus costs) discounted by the interest rate. As with bonds, falling interest rates boost stocks. So also do favourable macroeconomic environments. Inflation is not in itself bad for stocks. If inflation is balanced so that the price of goods sold rises by x% and costs such as wages rise by x%, then profits rise by x%. Inflation is only a problem for firms if the central bank responds by raising interest rates sharply, something we've seen in Figures 5.1 and 5.2, has not been the case for 40 years until just recently. In the same way, macroeconomic risk has been minimized by the 'Greenspan put' – whenever the stock market went down, it seems that Alan Greenspan's Fed put its foot on the accelerator (lowering interest rates to boost the economy). The key occasion was the 1987 stock market crash, when US stocks fell over 20% in one day – but this is hardly recognizable as an event in Figure 5.3. It is argued that the 2013 'taper tantrum' in response to the Fed's announcement of an anticipated reduction in quantitative easing caused Ben Bernanke to reconsider and back down. Given the interest rate policies followed by the Fed, it should be no surprise that a broad-based index of US shares has marched inexorably up.

The fall after the 'dot-com crash', after the 'financial crisis' and then after the pandemic was shortly reversed. The Trump tax cuts lowered taxes on corporations, imports kept material and production costs low and wages have been stagnant. Finally, the 'Greenspan put' has meant the disappearance of the risk premium previously applicable when stocks as a class were viewed as risky. As the stock market adage goes, 'don't fight the Fed'. And for 40 years, the Fed said up, up and away.

Figure 5.3: Wilshire 5000 Total Market Full Cap Index

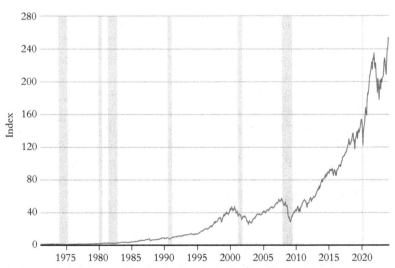

Source: Wilshire Associates, Wilshire 5000 Total Market Index [WILL5000IND], retrieved from FRED, Federal Reserve Bank of St Louis; https://fred.stlouisfed.org/series/WILL5000 IND, 27 February, 2024.

The housing market

Nothing represents the divide between the generations as much as housing, particularly in urban areas. House prices in London are roughly 12 times average incomes, compared to a traditional valuation (and what used to be the traditional mortgage lending ratio) of three times. The conventional wisdom is that we need to build more, even on the green belt, suggesting as with other aspects of policy that the solution to the newer generations' needs is to destroy the planet where they intend to live in 50 years' time. We will discuss housing in greater depth in Chapter 10.

But people are already living somewhere, so the issue is primarily one of housing tenure – we have too much privately rented housing and too little ownership. Margaret Thatcher, with the 'right to buy' policy, at a stroke turned public renters into private owners. Given that the public housing stock is now decimated from that policy and a lack of subsequent funding, the change in the future needs to be turning private renters into private owners. Like all the issues in this book, there are straightforward solutions once we deviate from the conventional wisdom. Quite simply, we need to drive speculators out and tenants in to home ownership. But central banks and governments have been doing exactly the reverse, sometimes disguised as helping out 'first-time buyers' but almost invariably further enriching the well-off.

The value of housing is not unlike that of the stock market and other real assets. In this case, owning a house entitles you to 'housing services', the residential use of the house. There are maintenance costs and depreciation. These go up with inflation, but the 'locked-in' house price provides a potentially good hedge against inflation. In effect, you freeze your rent levels into the future. As with stocks, there are macroeconomic risks. If the economy is booming, people have more income and wealth to spend on housing, and bid up the price of houses.

Even more than with stocks, the biggest determinant of house prices is the interest rate. In the UK, given the short duration of mortgages (either fixed for two or five years, or variable), Bank of England policy quickly impacts on all actual mortgage-holders and potential homeowners. In contrast, in the US, mortgages are typically 30 years long, locking in today's 30-year interest rate. The increase in interest rates in the last few years (with the high inflation that has been occurring) is seen in the US 30-year fixed mortgage rate (see Figure 5.4).

The effect of interest rate rises on current owners in the UK (except for the remarkably high one-third of owners who own outright without a mortgage) tends to be immediate and impactful. For owners with limited equity in their house (and therefore a high mortgage to value ratio), a doubling of rates – such as we've seen after the pandemic – has a major impact on their

Figure 5.4: Thirty-year fixed rate mortgage average in the US

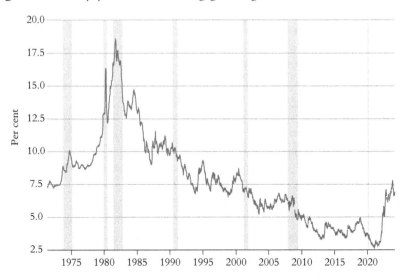

Source: Freddie Mac, 30-year fixed rate mortgage average in the United States
[MORTGAGE30US], retrieved from FRED, Federal Reserve Bank of St Louis; https://fred.stl
ouisfed.org/series/MORTGAGE30US, 27 February 2024.

household budget. In some ways, however, short-term fixed mortgages are a good thing – buy-to-let landlords, for example, may have to sell their property because of difficulties in meeting the new mortgage interest payments, putting more property back on the market for owner-occupiers. In contrast, in the US, with a typical 30-year fixed rate that is generally not portable to a new house, owners are locked into their property. If they moved to a new house and a new mortgage, they would be paying much higher interest rates.

Another major distortion from the 40 years of falling interest rates, and rising house prices, is that baby boomer homeowners are frequently sitting on very large capital gains. Rather than downsizing to a more convenient size of house (and probably one in a sunnier location), they want to avoid paying capital gains taxes on the sale of their house. Ironically, this is typically to benefit their children (given the low rates of inheritance tax in the US and high thresholds in both the US and the UK), reminding us that there are substantial within-generation as well as intergenerational effects of the policies we criticize in this book. The net effect is that the boomers over-consume housing in their later years.

Where are the bond vigilantes?

The policy (whether explicit or not) of falling and falling interest rates over the last four decades had to come to an end when the zero interest rate floor was hit. You have driven your car down a blind alley and come upon a brick wall. You cannot turn the car around – what do you do? Monetary policy to fight the post-pandemic inflation has had the effect of backing the car up a bit in the alley, but the wall is still there and not that far away from 5% interest rates.

Economists and financial commentators are falling over themselves encouraging the Fed and the Bank of England to lower rates immediately, now that inflation has fallen to 3–4%. By the time this book goes to press, the inflation rate could be higher or lower (although in general, the safest prediction in most cases is to assume it just stays where it is). This is well above the mystical 2% target adopted by central banks, so on that basis, rates should certainly not be lowered. It is only because of the 'long and variable lags' that are part of monetary policy tradition that an argument can be made against raising them further. The 5% rates may be having a continued deceleration effect on inflation (long lags), or – then again – they may not (variable lags).

The problem with the zero interest rate floor is understood in the conventional wisdom to be the inability to lower interest rates once you hit the floor. In their perceived world of 'global savings glut' and 'secular stagnation', we might want to lower interest rates below zero to keep the economy ticking over. In fact, the problem is a different one if it is recognized that the central bank policy of the last decades was not just for very low interest rates, but required interest rates actually to be predictably falling.

Bonds are the Achilles heel in a low or zero interest rate policy. Along the path of declining interest rates, bond holders (along with other asset holders) did extremely well. With lower interest rates, the direct return in the form of an interest payment (on new bonds) was less and less each year. But each year there was a capital gain on existing bonds. Another way of looking at this is that, if I bought a bond ten years ago, I locked in the interest rate at the time. If the rate declines, I neither gain nor lose.

But once the zero interest rate floor has been reached, the capital gains are over. Long-term bonds become a one-way negative bet. If interest rates rise, you lose. If they stay at zero, you neither win nor lose. We are now seeing capital losses on bonds that are having impacts on bank and other balance sheets. This particularly affected pension funds (who had in fact not only bought government bonds in large percentages, but actually leveraged up the impact of interest rate changes through associated financial instruments) and banks, such as the Silicon Valley Bank which collapsed in 2023.

Other assets, such as stocks and real estate, do not suffer the same one-way bet effect as interest rates move towards zero. The reason is that they are generally positively affected by growth induced by very low interest rates, and they are generally positively affected (if interest rates do not rise to counteract it) by inflation. Even if wages and inputs rise at a common rate of inflation as the output price of the firm, profits rise at the same rate in that balanced inflation. Other things being equal, house prices rise with inflation. Maintaining a zero interest rate policy, if it can be done, is great for other assets, if a potential disaster for bonds.

A mystery over the period is the absence of the 'bond vigilantes' – a posse of self-appointed individuals (in this case, banks and market traders) who enforce the law when the authorities are absent. Given that bonds had become a one-way losing bet when long-term rates approached zero, where were the vigilantes? Why weren't bonds dumped on the market, precipitating drastic falls in their value and – in that way – putting back up the long-term interest rate?

In large part, the debt market has not collapsed since only a modest part is held by private investors, who have over the decades of the low interest rate policy moved into more lucrative 'risky' investments including 'buy-to-let housing' and even cryptocurrencies. Out of the over $28 trillion in US Government debt in 2021 (of which only $1.6 trillion is inflation-protected, to be discussed further later), $11 trillion is held by government agencies such as Social Security and the Fed. Another $7 trillion is held by foreign countries, notably China ($1 trillion) and Japan ($1.2 trillion). Private pensions account for $800 billion, state/local government pension funds hold about $300 billion, insurance companies $400 billion, mutual funds $3.5 trillion, state/local governments $1 trillion, leaving about $2 trillion for other investors (individuals, corporations and other enterprises).

Traditionally, private investors were advised to have a portfolio that varied over age. For example, there was a rule of thumb that the percentage of your portfolio in stocks should be 100 less one's age. At age 50, one would have a 50/50 split in the portfolio between 'safe' bonds and 'risky' stocks. Compare the figures above to the total roughly $50 trillion value of US stocks and when you last heard a private individual talk about buying bonds rather than stocks or real estate.

So, a large part of the answer as to why the debt continues to be bought at very low interest rates – where it becomes a one-way bet that rates will go up not down – is that the bulk is sterilized in government holdings, the Fed and overseas. Overseas debt holdings are guided by the interests of the foreign entity – for example, China is unlikely to want to destabilize its largest market. At home, pensions are largely required to hold some of their portfolio in government debt. Pension holdings are a larger percentage of the extremely high debt levels in Japan, and explain in large part why the Japanese bond market hasn't collapsed.

But, like any unsustainable policy, it works until it doesn't. In the UK, many can remember Black Wednesday when, in 1992, Britain crashed out of the European Monetary Union. During the day, the government drove interest rates up to 18% before they gave up the game. The government strategy worked until it didn't. That the interest rate policy was very differential in its impacts – charging the future to benefit consumption (rather than investment) today – would have led many – if there had been full disclosure – to call halt, rather than voting in one government that raises expenditure and cuts taxes followed by the opposite party government that raises expenditure and cuts taxes, and with a central bank that silently monetizes the debt.

Getting out of the ditch

In our no label economics, we don't have a biblical injunction against the government borrowing even to finance current expenditure (much less needed investment in the infrastructure and the green economy) or even about the central bank printing money to finance the debt. Keynesian economics tells us to lower interest rates and run deficits during recessions to mitigate their effects and smooth the adjustment process. It may even tell us to err on the side of 'running the economy hot' to help workers, particularly those from less favoured backgrounds and who might suffer from discrimination when employers have too much choice across job applications. Running a sustained policy of lowering interest rates by printing money, while running government deficits, is another story and not perhaps one to be found in Keynes's *The General Theory* (1936).

Given that interest rates at the time of writing are 5%, what should happen next? Since 5% has been the standard rate of interest historically, it seems natural to view it as the 'normal' or – in preferred economic parlance – 'natural' rate. Even if inflation were to return to its 2% target (by no means guaranteed), there is full employment, so where is the economic argument for the observed urgency for lowering interest rates?

Cynical economists (clearly, the best kind to have) look at the winners and losers of a policy. Two-thirds of US households (50% in the UK) own their home. Someone who bought a $1 million house with a mortgage interest rate of 2% will still pay the same amount each month, provided they are in the US and locked in the rate with a long fixed rate period. But a potential buyer will now be financing at perhaps 6%, so that the interest repayment has tripled. If that marginal buyer could previously have just afforded to pay $1 million, they must now lower their sights to a $350,000 house. Over time, the price of houses will significantly fall. Stocks will similarly plummet in value as their future earnings are discounted at the new, higher interest rate. It would take a courageous Fed to maintain its 5% rate in the face of that political imperative (particularly in an election year) to lower rates.

The government itself is not immune in that the central bank is holding huge amounts of government debt, a large amount of which was bought as 'quantitative easing' during the financial crisis and the pandemic. It is also paying 5% on the cash reserves held by financial institutions at the central bank. Instead of declaring a profit (remitted to the Treasury) each year, the central bank will have to declare a loss on its holdings of government debt and paying interest on reserves. The government – assuming (as seems the case for both conservative and liberal governments) that it won't want to raise taxes or cut expenditure – will have its deficit significantly increased even without raising expenditure.

Macroeconomic and monetary imbalances get resolved in different ways. If the bond vigilantes don't show up, the economy may crash (the dot-com bubble, the financial crisis and the pandemic) or inflation may arise (the post-pandemic period). When the Soviet Union collapsed, Russian inflation soared. Michael Kaser (1999) reported that 'consumer prices rose 16-fold ... in 1992 alone'. Inflation is a way of devaluing savings (and government bonds) and other forms of nominal debt in the economy to restore balance.

A clear imbalance in the UK economy, in particular, concerns the house price to incomes ratio, currently about 7–9 times, depending upon just how you measure house prices and incomes. There are equity issues within a generation (between homeowners and renters) and across generations (since the baby boomers are often sitting on extremely large capital gains). One way of bringing this down significantly is to have house prices actually fall, but another way is to have incomes rise. For political reasons and to avoid a chance of another financial crisis, a severe fall in house prices is both unlikely to occur and potentially undesirable. Over the last four years, house prices in the UK have risen about 20%; in the last year (2023) they were flat. The most that a 5% interest rate can do is continue to cap further rises in the price. But that allows the possibility of restoring a balance through inflation in incomes. An inflation rate of 5% in incomes would – if house prices were flat – bring the house price to income ratio back down towards realistic levels in the medium term.

The government has tools to raise income inflation other than through monetary policy. We will discuss these further in Chapter 7 on the labour market. They range from raising the minimum wage through to increasing trade union bargaining power.

6

Smart Motorways

There be monsters there

When an economist – of almost any persuasion or field of study – goes down the list of Nobel Prize winners since 1968, they see a mountain of progress in the subject. A lot of it is 'inside baseball' whose importance might not be readily accessible to non-economists, and it might not add up to technological progress as observable as mobile phones and laptop computers, or advances in medicine. Because of the nature of economics as already described – storytelling that is not particularly testable – different economists in different fields and of different political alignments will like some of the work, and not like some of the work. For me, the research on information asymmetries showing how unregulated markets don't work well – even in terms of productivity – is particularly important. It also highlights the role for implicit and explicit contracts, in other words 'good behaviour', ideally enforced without the expenses of the legal system. As we will argue, the adherence to norms is valuable not least for a central bank.

But what one won't find is any discovery that is so earth-shattering in its policy impact that it can be the explanation for a new world order of permanently low inflation and interest rates. There has been no polio or smallpox vaccine in economics research. 'Forward guidance' in monetary policy may or may not be new (it may just be a variant on old-fashioned 'jawboning' as a policy tool) but it's hard to imagine that anyone would say that it changed the shape of monetary policy to the extent necessary to explain a fundamental shift in outcomes.

The rise of China, and the opening of the world to free trade with China, has been of large magnitude. Deregulation, the weakening of trade unions and employee rights, increased university enrolment rates, lowering of taxes on corporations and the well-off, increased female participation in the labour market – all of these were of sufficient magnitude that they had significant impacts, some good and some bad; even leaving aside that they have left us with a world on the brink of environmental disaster.

Rather than thinking that the policies of the central banks were novel and based upon unobservable but dramatic improvements in economic analysis, maybe what's gone on is something much simpler. Policy makers ignored the map markings that 'there be monsters there'. Maybe – like Columbus not actually falling off the end of the world – our 'courage to act' took us to new frontiers of monetary policy and we avoided the mistakes that may (or may not) have been made by previous central banks. Maybe – by going into uncharted territory – the modern-day Fed avoided the financial crisis changing from the Great Recession into a second Great Depression. Or maybe the 'automatic stabilizers' set up during the Great Depression (bank deposit guarantees, social security, progressive taxation, unemployment insurance) did what every economics textbook predicted they would do – prevent another Great Depression.

Current valuations of stocks and bonds seem to be predicting a return to the low inflation, low interest rate environment. The inflation of 2022/23 might be a transient effect of the pandemic (supply chains and a disrupted labour market) and the invasion of Ukraine. But maybe we have awakened the monsters, and – once awakened – perhaps they are not easily returned to sleep.

Golden guardrails

John Adams composed the opera *Nixon in China* about the 1972 visit of President Nixon and his wife to Mao's China, an example of the impact of the visit on the world. It is hard to over-state the importance of China, and in particular the opening of China – China joining the World Trade Organization and gaining most favoured nation status in 2001 – in the equilibrium of the last 40 years. We have already argued that, despite the claims of Ben Bernanke, there was nothing inevitable about the macroeconomic and monetary equilibrium that followed. The US Government did not have to run large deficits, created in significant part by tax cuts on corporations and the wealthy. Any excess savings that might have been associated with an insufficiency of aggregate demand could have been channelled into massive investment in the infrastructure, in housing and in protecting the environment. Of course, these alternative policies might not have gained favour from the wealthy, from those owning shares and houses (particular buy-to-let empires), or a whole generation benefitting from low interest rates.

To reiterate a central thesis of this book, we give policy makers credit for having knowledge and intelligence such that the equilibrium observed is largely one that they have chosen, not one that arose through shocks out of their control. What made the zero interest rate equilibrium possible was not just the opening to China, but the removal of guardrails that would have prevented the Fed's extreme expansionary policies. A very powerful guardrail was the historical gold standard.

Figure 6.1: Gold fixing price 10:30 a.m. (London time) in London bullion market, based in US dollars

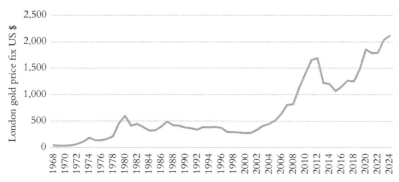

Source: LBMA (www.lbma.org.uk/prices-and-data/precious-metal-prices#/table). Accessed 9 March 2024.

Prior to 1971, the agreement signed at Bretton Woods in 1944 tied the value of the US dollar to gold. Keynes was the British negotiator at Bretton Woods, and it might reasonably be thought that the fixed exchange rates developed (supported by the establishment of the International Monetary Fund to stabilize national and the world economy) were not therefore anti-Keynesian. The IMF came to play an ongoing role in perceptions of the Labour Party's financial imprudence in that Harold Wilson in 1967 had to devalue the pound, and again in 1976 when James Callaghan went cap in hand to borrow from the IMF and adopted a policy of austerity at home. Bretton Woods set the price of gold at $35 an ounce. Under the gold standard, the US was required to support that price level by allowing governments to convert dollars into gold at that rate.

Richard Nixon suspended the conversion of dollars into gold on 15 August 1971. During the 1970s/80s inflation, the dollar devalued to a tenth of the gold standard rate – that is, gold went up to $400 an ounce (Figure 6.1). The everything bubble has led gold to further rise up towards $2,000 an ounce.

If the dollar had remained pegged at $35 per ounce, then the everything bubble could never have occurred. The Federal Reserve would not have printed all the money that sent interest rates towards zero, or – if it did – it would have quickly depleted all the gold stored in Fort Knox reserves buying back the dollars to maintain the gold price at $35.

The Taylor rule

Under fixed exchange rates, central banks and governments needed to follow a 'responsible policy' in the sense that the foreign exchange markets saw the policy as prudent. We have already described the runs on the pound in 1967 and 1976, and the crashing out of the European Monetary Union (under a Conservative government in 1992, also the event which brought George Soros to notice as a very successful investor). But with the tight guardrails of the gold standard and fixed exchange rates dropped, what could replace them? What would make central banks follow the dictum of the Fed Chair, William McChesney Martin, who famously said the job of the Fed was "to take away the punch bowl just as the party gets going".

The 'Taylor rule' of John Taylor became the informal answer. If the job of central banks is to stabilize the economy (not to seek to perpetually accelerate the economy, not to provide a guarantee on risky assets so that they were no longer risky, not to monetize the debt by purchasing a very large percentage of the debt that was issued by the government, not to seek to run the economy hot to raise real wages, and so on), then the central bank should follow rules that centre their policy over time as broadly neutral. If inflation is above the long-run norm (defined by the Fed and other central banks as 2%), other things being equal, interest rates should be above the long-run norm. If unemployment is below the long-run norm (traditionally about 4%), then interest rates should be above the long-run norm. This would gently push the economy back into the long-run equilibrium.

The important feature of the Taylor rule is not to give specific policy numbers for the interest rate, but to effectively commit to a symmetric policy – raise rates when the economy is running hot and lower rates when it is running cold. The Fed, during the first period of zero rates – in response to the financial crisis – at least felt the need to give lip service to the Taylor rule.

As an example of this, Ben Bernanke wrote in 2015 (for the Brookings Institution) that, under what he viewed as reasonable modifications to the Taylor rule, it actually generated negative interest rates for the post-financial crash period (Bernanke, 2015a). In particular, Bernanke hypothesized a higher weight on the output gap than on inflation, compared to the original formulation. But this misses the whole point of guardrails – they are not meant to be moveable as soon as they become binding. Further, this sort of reasoning has led some macroeconomists to claim that the main thing they got wrong – in determining monetary policy frameworks for the past decades – was not to recognize that the zero interest rate floor would become binding. This is something like going to an interview and facing the question 'What is your main weakness?' and coming up with the answer 'I tend to be too successful'.

But at a certain point in the Fed's monetary policy, it appears that the Taylor rule was abandoned. In December 2019 (therefore, before the pandemic was influencing policy), the US unemployment rate was 3.5% and the consumer price inflation over the year had been 2.3%. Under no traditional calculation could this situation – low unemployment and target inflation (by the 2% rule) – warrant expansionary monetary policy. Yet the Fed meeting of December 2019 maintained the target rate for Fed funds at between 1.5% and 1.75%, rates that historically can be viewed as extremely low.

The Taylor rule had failed in its function, recentring monetary policy back to neutral once the heavy lifting for the financial crisis was done. Once the pandemic had taken centre stage, there was no holding back and, in March 2020, the Fed funds rate was dropped to between zero and 0.25%.

From there to now (March 2023), we have had either the natural denouement of the Fed's monetary policy excesses after the guardrails were weakened and then removed, or the impacts of a series of large shocks – the supply shocks following the pandemic and the invasion of Ukraine. Mohamed El-Erian (2023a), in the *Financial Times* on 21 March 2023, put it succinctly:

> The [Silicon Valley Bank, Signature Bank and Silvergate] failures were also a reflection of the mishandled shift in the country's interest rate regime. After allowing financial conditions to be too loose for way too long, the Fed slammed on the brakes only after a protracted and damaging mischaracterisation of inflation as transitory.

Rather than anchoring inflationary expectations to 2%, as the Fed sought to do with its monetary policy, it had instead anchored interest rate expectations to zero. Consequently, when inflation rose and the Fed needed to respond with contractionary monetary policy – raising interest rates – banks, corporations and individuals had all constructed their balance sheets and strategies based upon extremely low interest rates and the absence of macroeconomic risk.

In the final chapter, we will discuss how to get out of this impasse in a way that takes account of the interests of future generations, following the line we have already given. Interest rates should be anchored at a normal level of about 5%, but inflation should be predicted to run at a higher rate than 2% for the next few years.

Why is the Fed frit?

One answer is historical. Ben Bernanke followed Milton Friedman in having the monetary authorities take responsibility for the Great Depression:

> 'Let me end my talk by abusing slightly my status as an official representative of the Federal Reserve. I would like to say to Milton and Anna: Regarding the Great Depression. You're right, we did it. We're very sorry. But thanks to you, we won't do it again.' (Bernanke,

2002; at the conference to honour Milton Friedman, University of Chicago, Chicago, Illinois, 8 November 2002, on Milton Friedman's 90th birthday)

As we've already discussed, it's not really possible (and maybe not desirable) to go back into history to try to determine what really happened. The Great Depression was just as likely (we would argue, rather more so) to have been caused by the Federal Reserve standing back during the roaring 20s and not intervening to control the excessive zeal that appeared, not least in the financial markets. Indeed, it is likely that the same mistake has been made again, for the same reasons, during the dot-com bubble, the mortgage mayhem that led to the financial crisis of 2007/08 and finally the high inflation during and after the pandemic. That instead the problem was the failure of the Fed to adopt sufficiently expansionary monetary policies seems to be quickly refuted by the data on interest rates (see Figure 6.2).

The discount rate (the short-term borrowing rate from the Fed) fell substantially and fairly consistently during the 1930s. In particular, while there is a jump from 2.5% to 3.5% in the second half of 1931, there is no apparent tightening in 1936 leading up to the recession in 1937. But the myth persists: 'Ancient history is worse. In 1936, the Fed tightened rates

Figure 6.2: US basic discount rate (discontinued)

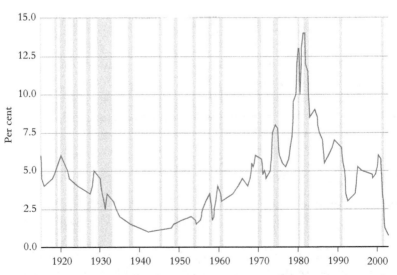

Source: Board of Governors of the Federal Reserve System (US), Federal Reserve Bank of St Louis Basic Discount Rate (DISCONTINUED) [DISCNTD8], retrieved from FRED, Federal Reserve Bank of St Louis; https://fred.stlouisfed.org/series/DISCNTD8, 27 February 2024.

when the economy was already in recession, contributing to the second part of the Great Depression and a 50 per cent collapse in the Dow Jones Industrial Average' (Das, 2016).

Bernanke's own view seems to follow from his research in 1983 on the 'Non-monetary effects of the financial crisis in the propagation of the Great Depression'. Looking at monetary variables (either the money supply or interest rates) doesn't tell the full story since bank behaviour may well affect the availability and cost of credit to the private sector. The lending system may simply break down. The pandemic represented an extreme case where risks could not be judged. During the pandemic, it was unclear what businesses might survive and what individuals might lose their jobs. In effect, it became impossible for the private sector to provide loans that weren't guaranteed by the government. The UK Government ran loan schemes through the banks – the 'Coronavirus Business Interruption Loan Scheme', the 'Coronavirus Larger Business Interruption Loan Scheme', and the 'Bounce Back Loan Scheme'. By 31 May 2021 (House of Commons research briefing), over £79 billion had been lent, with an estimate that 37% would not be repaid.

That the Fed is 'frit' is evident from the 'taper tantrum' in 2013, already described. In 2013, the Chair of the Fed discussed that the central bank could 'taper' its purchases of bonds. Ten-year bond yields quickly moved up – even though no actual 'tapering' had yet occurred – from 2% to 3%. Either as a consequence, or not, the Fed did not carry through on this until December, when it modestly lowered its bond purchases from $85 billion to $75 billion a month. With the failure of the Silicon Valley Bank in 2023, there were quick calls for the Fed to reverse its tightening policy on interest rates and the associated quantitative tightening.

Left-wing trickle-down

During the financial crisis, the large bank bailouts and government fiscal support were carried out under the Obama administration in the US and the Labour Government in the UK. While it might seem obvious that a Conservative administration would support the banking and business sectors, it is less obvious why a centre-left government would do the same. While our inherited memories of the Great Depression show Wall Street brokers jumping from New York City skyscrapers, they also show Hoovervilles of unemployed and homeless working-class inhabitants. When the banks fail, and corporations go bankrupt, it is a short journey to high unemployment. As we will discuss in the next section, bailing out the banks is one thing if the problem is indeed asteroids from the sky, unpredictable shocks that can neither be prevented nor mitigated in advance. It's another thing if 'moral hazard' either creates the 'shocks' or amplifies their impact, as seemed clearly the case in the sub-prime mortgage crisis of 2007 leading to the Great Recession.

But before looking at that, let's consider the argument on some parts of the left to 'run the economy hot'. As we have described in a preceding chapter, former Fed Chair (now Secretary of the Treasury) Janet Yellen argued at the Brookings Institution in 2019 that "[a]llowing the labor market to run hot could bring substantial benefits", citing a paper by Arthur Okun (1973) on how upward mobility is enhanced in tight labour markets. But Yellen has displayed mixed views on the subject, previously arguing at Stanford in 2017 that "allowing the economy to run markedly and persistently 'hot' would be risky and unwise".

Of course, these statements are not necessarily in contradiction. There is no reason to think that a 'hot' economy benefits workers as a whole – to the contrary, a hot labour market is often because real wages are low so that firms seek to hire cheap labour rather than invest in expensive machinery. This has been seen in the recent inflation in the UK. Even though firms (notably in the hospitality sector) have decried labour shortages, exacerbated by Brexit, wages on average in the UK have not kept up with inflation. But there is considerable evidence that, when labour markets are tight, firms have to consider hiring those (often from minority groups) whom they would otherwise have passed over due to discrimination.

David Blanchflower was noted for an expansionary view while on the Bank of England Monetary Policy Committee during the financial crisis. With Richard Murphy he has (March 2023) given testimony to the House of Commons Treasury Committee. They describe what they see as the successes of the quantitative easing policy, not least countering contractionary government policies of austerity. Ironically, perhaps, they take the opposite view to the idea that monetary expansion has been of particular benefit to the less well-off, noting that the big winners have been the owners of assets, not the sellers of labour. With that caveat, they support the continuation of the quantitative easing policy.

There is however a danger that monetary expansion may have become the trickle-down economics of the left, with monetary expansion filling in when governments fail to provide baseline support for the less well-off. Expanded unemployment insurance during a recession, rather than low interest rates or bailing out the banks, might prove more effective in terms of sustaining wages and directing government funds to those needing support.

Zero interest rate debt overhang

Richard Koo has written influential (but perhaps unfortunately not with the policy makers) books on the balance sheet recession, where high debt necessarily impacts on the current behaviour of businesses (see, for example, Koo, 2003).

Figure 6.3: US gross federal debt as percentage of gross domestic product

Source: US Office of Management and Budget and Federal Reserve Bank of St Louis, Gross Federal Debt as Percent of Gross Domestic Product [GFDGDPA188S], retrieved from FRED, Federal Reserve Bank of St Louis; https://fred.stlouisfed.org/series/GFDGDPA188S, 27 February 2024.

What is probably not a huge worry is government debt. This is not because it isn't extremely large. Government debt in the US is $28 trillion and in the UK £2.2 trillion. In both cases, this is over 100% of annual GDP, over the levels highlighted by Reinhart and Rogoff (2010) as leading to lowered growth (see Figure 6.3). Further, by historical standards, as a percentage of GDP, this is back to levels last seen during the Second World War.

However, the level of debt from the Second World War did not lead to low growth. Through a combination of inflation and growth, debt declined regularly and substantially after the war. It was back to 30% by 1980. This failure of the debt to hamstring the economy is partly because the comparison of debt to GDP, and focusing upon a figure of 100%, is bizarre. Even at 'normal' interest rates of 5%, the interest costs on that level of debt are just 5% of GDP, hardly an unsupportable amount. But in fact, a lot of the debt is at lower rates, averaging about 3%. Further, a lot is now held by the Fed or by government agencies such as social security, so it is the government paying interest to itself.

What might be of more concern is private debt to GDP (outside of the financial sector). This figure currently stands at over 200% in the UK and 235% in the US. There is as yet little evidence perhaps for Richard Koo's belief that this will lead to particularly prudent and conservative financial policies within firms. To the contrary, the private equity model is one of increased leverage of firms. Private equity buys a business, engages in cost-cutting and leveraging up the balance sheet before potentially selling it on.

For this reason, and the general availability of low interest rate finance over the last two decades, there has been a rise in 'zombie' firms (Favara et al, 2021) that are only kept alive because low interest rates mean that the repayment sums are small. Consider a firm with losses (taking account of depreciation) of £1 million, cash-flow of £500,000 a year and £10 million of debt (structured with a balloon repayment of the principal at maturity, sometimes decades away) at 5%. The interest payments are covered from the cash-flow, so there is no imperative for management – other than accounting good practice – to declare the firm insolvent. Management would lose its salaries and bonuses when it could just keep going. This is a 'zombie' firm that has little rationale in economics, but nothing forces its closure. The lenders try to get around this – to cut their losses – by having covenants in the loans that make them payable if they are not met, but this becomes a negotiating game since it is not generally in the interest of the lender either to book the loss.

It is generally believed that the leverage of monetary policy – interest rate rises – may be much higher than the historical norm after decades of low interest rates. A modest slowing of the economy may cause large numbers of 'zombie' firms to crash when the cash-flow (rather than profits) constraint becomes binding.

Aeroplane analogies

The central banks – the Fed and the Bank of England – are now expected by the financial markets to achieve 'soft landings' by analogy with aeroplanes. Somehow, in the UK, the Bank of England is expected to bring down double-digit inflation without a serious recession, and the US Fed is expected to bring its 6% inflation down to the target 2%, again without a serious recession. Traditional monetary policy, operating through the Phillips curve, says that this won't happen, it cannot happen. It is only the recession that brings down inflation.

Ironically, the aeroplane analogy suggests why 'soft landings' don't exist. Instead, passengers have different degrees of fright as the plane touches down at speed (about 170 mph) and the pilot slams on the brakes. The unavoidable reason for this is to avoid stalling, to maintain sufficient speed that the aeroplane remains airborne until it touches the ground. In the same way, an economy may not be able to achieve a smooth glide into low inflation without a recession with increasing unemployment.

Monetary policy in the last four decades has been based upon the idea that the central banks can prevent recessions, rather than – as in earlier vintages of monetary theory – smooth out transitions. Central banks argue that they were restoring policy normalcy after 'doing whatever it takes' to prevent the financial crisis from turning into a Great Depression, and then the pandemic hit. But 'doing whatever it takes' is almost never the right policy. After Dunkirk, Churchill had to go to the Commons to, in part, explain the role of the Royal Air Force (RAF). It has been suggested that Churchill, expecting to lose the bulk of the British Expeditionary Force (BEF), kept the RAF in reserve to avoid losing a vital part of the future defence of the UK. Whether or not he did so, it would have been a totally explicable decision. Losing both the BEF and the RAF would have left the country in an extremely unfortunate situation. Economically, that is where we are today. Central banks should never have used up their arsenal by going to zero interest rates and should – as soon as the opportunity presented itself – have rebuilt their arsenal by raising rates after the worst of the housing crash was over.

Car analogies

When macroeconomists don't use aeroplane analogies, they use car analogies. 'The economy is running on all cylinders.' For policy, we use the analogy of 'smart highways', introduced in the UK.

According to the UK Department of Transport (2020) report on 'Smart Motorway Safety', controlled motorways with dynamic speed limits (adjusting to circumstances) came into play in 1995. Dynamic hard shoulders (with circumstances determining when the hard shoulder is used for traffic) arrived in 2006, and 'all lane running' motorways without hard shoulders – but with safety bays every so often – in 2014. All this was to allow for greater capacity without actual expansion of the motorways. The report confirms intuition that collisions between moving and stationary vehicles have increased without hard shoulders, while collisions between moving vehicles are lessened due to the dynamic controls and increased capacity.

The report supports smart motorways, but favours 'all lane running' over 'dynamic hard shoulders', since these are seen as creating confusion for drivers. There should be more emergency areas to allow drivers in difficulty safe places to stop (at no more than a mile distance), and improved methods of notification and response. There would be automatic displays of obstruction.

In effect, smart highways were intended to replace 'hardware' – building up the infrastructure with either more highways or (certainly preferably in the environmental crisis) other forms of transport such as rail – with 'software'. It didn't work. On 15 April 2023, the government announced that all planned new smart motorways would be cancelled.

To take a different example, for smartphones, improved distance pictures can be taken by having a telephoto lens in addition to a regular and a wide lens. Alternatively, to save money, software can attempt to fill in the pixels when there isn't an optical telephoto capacity, but it's clearly a second-best solution. Similarly, MP3 files for music streaming compress the sound content. An expensive traditional stereo system is higher quality, with a trade-off between hardware and software. It is perhaps not pure nostalgia that leads audiophiles to return to LPs and turntables.

In macroeconomics, there has been a similar trade-off between what can be done by aggregate demand management and what can better be done on the supply side. Much of the discussion was unfortunately side-tracked by a 'supply side' economics based upon low regulation and taxation, along with unfettered trade, that – in fact – had no clear supply side advantages and in practice considerable disadvantages over the previous model of a regulated mixed economy. In addition, there is little reason to think that the economic policy 'software' – the policy tools of central banks – has dramatically improved over past practice.

Go back to the question of whether we should run the economy hot in order to lower unemployment and bring disadvantaged (and discriminated against) groups into employment. Instead of trying to use monetary policy to achieve these ends, there are real, direct policies that can be put into play. Affirmative action and effective enforcement of equality laws can impact on discrimination. Effective job centres can better match the unemployed to available vacancies. Training and apprenticeships – funding further education colleges who provide direct training on a basis more commensurate with higher education, as argued for in the Augar Report (Augar, 2019) – can improve the productivity and thereby the employability of young people. Investment in the infrastructure and in physical capital (rather than the financial sector) can create good jobs. Having an effective NHS – without inefficient waiting lists – can keep the population in good health and increase labour productivity.

The restoration of guardrails

It is likely that historians 50 years from now will wonder, 'What were they thinking?' How could anyone think that house prices that were eight times household incomes were a good thing? How could people take flights for a weekend away in a time when the Paris Accord of 1.5 degrees temperature rise was in jeopardy? How could the UK go into a hard Brexit? How could some politicians seek to justify the storming of the US Capitol?

The rest of this book is therefore largely about restoring guardrails. Even if it were feasible, interest rates of near zero make no sense in a time when we need to consume less and invest more. Population growth is categorically a bad thing. Education is too important to underpay teachers, to starve further education of funding and put in policies that direct universities to strive for 'student satisfaction' rather than learning.

7

The Future of Work

The present of work

We have spent considerable time exploring monetary policy and – in particular – the role of low and zero interest rates. We've argued that these led the older generations to borrow from the future for consumption (and not investment) today, but with no intention of paying back the debt themselves, but instead handing it on to the younger generations. Dealing with the debt overhang is one major area of policy concern, but in many ways is less important than the real imbalances in the economy. In the next four chapters, we consider the labour market, population of humans and robots, university education and the housing market. We could have discussed other topics – the environment would be a book in itself – but these are indicative of the problematic policies that have been adopted, and suggest policies for the future. They also clearly impact different generations differentially.

One of the major issues for the future is how to organize and remunerate work. Do we continue with the gig economy? Do workers go back to the office or work from home? As demographics shift older, how do we most effectively utilize the relatively smaller groups of working age? Will AI provide the necessary stretching of human labour, or will it have negative effects, with the robots taking all the creative and interesting jobs?

At the Conservative Conference in 2021, Boris Johnson observed: "We are not going back to the same old broken model with low wages, low growth, low skills and low productivity." As can be seen in the Figure 7.1, real pay in the UK was stagnant for a decade from 2008 to 2018, after the financial crisis, only ticking up during the pandemic.

The US pattern differed in that stagnant wages had essentially run from the late-1970s through to 2015, when the Fed decided to 'run the economy hot'. From Figure 7.2, there is recent evidence that 'running hot' works in the short run, but at the risk – in theory and in practice – of inflation. US real wages turned down sharply as inflation rose rapidly in 2021 and 2022.

Figure 7.1: UK average pay in real terms

Source: Office for National Statistics – Monthly Wages and Salaries Survey.

Wages are a generational issue for the simple reason that younger participants in the workforce generally start out with limited assets other than their labour and their human capital. If wages are low (and profits and asset prices are high), workers will find it hard to ever acquire property and other assets, including pensions.

What determines wages?

The main point of this chapter is that the low-wage, low-productivity economy arose from poor public policy. The 'flexible' labour market espoused

Figure 7.2: US median usual weekly real earnings for wage and salary workers, 16 years and over

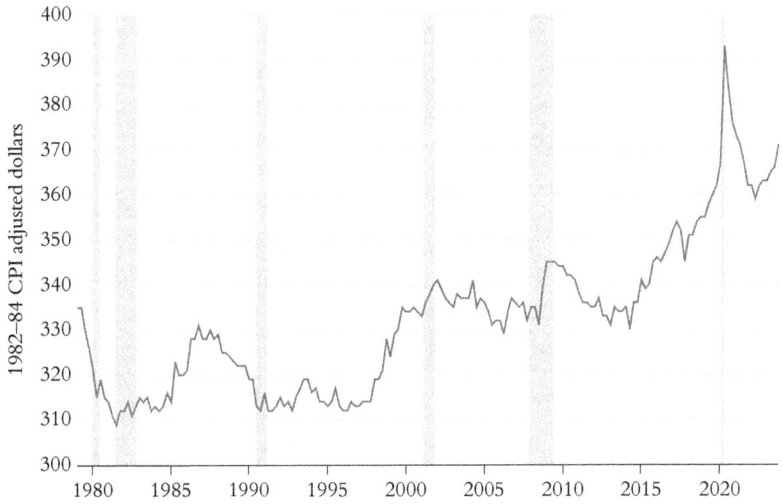

Source: US Bureau of Labor Statistics [LES1252881600Q], retrieved from FRED, Federal Reserve Bank of St Louis; https://fred.stlouisfed.org/series/LES1252881600Q, 27 February 2024.

by Thatcher and Reagan not only led to greater and greater inequality, but it also led to low productivity and growth. The reason is that it misunderstood the nature of the employment relationship and what makes for a productive workplace and economy.

The employment relationship is like any relationship – the benefits to an individual depend on group productivity, and on the division of the benefits across the participants. The group could be a family, a workplace or a community. If a soccer coach tries to build a team, they don't just focus on each individual player, but upon the effectiveness of the team.

In the workplace, workers and management at the firm use the capital of the firm (physical capital, brand reputation, social capital within the firm), along with their individual efforts, to produce and market output. How the surplus (think revenues less non-labour costs) gets divided is mediated by numerous factors such as the ownership of the firm (John Lewis, for example, remains for now 'owned' by its employees rather than shareholders or private equity), the presence or absence of effective trade unions and government regulation. Legislation can define the length of the working week and the rules for overtime, along with statutory maternity/paternity leave, sick pay and so on. Importantly, it can set redundancy pay. These statutes provide direct returns to workers, but also set the parameters for bargaining on the individual or union level.

Importantly, your productivity (as a worker or manager) depends upon the context, including the firm's culture (is the firm attuned to success?), the capital equipment given to you and the contributions of your fellow workers. If you're a desk-worker, being given a new computer and a pleasant working environment is likely to increase your productivity. If you're working in a restaurant, space to work and good equipment increase your productivity. So does having good co-workers. A brilliant server is limited if the chef isn't very good.

On your own, if you do the traditional walk into your boss's office and ask for a pay rise, they will consider your 'marginal productivity' – on the assumption you and just you would leave if your request is turned down, what is the loss to the firm? Even if you're a fairly average employee, it would take some time to fill your post and there are risks involved in any hiring process – 'better the devil you know'. But the supply of labour (how easy it would be to find a replacement) and your productivity enter into the determination. The firm has to also consider the effect on other workers, and might not want to reward individual pay demands since this will encourage other workers to make the same approach.

If your whole team walks into the boss's office and asks for a pay rise, the potential loss to the employer is much greater. This is the simple proposition behind organizing a trade union. While formation of a trade union is unlikely to be a welcomed event for the employer, since they will have to agree a higher wage rate, they can potentially see the bright side, that they can now negotiate productivity issues (such as a change in working practices) in an organized way.

If a policy maker wants to increase wages, there are essentially three ways to do so. One we have discussed under monetary policy – the central bank can try to run the economy hot. The problem is that this involves low interest rates which – as we've discussed – generally benefit asset-owners and penalize future generations. Further, this may or may not be sustainable. If it requires a constantly increasing money supply, this will either be self-reversing as the central bank raises interest rates to keep the money dammed up as reserves, or an eventual inflation – even if there are 'long and variable lags' – may call for an emergency change in monetary policy.

Investment in public and private capital, and in human capital through education, raises productivity and wage rates. Traditionally, expansionary monetary policy worked through an investment channel, as well as a consumption channel, and expansionary monetary policy could be more sustainable. Low interest rates in the past led to new plants and equipment, raising productivity. We will discuss in the next chapter why the investment channel seems to have disappeared from the impact of monetary policy. Investment in human capital through education and training, and equipping the next generation with extensive physical capital, also benefits the future generations. This does not have to be encouraged by low interest rates – the government can directly invest in the infrastructure and in providing low-cost higher education or skills training, or can subsidize firms to invest through tax credits.

Finally, the government can seek to increase the bargaining power of workers. This involves trade union power – both the rules of organizing and the rules for taking industrial action, the minimum wage, the benefits system, redundancy pay, health and safety regulations, overtime and work-week rules, pensions, and the whole tax system. Part of the false narrative of the economics of the 1980s is that all these – while they may be desirable from a redistribution or poverty-alleviation perspective – are economically inefficient. This is fundamentally misleading if not the opposite of the truth. Indeed, the low productivity growth since the 1980s should be indicative that the very reverse may be the case. The problem, instead, is that much of this may benefit consumption by current generations at the expense of the future. Trade unions, for example, may benefit primarily established workers with seniority – indeed, trade unions typically establish 'last-in, first-out' rules for redundancies as part of their contracts with employers, and typically negotiate pay scales that rise with seniority.

Trade unions

Early in his presidency, Ronald Reagan took on the Professional Air Traffic Controllers Organization, firing the members when they went on strike. Margaret Thatcher took on the National Union of Mineworkers. In both countries, trade unions have decreased substantially as a factor in the labour markets. The US Bureau of Labor Statistics reported in 2022 that union membership was 33.1% in the public sector but only 6% in the private sector. In the UK, the Department for Business, Energy & Industrial Strategy reports that 2021 membership was 50.1% in the public sector and 12.8% in the private sector. For the UK, trade union membership has halved since the 1980s peak as seen in Figure 7.3.

Rebuilding trade unions is one way of increasing bargaining power on the labour side. There have been some recent successes in gaining recognition, but it remains the case that corporations fight aggressively to maintain a union-free workplace.

Robert Reich (2021) wrote in *The Guardian* about the attempts to unionize Amazon, describing the poor working conditions of a hugely profitable company. He quotes Amazon as saying:

> Our employees have the choice of whether or not to join a union. They always have. As a company, we don't think unions are the best answer for our employees. Every day we empower people to find ways to improve their jobs, and when they do that we want to make those

Figure 7.3: UK trade union membership

Sources: Administrative data on union membership: Department for Employment (1892–1973) and the Certification Office (1974–2021). Data on employees that are trade union members in the UK and Great Britain: Labour Force Survey, Office for National Statistics.

changes – quickly. That type of continuous improvement is harder to do quickly and nimbly with unions in the middle.

In California, the *New York Times* reported on 23 August 2021 that Uber has sought to maintain 'gig' status for its workers as independent contractors (Conger and Browning, 2021). California passed a law in 2019 requiring those workers to be classified as employees. A Proposition was put on the ballot to have a vote of citizens to overturn the law. Proposition 22 passed strongly, was overturned in court and is now subject to appeal. It requires considerable naivety to believe, as with the claims by Amazon, that these large companies are motivated primarily by the well-being of their – well, we cannot say employees for the 'gig' workers until perhaps the appeal on Proposition 22 is heard.

At Starbucks, *The Guardian* reported on 17 November 2022 that unions have started to win representation ballots, but the corporation is viewed as resistant to bargaining (Sainato, 2022). This is despite having a clearly inefficient turnover rate of 65% of employees in a year, that might be lowered by higher union wages and better working conditions.

From an economic efficiency point of view, trade unions are viewed as a counter-balance to the power of monopsonistic (sole buyer of labour) firms. For example, in American baseball, owners of teams relied upon the 'reserve clause' that allowed them to renew the player's contract for a further year. With considerable stretch of the imagination, they viewed this power as renewing the contract in its entirety, including the 'reserve clause', so that the contract was essentially in perpetuity. This meant that the player could never become a 'free agent' to negotiate a better deal with another club, unless their original club chose to release them from their contract. Remarkably, the US Supreme Court in 1972 upheld the reserve clause. It was only through arbitration under a trade union agreement, and a subsequent contract that the reserve clause was rescinded.

A trade union can also counteract monopsonistic power at a less exalted level of the labour market. Alan Manning (2003) has developed many of the arguments as to how imperfect competition affects outcomes and desirable public policy. Empirically, the work by Card and Krueger (1995) can be taken to show that simplistic views – a higher minimum wage causes unemployment – are not validated in the real world.

Generally, economic models of bargaining argue that efficient outcomes are attained. In negotiations, it's in the interest of both sides – management and workers – to maximize the size of the pie to be divided. Whatever share of the pie their bargaining power (the ability to lock out workers or to strike) can attain for them, they gain from having that share come from a larger pie. As an example, consider the recent negotiations (2021) between the United Auto Workers in the US and John Deere which show the dimensionality – and efficiency gains – possible under negotiation. The contract gives sharp immediate wage gains (10%) and a ratification bonus, as well as further income gains over a six-year period. It also covers pensions (important in both the US and the UK) and health insurance (important in the US). But between the second and third company offers, the major tweaks were in the productivity bonuses.

But what about future generations?

If bargaining power for workers (either individual or organized as a collective) has gone down, is that a generational issue? Part of the answer is immediate. If Generation X worked half their careers on a higher wage, and then half their careers on a lower wage, they are doing better than millennials who may have worked their entire career on the lower wage. Further, Generation X could have used their higher wage period to build up savings, buy a house and start a pension if – as is becoming common in the private sector – there is no substantial workplace one. UK companies are required to offer a workplace pension to most employees, but only need to put in 3% of salary while you put in 5%, much less than traditional public sector pensions or what large private firms did in the past.

In fact, the situation is typically worse than described for newer generations, since wages over a career are back-loaded – wages and benefits rise with seniority. There are good economic efficiency reasons for this, that we will discuss shortly, but it means that – as for millennials – the failure of real wages to keep up with economic growth hits them during the part of their career when they might have hoped to have progressed into higher paying posts and to really build up their assets and pensions. This is particularly the case if career progression and pensions are precisely where the earnings stagnation has hit.

Go back to the firm which, either because it wants to attract the best employees or because it is under union bargaining pressure, wants to construct an offer that pays the higher remuneration in the most efficient way. One way of doing this is to have substantial progression during the career. By setting up a promotions process, the firm can induce high effort from its workers – the steeper the wage gains obtained from promotion, the more effort that workers will apply. Negotiations with trade unions often involve this sort of trade-off – the union would like incremental salary scales where workers' wages rise with seniority without any special effort, while the firm would like to tie the wage progression to promotion. But in bargaining, both sides can see a benefit to 'back-loading' the wage contract, paying higher wages and benefits to longer-serving workers. This is to encourage both sides to invest in the employment relationship, to develop the 'specific human capital' – experience and training – that is of greatest benefit to the firm and not to the outside labour market.

Perhaps surprisingly, final salary pension schemes are the ultimate way of back-loading an employment contract and make the point clearly on the advantages to the firm of having this sort of remuneration pattern. In universities, it was something of a commonplace that Dr X, a long-serving and conscientious (but sadly not brilliant) academic would be promoted from senior lecturer to professor in the twilight of their career. In the days of the final salary pension (curtailed for new entrants in 2012), this last-minute jump in their final salary (say, by 10 or 20%) would increase their pension by that percentage. The university had immense leverage over Dr X for much of their career, holding the reward in front of them for one or two decades. Dr X regularly served on the tedious committees that more brilliant colleagues avoided, and took on important but time-consuming teaching such as the first-year Economics Principles course. Dr X might, in their later years, be approached by the dean with an offer to become head of department or dean of students with the expectation of finally achieving the promotion that would permanently increase their pension.

Final salary pension schemes have largely disappeared, with little commentary on the efficiency loss (particularly to the employer). This was one of the consequences of the low and zero interest rate policies in an economy where the other institutions didn't adjust to the side effects of extreme monetary policy. In the case of pensions, there is an accounting anomaly that is nonetheless enforced by The Pensions Regulator. Pensions (both for good reasons of financial prudence and for regulatory reasons) need to invest in a low-risk portfolio, largely comprised of government bonds. With the interest rate on these at historical lows over the last few decades, the trajectory of assets is assumed to grow at the near zero rate of interest. This ignores that the funds over the last four decades have – even if fully invested in government bonds – gotten the large capital gains from the consistently falling interest rate. Ironically, the recent rise in interest rates has bailed out pension funds – the Universities Superannuation Scheme covering UK university employees went from a severe deficit to a large surplus when interest rates went up.

Without over-stating the extent to which companies have – now that interest rates have gone up – reconsidered the role of defined benefits pensions, IBM has for example reopened its frozen pension scheme in place of contributions to the US tax-advantaged individual 401(k) pension accounts (Sommer, 2024).

One of the ways the gig economy has hit productivity is through the elimination of the reward structure that encouraged investment – by both the firm and the worker – in the employment relationship.

The employment relationship

There are two extremes to structuring employment in an economy. One is the 'gig economy' where there is a casual relationship. Workers are hired for a specific 'gig' when it suits the firm and the worker. This could be at a fixed hourly or gig wage, or it could mimic Uber by having dynamic wages that change with supply and demand on an hourly basis. It is, however, hard to see that many jobs or workers need that kind of flexibility.

The other is the 'long-term relationship' model where the firm and the worker invest in the relationship with a view to maintaining it. This tends to arise automatically in a unionized workplace – wages are higher than in a non-union firm, so workers would not lightly give up their employment. Further 'last-in, first-out' redundancy rules protect workers as they gain seniority over time. As we've discussed, effective promotion schemes and pensions can maintain productivity in that sort of otherwise protected environment. 'Jobs for life' can enhance productivity as both the firm and the worker invest in the relationship in any firm. IBM had a no layoff policy until 1993. Japan was renowned for its paternalistic labour market practices during the boom years.

This doesn't mean that firms with these long-term relationship models for employment are 'soft touches' for new workers. Professional roles such as lawyers, doctors, investment bankers and professors are extremely hard on new entrants, with the rewards attained when the individual hopefully gains partnership, tenure or senior doctor status. Lorne Carmichael (1988) argued that tenure was a mechanism to ensure that 'informed' senior academics made the right decisions in hiring the best new lecturers. Since the senior professor could not be replaced involuntarily with a new entrant becoming a mid-career star, they did not have to fear hiring the best candidate. Renee Landers, James Rebitzer and Lowell Taylor (1996) show why law firms might require new hires to work extremely long hours in a 'rat race' to demonstrate their inherent effort levels. The payoff for all these overworked and stressed new entrants is that, provided they can stay the course and achieve partner/ full professor/consultant status, they have flexibility and control in their career activities. In the UK, for doctors in particular, they give up high remuneration (achievable in countries such as the US) in return for that influence and control of their workplace, something that benefits patients.

As with pensions and pay progression, removing that professional control from the employment structure – in favour of a more 'managerial' model – impacts negatively on productivity. An NHS consultant balances work in the public sector, and the ability to provide public service and support the development of junior doctors, with the much higher remuneration in the private sector. In the same way, an economics or finance professor forgoes considerably higher pay they could get in the financial sector, and King's Counsel barristers become High Court judges in part for the security of the pension scheme (a further argument for retaining generous pensions) but as well for the forum for serving the public interest.

The failure to recognize the desire of workers at each level to contribute, in a well-structured employment relationship, has led to many of the poor policy choices made over the last four decades. The pandemic unfortunately has moved us further from the relationship model of employment to an informal, less fundamental connection between employer and employee. The younger generation has been offered a work from home or hybrid model instead – for many workers – of going into the place of work. Just as with 'lecture capture' (recording university lectures so they can be watched from the comfort of home, rather than engaging in the classroom) and other disengagement devices at universities, this disengagement from the work environment will prove costly to younger generations. They will not be gaining the learning from experience and implicit mentoring that occurs in the workplace, gaining knowledge of the firm's culture (albeit that is not always a benefit, if the culture is toxic) and being able to demonstrate their contribution to team efforts.

Job security

While the oil cartel OPEC gains regular attention, the maple syrup cartel is less well known. A cartel is often noted as a way of raising prices, but it can also smooth out supply and prices, ensuring consumers that they can have a high-quality product to put on their pancakes at a substantial but predictable price. This came to the fore in 2021 during the pandemic when a combination of diminished supply and increased demand (if you're not commuting, you can have a better breakfast) would have led to a maple syrup shortage. However, it turns out that Quebecois producers maintain a strategic reserve of maple syrup as reported in *The Guardian* (28 November 2021) precisely to smooth out imbalances in supply and demand when they arise.

The 'contract' models of labour markets work on similar principles. Maple syrup, given the production process and geographical limitations, was never likely to be a mass-market low-cost commodity, but no doubt having even a partial cartel raises the average price over time. But this has potential benefits – even without reading the no doubt informative materials put out by the Federation of Quebec Maple Syrup Producers – in terms of consistently high quality, stabilized if high prices and supply reliability. The 'contract' models view the labour market as potentially benefitting from stabilization in the same way as the maple syrup market (or, for those who prefer to concentrate their grocery shopping towards later in the day, the market for Bordeaux wines, which similarly has a system in place to balance out supplies and demands, and production in good and bad vintages).

One way of providing this sort of stability over the whole economy is through monetary policy, using interest rates to ease adjustments over time and mitigate the impact of recessions and booms. As we've discussed, however, this comes with costs, particularly if – as has been the case over the last 40 years – the policy becomes asymmetric. Internalized at a firm or industry level, however, smoothing out is likely to be more symmetric in nature. A firm maintains a relationship with its workforce such that, in boom times, workers put in extra effort and, in recession, workers are not wantonly laid off. This can be because of union pressure (as we've noted, the government can adopt policies to encourage or discourage unionization) or it can be because the firm takes a long-term view.

The government can also support these sorts of automatic stabilizers into the economy. Rather than addressing issues in a panicked mode, as occurred during the pandemic with considerable waste and fraud, the system can be designed to be more efficient in smoothing out the 'shocks' that conventional economists now see as perpetual asteroid showers. In the UK, you are entitled to statutory redundancy pay from your employer of more than two years if you are laid off from your job and no suitable alternative is provided. This pay occurs at the rate of one week's pay per year of service for mid-age workers, but is capped in total at about £16,000. The government chips in by making this free of tax. Rather than putting the burden on the monetary authority or solely upon the taxpayer, the firm automatically is made to chip in or to help stabilize the economy by limiting layoffs.

Alison Booth and Gylfi Zoega (2003) argued that there are externalities arising from firms being too ready to fire workers in a recession, so this sort of government intervention can be efficient. J. Kenneth Galbraith (1958) proposes that unemployment benefits should vary according to the general state of the economy – arguably the same should hold for statutory redundancy pay, being higher and thereby discouraging layoffs when unemployment is high.

Rather than spending hundreds of billions of pounds during the pandemic, more reliance on the automatic stabilizers we already had, and amplification of existing ones (a pandemic increase in unemployment insurance rather than a poorly targeted furlough programme) – all designed to solidify the employment relationship – could be economically efficient. We've already questioned whether the extraordinary policies undertaken to keep the financial crisis from becoming a second Great Depression were necessary at all, given the automatic stabilizers instituted in the Great Depression.

A two-tier society

Wages and employment relationships are also affected by the tax and benefits system in place. These can be designed to support work – a well-funded NHS, social housing, quality education and universal services from parks to broadband and libraries, museums and public theatres – or can become substitutes for an efficient and productive work environment.

When Rishi Sunak became the third Conservative prime minister within a year, he tilted the rhetoric away from 'levelling up' to: "This government will always act to protect the most vulnerable in our society." As an example, the prime minister – in that tweet of 3 January 2023 – referred to the 'Cost of Living Payment' of £900 for means tested benefit claimants, on top of the £400 energy bill discount in 2022, the £1,200 payment to eight million low-income households in 2022, and the £1,300 for all households on their energy bills.

While protecting the vulnerable is unobjectionable, this agenda to help people pay their inflated gas and electricity bills is a modest one compared to the post-war efforts to bring society together through policies such as the establishment of the NHS. Further, it is essentially wasted money compared to lasting improvements to insulation and heating systems. As the fuel crisis hit, professional class households throughout the country put in new boilers, avoiding much of the impact, while the less well-off struggled on the energy support schemes.

The hapless Jeremy Corbyn, in his 2019 campaign, actually began with a good idea, providing free high-speed broadband to everyone in the country. Universal benefits like this have the advantage of economic efficiency – since everyone in this century needs broadband, there is no reason for having a market to ration it, and there is little reason for digging up streets several times to lay cables for different broadband companies. But also, since everyone is using it, politicians have a strong incentive to provide a high-quality service.

In fact, much of a reasonable standard of living can be provided by universal services such as high-quality education and the NHS, public parks and leisure facilities, public transport, child and elder care, and so on. By providing universal services, stigma is removed from using them – it is hard to think of something crueller, for example, than 'means testing' free school meals, when they could be provided for all (and are being provided in London for all primary school children from 2023/24).

A further category is more expensive to provide, such as housing. Besley and Coate (1991) made the important point that redistribution by providing goods could be more efficient than simple cash benefits, since the level of provision would cause only a proportion of the population to choose the public provision. Quality council housing, built after the war, could be chosen by working-class households, while the better off could remain in the private sector. They would benefit indirectly since the option of having a council house would keep private rents and house prices down.

Beyond the provision of goods and services, the government might also address poverty (particularly child poverty) with direct support payments. Politically, however, there has been limited support for programmes such as a universal basic income where everyone receives a basic level of government support that is funded from general tax revenues. To economists of all stripes, this is an efficient system in that work decisions are neither incentivized nor disincentivized. To take an example, suppose that there is a universal basic income of £3,000 a year funded by an increase in the average tax rate. UK GDP per capita is about £32,000. Hence taxes would have to go up by ten percentage points to fund this system. But people wouldn't lose their basic income by going to work, so wouldn't be disincentivized from doing so.

The political objection is that individuals or households could choose not to work. Consequently, policies were adopted that provided benefits (not least, to limit child poverty) but that were tied to at least part-time work. The UK introduced the Working Tax Credit in 2003, while the US has had the Earned Income Tax Credit since 1975. In the UK, claimants without children needed to work 30 hours a week. Single parents needed to work 16 hours to be eligible.

But the credits were limited to low-income individuals and households. For a single individual without childcare responsibilities, there is claw back above an income of £6,770 at the remarkably high rate of 41%. In the US, the credits rise with income – for a married couple with three or more children, up to about $60,000 – and then taper back down to zero as income rises. In the UK, Working Tax Credits are being replaced by Universal Credit. Despite the name, this misses out on the important point of universal benefits, that they don't distort the work decision since there is no claw back – one continues to get the benefit amount as one goes to work. Universal Credit instead claws back at the remarkably high rate of 55%. Not surprisingly, given this disincentive to work, Universal Credit comes with coercion in the form of a 'claimant commitment' and regular appointments with a 'work coach'.

In effect, these policies subsidize poorly paid jobs. Rather than encouraging individuals to get training (for example, following the traditional route of night school as – in the UK – offered by institutions such as Birkbeck College of the University of London) and put in effort to gain promotion, they face exceptionally high marginal tax rates as their credits are clawed back. A self-policing system would seek to make work attractive, with low marginal tax rates on low incomes, ample free education, training and apprenticeships, and high minimum wages. Childcare could be provided through workplace creches.

Why does the public support the large corporations rather than the workers?

We have emphasized throughout this book that the economic pathways we have taken, and are taking, are policy choices. Governments and central banks, along with international organizations, have either deliberately chosen one equilibrium over time, or they have watched things move in a consistent direction without intervention. Governments in the US and the UK deliberately chose the gig economy and the decline in unions, with the not surprising result that real wages have been going down. They've chosen inefficient safety-net payments to some of those in poverty, rather than providing top public services and effective education and other routes into well-paid employment.

Given that many voters are not benefitting from the current equilibrium, how can it politically persist? One answer is that some of the losers from the policy do not have the vote. Many members of older generations have assets (houses and stocks) that benefit from the overall policy mix of lower interest rates and – for stocks – higher profits as wages decline (at least as a share of GDP). Younger generations, who will suffer from the lower wages but don't have assets that gain, haven't had the vote. Another way in which the equilibrium will become unsustainable is politically as the younger generations become of voting age, and the ratios of winners and losers shifts.

Sometimes, however, things look beneficial until considerable thought goes into them. For example, why do we have laws on marriage? Why not instead have 'gig' arrangements where family relationships are by the hour or minute? If one of the adult parties to the arrangement has a bad day with the kids, why not go on the internet and find a better parent? The reason is that we want the parties to relationships – families, communities, workplaces – to invest in them, not to engage in short-term behaviour. Whether it's the builder we use, the doctor, the restaurant, we try to develop an ongoing relationship. It would be surprising if we didn't do that in our employment.

Economists have not done enough to clarify the underlying realities. An interesting example is 'net neutrality', the principle that the internet service provider cannot charge or favour one website over another. On the face of it, this looks great for the consumer. You will not have to pay to use Facebook as a 'premium channel' on your internet service. Of course, websites can and do charge you for access – typically now newspapers are behind paywalls, you can pay to have YouTube without advertising. What would happen if instead of 'net neutrality', the ISP could charge Facebook for fast access? Facebook would pay up and profits would be transferred from Facebook to the ISP and – since the ISP market is more competitive than the big social media firms – the cost you pay to the ISP would go down. It would be like 'terrestrial TV', low-cost to access but with lots of commercials. Or you could buy a premium service without advertising.

Nonetheless, it's hard to understand why, in the 21st century, a deference to the financial sector in particular and corporations in general has taken over. There is no bank that, in reality, is 'too big to fail' since it can continue to run in administration and – from the Great Depression – there are in place protections for depositors (to certain pound or dollar limits). Well-off investors had an unpleasant weekend when the Silicon Valley Bank was in the process of going under, but all the behaviour of the Fed and government agencies ended up demonstrating that once again the financial sector would be bailed out.

Apple computer has been perhaps the prime example of a company that managed to engender considerable 'hipster' brand identity while growing to be the highest market value business in the world with astronomical profit margins. Through the '1984' ad, and the 'I'm a Mac' ads, Apple reinforced that it was the 'counter-culture' and 'cool' alternative to the corporate world. But that worked precisely because Apple was setting itself in opposition (true or false) against the grey corporate world while at the same time aggressively maximizing profits.

The opioid crisis and the climate emergency have reminded us that – while private sector companies are vital to a productive economy – they do not necessarily come with the public's interests at the forefront. Campaigns seek to remove problematic donors' names from museums and museum exhibitions.

Newer generations are entitled – because the underlying resource is common property, not least social capital – to have good jobs in organizations that are not destroying the environment or creating social crises. In the US, life expectancy at birth has dropped to its lowest level since 1996 (National Center for Health Statistics, Centers for Disease Control and Prevention, 2022). While the pandemic caused much of the decline since 2019, suicides and homicides remain high among young males. There were over 100,000 deaths due to drug overdoses between April 2020 and April 2021, primarily from opioids.

In *The Ox-Bow Incident* (Clark, 1940: 40), it is observed as a lynch mob is put together to catch suspected rustlers:

> Thinking about it afterwards I was surprised that Bartlett succeeded so easily. None of the men he was talking to owned any cattle or any land. None of them had any property but their horses and their outfits. None of them were even married, and the kind of women they got a chance to know weren't likely to be changed by what a rustler would do to them. Some out of that many were bound to have done a little rustling on their own, and maybe one or two had even killed a man. But they weren't thinking of those things then, any more than I was.

The lynch mob ended up killing innocent men.

8

People and Robots

The population bomb

The UN has estimated world population in 1950 as being 2.5 billion people. In 2022, it had risen to 8 billion. Population growth is concentrated in low-income countries. High-income economies in Asia, such as Japan, South Korea and Singapore, and in Europe now have fertility rates well below the level that would maintain their existing populations.

Looking forward from 1950, would this greater than three-fold population growth have been the subject of utopian or dystopian novels and films? Would an effective United Nations after the Second World War have argued that the greatest need of the planet was for dramatic growth in the world population?

William Morris is now primarily known as a Victorian-era wallpaper designer, employing the classic forms of arts and crafts in flowing leaves and designs of natural foliage. He was also a socialist. His 1892 book, *News from Nowhere*, represents a particular agrarian view of socialist life. Fundamental to this lifestyle was an emphasis upon crafts, but also upon a severe diminution of London's population to return to a city of villages. If that was the case in 1891, surely it held with greater impetus in 1950 and in 2000.

In 1968, Paul and Anne Ehrlich wrote *The Population Bomb* on the dangers of over-populating the Earth, and the Zero Population Growth movement grew over the 1970s. Yet the world population has doubled from roughly 4 billion in 1970 to roughly 8 billion today. GDP per capita is measured as over $60,000 in the US, $5,000 in South Africa and $500 in Afghanistan. It does not seem unduly naive to suggest that international development efforts and policies in countries concerned about the well-being of their future populations might have been better directed at increases in output per capita than dividing output and the natural environment across an expanding population.

China of course did exactly that with the one-child policy introduced in 1980. GDP per capita was $194.80 in 1980 (according to the World Bank) and achieved $12,556.30 in 2021. India did not follow that policy and is now projected to have overtaken China in population. India GDP per capita was $267.40 in 1980 and $2,256.60 in 2021. For those of us who believe in democracy, something has gone seriously wrong. India (China) population in 1980 was 696.8 million (981.2 million) and in 2021 was 1.41 billion (1.41 billion). It would be naive not to associate China's success, at least in part, with its relative population control.

We have argued that an equilibrium such as this – exponential growth in the world population – is either positively chosen by beneficiaries or, at least, is not sufficiently disliked among decision-makers to cause them to change the growth path. China has shown that a different choice is possible, although a democratic country might wish to achieve a similar end through less draconian measures.

From an economic viewpoint, population growth provides a large pool of labour and – insofar as population growth is at the expense of individual education and human capital development – a less skilled source of workers. Whether this labour is born in your home country, migrates to your home country, or arrives embodied in the form of produced goods, it increases the supply of labour relative to both human capital and physical capital. Those who have attended prestigious universities, and those who own assets, benefit while basic wages stagnate, as described in the preceding chapter. There may be a case for all of us to read Marx's theories of labour, which we had hoped were outdated in the post-war consensus on the mixed economy, but which involve how beneficiaries create a 'reserve army of labour'. As we discussed in Chapter 7, looking at wage stagnation in the US and the UK, established generations that own capital (houses, shares, bonds) gain from lowered wages that might arise from the diminution of the role of trade unions in the economy. They also benefit from lowered wages from population growth. Those who attend prestigious universities benefit as the return to human capital rises relative to simple labour services.

Despite the recent decades of wage stagnation, many commentators nonetheless claim that population growth is vital and point to Japan as an example (being quickly followed by parts of Europe) where low population growth has led in their view to 'lost decades'. Expansion of the number of young workers is needed, so the story goes, in order to pay the pensions of the elderly, who are living longer and also – due to medical advances that can prolong life even when they cannot cure illness and prevent dementia – need more medical attention and nursing and other care.

At the risk of offending again those who decry comparing a society to a family (but we have probably permanently alienated them in Chapter 2, so they are unlikely to still be reading), let's see how this argument works in a family located in London or New York, deliberately chosen examples. We have a single parent (you can do the exercise for your preferred family structure) with two children. The single parent works in a shop. Should they have more children in the hopes that the children will support the parent, help out at home and then get jobs at 16 and pay rent at the family home, and eventually move out but still support the parent with part of their earnings? Or should the parent put in the maximum effort seeing that the children do as well as they possibly can at school, and potentially go on to university? Does it matter whether our single parent is male or female, Celtic from Wales or a first-generation immigrant from India? If we give a different answer for society as a whole, or for other less well-off countries, we are fundamentally saying that what we want for our children is not what we want for other people's children.

Ironically, the same people who tell us to have more children to pay for our pensions also worry about how AI and robots will take over the workplace, creating unemployment. Return to the previous paragraph and now, after the two human children, the parent is offered the chance to adopt a cuddly dog-like but very hard-working and productive robot. The children with their university degrees can watch while the robots do the grunt work on the factory floor and cleaning the streets, in place of a potential younger sibling who could do that work. In light of the environmental crisis, it seems obvious to this author that freezing (and reversing) human population in favour of more robots is supremely desirable. Further, if in fact robots and AI can take over many routine jobs, or even less mundane ones from humans, this is even better. Economists have long predicted substantial declines in the working week. The pandemic has reminded people that they would rather spend more time away from the workplace. Given the simple choice between more robots and more people, there is much to be said in favour of robots.

To be fair, there are more subtle arguments for having children expressed by William MacAskill (2022: 234): 'Although your offspring will produce carbon emissions, they will also do lots of good things, such as contributing to society, innovating, and advocating for political change. ... I think that an impartial concern for our future counts in favour, not against.'

Guilds and clubs

Look at a country as a guild or club. Current members (who may not all have equal status in either decision-making or sharing the benefits of the club) will decide upon the numbers and terms for new members. They can also decide on capital and other expenditures. A club may take in new members (perhaps with a joining fee and different membership rates), particularly if it is facing a major expense such as a new clubhouse. But in general, a club will be rigorous in defending its membership rules.

First let's go back in time to the Middle Ages. Patrick Wallis (2018: 3) has re-examined the role of guilds in England. He observes that:

England's guilds were largely urban organisations that exerted control over various occupations, limiting full economic participation in specific sectors to their members, regulating product quality and market access, raising funds for city and crown, resolving disputes, registering apprenticeships and forming a social, convivial and spiritual thread in the lives of (at least some of) their members.

For its members, and in some ways the broader public (quality control of products and services is generally a good thing), the guilds were welfare improving. They even provided insurance services covering, for example, sickness or old age. Wallis finds that, instead of defined insurance benefits, the guilds operated through charity, significantly but not exclusively to members, and then in part taking account of seniority of membership. A separate institution, friendly societies, providing clear benefits in return for dues, arose subsequently. By 1870, 'more than half of adult males in Britain belonged to a society' (Wallis, 2018: 19).

We can consider the citizens of a well-off country in this light. The government provides all sorts of positive services, predominantly (but not exclusively) for its citizens. Guilds treated their members differently depending upon whether they were apprentices, journeymen or masters. In the same way, countries don't treat all citizens equally, perhaps depending upon their region within the country, their ethnicity, their sex, and their parents' social class. 'Levelling up' in the UK may be a political slogan, but it reflects a real difference in the standard of living, and even public services, between the affluent South and London, and the de-industrialized North.

'Citizens' of a colony often have different status, as codified for the UK by the introduction of the 'British overseas citizen' status in 1983. Even being born in the UK does not automatically entitle you to citizenship with the right of residency, unlike the bulk of countries in the Americas. From January 2021, however, Hong Kong residents were given the right to settle in the UK, leading to full citizenship, in response to political actions taken by the Chinese government. From 1941, those born in Puerto Rico had full US citizenship.

The difference between 'charity' and 'insurance' is an important one. For largely historical reasons, important social welfare programmes in the US and the UK were set up as 'insurance' programmes. To gain the full state pension, you need to have paid contributions over the years that built up your entitlement. The historical background leads in the US to the fiction of the Social Security and Medicare Trust Funds with the idea that accumulated contributions are there for disbursal and – if the funds were to go into deficit, as is constantly predicted – expenditures must be cut to fit the cloth. It also has led to an anomaly in both countries that social security (national insurance) taxes only go up to a certain relatively modest level of income. In the US in 2023, employers and employees each pay 6.2% up to an income of $160,200. In the UK, the national insurance rate drops from 12% to 2% for incomes over £967 a week (although the employer's rate remains 13.8%). One of the easiest fiscal reforms – from an economics point of view – that would put the funds sharply into surplus would be to remove the regressive cap on contributions.

Clubs

Guilds represent one form of a 'club'. Todd Sandler and John Tschirhart (1980) provide an extensive review of the issue of the economics of clubs. They note the importance of the assumption of whether or not all members have to pay the same dues (and how much of the literature implicitly makes this assumption and ends up with homogeneous membership of the clubs as being second-best optimal). In practice – and because it is generally efficient – members do not pay the same dues in clubs. Sometimes, out-of-town members pay less because they are expected to use the facilities less. There are also potential seniority rules. If we view a workplace as a 'club' – and the suggestion is to view everything in this way – more senior workers get higher pay and protection from redundancy. As we have discussed, 'back-loading' contracts in this way is typically economically efficient, rather than an issue of 'fairness'. It causes members to have a commitment to the 'club', since the benefits increase over time.

A club has the ability to choose its members, which can often lead to discrimination. The plot in George Orwell's 1934 novel *Burmese Days* revolves around pressure for the European Club in a modest sized town in Burma to admit a native member. The Garrick Club in London has engendered controversy over its exclusion of women from membership.

The first rule of a club is that new members are admitted not because they want to be, but because it benefits the existing members. In the university sector, Oxford and Cambridge have not really expanded their undergraduate numbers, while the rest of the sector has expanded dramatically. An economist would observe that existing graduates gain very large economic rents because of their degree (largely paid for by the taxpayer). At Oxbridge, as at US universities such as Harvard and Yale (that also haven't expanded undergraduate numbers), the university gains donations from alumni and these become major stakeholders. 'Legacy admissions' – where descendants of former graduates gain preference in admission – maintain this equilibrium. Some have argued that the only way to break up this club is by making Oxbridge postgraduate only. In the US, particularly with the recent Supreme Court ruling against affirmative action, there are proposals to eliminate the legacy admissions that benefit those already from privileged backgrounds.

Let's suppose that the club rules stipulate that all members (when newly admitted or having been members for decades) are treated equally. Adding new members allows for greater cost-sharing of the fixed costs. It also potentially allows for new facilities, since there are more members to share the increased expenses. Consider the Garrick Club in its building in Covent Garden. If membership is expanded – for example, if a significant number of women are admitted to achieve some balance – the fixed costs of the building will be divided among a greater number of members, but at the cost of over-crowding. It is therefore possible that some of the members voting against opening up membership to women are not misogynistic at all, but just balancing their economic benefits. Given the very large endowment of the club (arising through the inheritance of part of the rights to the Winnie the Pooh books), equilibrium is to err on the side of a smaller membership.

On the other hand, if the new members can be charged an initiation fee or higher dues, or have less access to facilities, then the equation shifts in favour of admitting more.

Choose your migrants

The Brexit referendum can be viewed in significant part as being about migration (the issue of potential Turkish migration sounded loudly in one of the debates) and the 'leave' vote in some constituencies can be seen as following their economic well-being in limiting competing labour. With the end of the free movement of labour from Europe, there are shortages in the skilled labour categories (notably, during the pandemic, in truck drivers). The government offered 5,000 three-month visas to try to deal with the immediate shortage of drivers (notably the garages sold out of petrol), and were surprised that only a handful were taken up. But this shortage is precisely what is needed to drive up wages and increase the number of citizens and settled residents training for HGV licences. It also, in an era of extreme environmental stress, may be no bad thing if alternatives to road transport are developed.

The *Meet the Press* episode on 14 November 2021 involved a discussion of inflation. Brian Deese (Director of the National Economic Council) was challenged by the moderator Chuck Todd about inflation. Chuck Todd asked, and repeated to ask, about whether immigration was needed to resolve the truck driver shortage. Deese adamantly stuck to his line that we needed to improve truck driver wages and train more drivers. In the short run, the testing centres could remain open long hours to speed up the licensing of new drivers.

While Red Wall new Tory voters might well have been attracted by the claim that Brexit would restrict inward migration, traditional middle-class Tory voters, on the other hand, relied on builders coming from the new EU member countries, along with nannies and teachers, and for European PhDs and lecturers to teach their university age children. Even if they wished to limit immigration from parts of Europe, the overall package involved limitations on their travel in Europe (potentially including free mobile phone calls and health care) and the ability to work and live there (or have a second home). Indeed, one of the ironies of the current political structure is that the formerly centre right parties in the US and UK have abandoned their 'suburban' voters in favour of populism.

The current Tory policy focus is upon economically valuable migrants who can apply for a 'skilled worker' visa, who must be paid roughly the 'going wage' in their profession. This is cynical in that it often is at the expense of the origination countries who lose their best trained and educated workforce. The skilled worker visa can cost £610 plus a health surcharge of £624. But more substantively, you need to bring 'the tools of your trade' in the form of human capital. If you wish to bring your family, there are substantial additional visa and health costs. In effect, there is an entry fee to joining the club.

Suppose there is a given population in the UK – the current members of the club – who consider admitting new members. There is an existing capital stock in the country, both private and public. Do the proposed new members represent a net benefit to existing members? If migrants are highly skilled, then they will drive down wages in those areas (and the return to human capital) and benefit the owners of physical capital, who can easily recruit more trained and educated workers at lower wages. As we have discussed, it is older generations that own the bulk of the capital assets, so they gain at the expense of younger generations from that effect. If migrants instead are pegged into low-skilled jobs (irrespective of the actual skills and human capital held by the migrant – a medical doctor from abroad, who doesn't have British qualifications, may have to take up unskilled work), it is wages at the low end that are depressed. The argument is often made that immigration is necessary to fill the jobs British workers decline to accept. But that is misleading since a sufficiently high wage would no doubt sort out the recruitment problem. There is no reason in economics why an unpleasant job which does not require a university degree should pay less than a pleasant graduate job.

It is in any case distasteful to make the argument about migration, particularly of refugees – who are oppressed because of their religion, sexuality, ethnicity, gender or other characteristics – predominantly an economic one. We have an obligation under treaty to admit refugees who are suffering persecution in their country of origin. Family members gain priority in membership of our national club. Finally, we might want to increase the diversity of the membership either for political reasons – as in Orwell's *Burmese Days* – or to enrich our culture. This is particularly important for those of us who work in universities or the arts – while we might want to maintain a British perspective on our field of research in areas such as economics, it is hard to conceive of a vibrant university department whose members all obtained their PhDs in British universities.

Paying pensions – population or capital

In the same way, the 'generation gap' is not just about financial resources. While finances may create stresses across generations – notably at the moment, when younger generations are being priced out of housing – the dynamics of society depend upon a creative tension between generations. University students should develop independence of thought and action and not replicate their parents. The 'generation gap' that was popularized in the 1960s was neither unique to that period, nor at all a bad thing. In the 1960s, in the United States, it was exemplified by parents voting to have a draft to send their sons to Vietnam. That subsequently there was a switch to a 'volunteer army' with both men and women – populated disproportionately by those from a less well-off background or less favoured ethnicity – did not change the fact that one generation went to fight a war in Iraq decided upon by an older generation in the time-honoured ways that wars are generated and fought. Generations do not have the same interests, and often – for better or worse – they do not have the same values.

But, as with migration, arguments abound that we need population growth in order to pay the pensions of older generations; as with migration, those arguments are misleading. Let's suppose that people on average spend a quarter of their working age life in retirement, and on state-provided pensions of half their working age incomes. Further, suppose that there is no growth in either population or productivity. Then a tax on income of about 16–17% would be necessary just to cover pensions (not that much more than the total 12.4% contributions, half covered by firms and half by the worker, in the US Social Security system). If either population or productivity is growing over time, the tax rate can be less.

The idea of balancing the books by population growth, however, is something of a Ponzi scheme – the population presses against the limits of the environment, as we are now learning in dramatic ways. Population has to grow faster and faster to offset this effect. World population has increased by a nearly a third in the 20 years between 2002 and 2022. The alternative – if we feel that we cannot afford to pay an ongoing social security tax of 16–17% to cover pensions – is to increase our investment in human and physical capital. This comes at a current cost in lowered consumption, but on a more sustainable basis. But it also has a generational impact of the sort we have discussed. If population is not growing, so there are fewer workers than otherwise would have been the case, and the capital stock is growing, then it is likely that wages are higher and the returns to assets are lower. The magnitude of this effect depends upon whether capital is a 'complement' to labour. For example, if we increase investment in the tools that are used by a craftsperson – then wages definitely rise with investment. If the painter rents scaffolding for the house, and there is a lot of scaffolding about, then the cost goes down and the painter's net income goes up.

A different extreme of capital is where it is a pure substitute for labour. Think of robots that are sufficiently endowed with AI to be a perfect replacement for the economics lecturer. For about $3,000, you can buy the latest model of the Sony Aibo robot dog in most of the US. The puppy develops a personality and 'forms an emotional bond with members of the household'. Aibo is generally cute and cuddly, but comes with a warning that might also be attached to economics lecturers: 'Your Aibo™ robotic companion may dislike you depending on how you interact with it.' When AI creates robots that are fully interchangeable with lecturers, this will lower the wage (compared to a world with the same number of human lecturers but no robots). As such, there may in time be a generational conflict on the adoption of robots with – ironically – the older generations favouring the greater use of technology.

In terms of paying the state pension to the already retired, it doesn't matter whether there are 100 million people working and no robots, or (if productivity is the same – robots have developed just to the point of humans, and no further) 50 million people and 50 million robots. But the allocation with robots is better for the environment and lowers the pressure on pensions going forward. As has been observed in analyses, however, the state may decide to start levying national insurance charges on robots so there is a direct contribution from robots to the pensions of the human workers and provide the right incentive to firms deciding on how many of each to hire. Given the state pension will have to be paid to all humans – whether or not they lost their job to a robot – equal national insurance rates might level the playing field.

Darin Acemoglu and Pascual Restrepo (2020) present recent evidence on how the adoption of industrial robots may affect your job and wages. They find that robots reduce employment (relative to population) and wages. A summary measure they present is that one robot ends up costing six human jobs. Looking at international comparisons, Georg Graetz and Guy Michaels (2018) find that robot use is associated with increased labour productivity. Policy can restore wages by, for example, limiting the working week for humans in those jobs where they are required. As we have emphasized throughout the book, the government has incredibly strong powers if it utilizes them effectively.

While Aibo is available in most of the US, it is not sold in Illinois and Baltimore due to its use of facial recognition and the danger that data protection laws will be violated. Possibly because of the film *2001: A Space*

Odyssey, we have a fear that every robot – even the cuddly Aibo – is a HAL9000 in disguise.

What happened to investment?

Given that investment is arguably – along with technology, which itself is both generated and implemented through investment – the route out of our problems, the question immediately arises: what has happened to investment?

A student taking their first finance course quickly learns that finance markets are essentially arbitrage markets. Investors cannot (by definition) on average out-perform the market. Instead, retail investors should invest in index funds and money market funds, choosing a mix of stocks, bonds and cash that give the right amount of macroeconomic risk. Early in your savings path (for your retirement, for example), you can optimally take more risk simply because – if the economy goes into recession and your portfolio suffers – you have time to save and invest more, making up the losses. The legendary investor John Bogel (author of the 2008 book *Enough*) made index funds (a diversified portfolio of underlying assets) generally available to retail investors in 1975. Since you couldn't beat the market, it was best to minimize investing costs.

On the other hand, the legendary investor David Swensen revolutionized endowment investment at Yale by broadening the nature of assets, achieving out-sized returns for the university. Universities had previously adopted extremely conservative strategies. The Yale model emphasized risky assets such as stocks, venture capital and private equity.

That model, and in general the emphasis in the finance sector over the last decades (coinciding with the zero interest rate policy), may have been a product of its time. Not only did the Fed have a policy – as we have discussed – of ever-lower interest rates, but (along with governments) of providing insurance for risk. In addition, wages were stagnant and corporate taxes declined. In the US, the headline corporate tax rate was about 50% in the 1950s, falling to 21% under the Trump tax cuts in 2017. As we've discussed, all this benefitted older generations who owned assets at the expense of newer generations. It also benefitted those who took on risk before the rest of the market realized the full impact of the 'Greenspan put' and other government actions to insure asset prices from falling.

The underlying rationale for the finance sector is that it efficiently allocates savings from individuals and organizations to investments. But in fact, most of this can be done – and was traditionally done – with little involvement of the finance sector at all, through cash-flow and retained earnings at firms. A successful firm that is benefitting from good management and innovation will generate significant cash-flow. There is no need for an intermediary to be involved, no need for banks, venture capital or private equity – the firm generates its own funds for future investment.

Figure 8.1: US net domestic private investment and corporate profits after tax

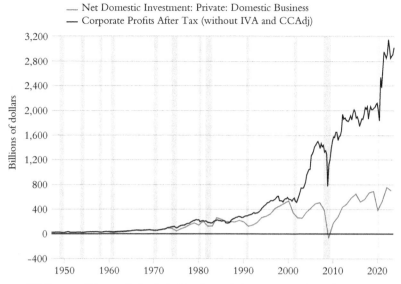

Source: US Bureau of Economic Analysis, Net domestic investment: Private: Domestic business [W790RC1A027NBEA], retrieved from FRED, Federal Reserve Bank of St Louis; https://fred.stlouisfed.org/series/W790RC1A027NBEA, 28 February 2024.

Steven Fazzari, Glenn Hubbard and Bruce Peterson (1988) divide firms into three classes based upon their dividend pay-out ratios (as a measure of their generation of excess capital). They find that cash-flow is an important explanatory variable for investment over the period 1970–84, and in particular that it is a bigger factor for those firms with low dividend pay-outs that are thereby demonstrating a need for capital.

Figure 8.1 shows aggregate historical data on how investment relates to after-tax corporate profits for US domestic accounts.

Up until the millennium, investment and profits traced each other. After the unconventional monetary policy adopted after the millennium, they diverged – investment was flat, while profits soared. Figure 8.2 focuses on the period after 1960.

We have scaled such that the percentage of gross investment, net investment and after-tax profits in GDP at the turn of the millennium was set at 100, in order to see the progression afterwards. It is seen that profits have risen sharply as a percentage of GDP, while investment (net and gross) has been flat.

We have discussed why profits soared – wages were stagnant, finance costs and taxes were cut. The conundrum is why investment didn't follow. Low interest rates had two channels of operation in the past. One is through increasing consumption, particularly of interest-sensitive goods such as automobiles and housing-related products such as furniture. But the

Figure 8.2: US net domestic private investment, corporate profits after tax and gross private domestic investment

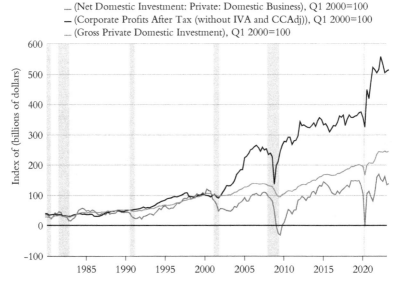

Source: US Bureau of Economic Analysis, Net domestic investment: Private: Domestic business [W790RC1Q027SBEA], retrieved from FRED, Federal Reserve Bank of St Louis; https://fred.stlouisfed.org/series/W790RC1Q027SBEA, 28 February 2024.

other – and the one that potentially raises productivity, keeps inflation down and benefits future generations – is investment. The screaming alarm that should have sounded at the central banks after 2000 was that their policies were not having a desired investment effect – they were a consumption boom of the sort that have regularly caused inflation. The Barber Boom of the early 1970s led to Britain going to the IMF 'cap in hand'. The Lawson Boom of the late 1980s repeated the pattern and eventually led to 'Black Monday' in 1992, when sterling crashed out of the Exchange Rate Mechanism.

We have not mentioned guardrails for some time. One of the guardrails that was removed in the UK in 1981 and in the US in 1982 was the prohibition in share buybacks. Instead of investing in the business, a firm can just buy back its shares. Finance theory provides little justification for share buybacks. If used in place of dividends, they effectively can translate dividend income – often taxed fully as income – with capital gains typically taxed at a lower rate. Alternatively, if the firm takes out loans in order to buy back shares (or uses existing cash), it increases the risk of its shares.

On 28 December 2021, the *Financial Times* reported: 'Companies raise over $12tn in "blockbuster" year for global financial markets.' But, at the same time as increasing their debt in this way, they also bought back shares. In the third quarter of 2021, the *Financial Times* reported: 'US companies authorise more than $870bn in stock buybacks' (11 October). Rather than having reserves to cover potential setbacks in the economy, or investing heavily in new technologies, firms have leveraged up for no purpose at all, but in the belief that central banks and governments will bail them out again and again.

'Works according to design'

We have already mentioned Jennie Bristow's (2019) book, *Stop Mugging Grandma*. Each time we have mentioned an issue – such as zero interest rates and asset prices – that have major generational effects, it is important to note that not everyone in a generation is the same. The Census Bureau in the US reports that non-Hispanic whites had (in 2022) a median household wealth of $187,300 and Black households had a median wealth of $14,100. In the UK, white British households had (in 2016–18) a median wealth of £314,000, while Black African ethnicity households had a median wealth of £34,000.

Ijeoma Oluo (2020) observes that the system 'works according to design'. We have described equilibria where those making decisions either deliberately choose a particular outcome or, in any case, do not take steps to change the outcome. An important part of the policy issues to do with population involve differential outcomes by gender, sexual orientation and gender identity, ethnicity, disability, and other demographic characteristics. Economists generally explain these differences on the basis of a 'taste for discrimination' or 'statistical discrimination'. In the former, managers of a firm may – for example – view Black people or gay men or women as less desirable than married straight white men. In the latter, in equilibrium, managers may use group statistics to judge people rather than individual assessment.

Sociologists, perhaps surprisingly, apply economics to these issues better than economists do, with concepts such as 'institutionalized racism'. The Macpherson Report into the killing of Stephen Lawrence was published in 1999 and highlighted the 'institutional racism' in the Metropolitan Police. The Casey Report was published in 2023 and highlighted that the Metropolitan Police was 'institutionally racist, sexist and homophobic' and 'institutionally corrupt'. These equilibria persist because sufficient people of sufficient influence gain from the equilibria compared to the likely alternatives. Economists are now starting to recognize these concepts, following the publication of the article by Small and Pager (2020) 'Sociological perspectives on racial discrimination' in the important *Journal of Economic Perspectives*.

If 'institutionalized discrimination' is the equilibrium, popular equality devices such as 'subconscious bias training' or 'formal hiring and promotion criteria' are unlikely to work; a point made by Frank Dobbin and Alexandra

Kaley (2018). To put it bluntly, all bias training does is reinforce to 'mediocre white males' (to use Oluo's terminology) that they benefit from the current equilibrium. What works (to use the title of the influential 2016 book by Iris Bohnet) is hard, direct policies. In my (2020) paper on 'The persistence of the gender pay gap in British universities', I show that the policy adopted by the University of Essex – simply raising all women professors' salaries by the average gap, removing the gender pay gap at a stroke – did work. Further, it wasn't a one-off effect, but persisted over time. In the UK Labour Party, women-only shortlists for parliamentary seats were introduced for the 1997 election for seats where a woman was vacating the seat and in half of other seats. The policy has now succeeded to the point (with women being represented not only above 50%, but above their representation in the population) where it is potentially no longer legally sustainable under UK equality legislation.

But individuals and groups advantaged by the current equilibrium are persistent. Policies and efforts to achieve equality are being co-opted by the usual suspects, for the usual purposes. 'Family friendly' policies are being adopted under the guise of helping women, who typically bear a disproportionate share of the burden of child-raising. But there is every likelihood that this is 'mediocre white men' co-opting the real issues of child-bearing and raising to shift rewards in their favour, the bulk of women in this circumstance being the partner of (in the UK) a white man. In a paper I co-authored with Alison Booth, we found a substantial marriage premium for male administrators (but not academics) (Booth and Frank, 2008). There was no such premium for married women or for partnered gay men or (lesbian or heterosexual) women. An equilibrium that was once sustained by explicit marriage pay increases for men (and often discharge papers for women upon marriage) is now sustained implicitly.

Alison Wolf's (2013) book *The XX Factor*, which seems to be alternatively sub-titled *How the rise of working women has created a far less equal world* or somewhat more positively *How working women are creating a new society*, makes the point that in developed economies, the benefits of greater gender equality have been concentrated upon the well-off. Professional women have gained, certainly in participation rates, in high-paying jobs in finance, law and education. But, on the other side, women who work part-time as cleaners or carers have not gained, even as they take on jobs as nannies for the well-off professional women.

Hard policies

When we come to the concluding Chapter 11, we will come back to the issues of politics and how to construct support for sensible policies in a now extremely threatened world. While some of the hard policies – for example, ending the reliance upon fossil fuels – may be extremely costly, it may alternatively turn out, due to technological progress, that in fact they do not cost more to implement. At the same time, ancillary benefits to saving the world from the climate crisis may arise in terms of health and pollution. One can imagine Los Angeles without smog, as electric vehicles take over. The point is that, relative to extinction, the cost cannot – for future generations that may or may not exist – be too high.

Perhaps the most distressing element of the conventional wisdom among economists is that growing populations are necessary for economic well-being. When one sees a headline about 'population crisis', it often refers to concerns that the fertility rate has declined below the replacement rate, rather than the all too real crisis that the world is simply over-populated. Fortunately, in developed countries, individuals and families have internalized the externalities of the over-production of children. Millennials and Generation Z are freezing embryos to allow them to defer child-bearing without precluding it at some future date, but it is unlikely they are planning at any time to have the large families that would compensate in population size for the delayed births.

Something we have not gotten into much in this book is the role of culture and religion in these issues. On the one hand, some cultures have emphasized the importance of education and knowledge, and (perhaps particularly for new immigrants in the US and the UK) in the context of having their children better integrate into society. On the other hand, some religions are demanding (and the Supreme Court has followed their lead in the overturning in 2022 of *Roe v Wade*) that society follow their particular personal beliefs. Since birth control technology has made population control much easier, and abortion has limited unintended births, religious removal of these mechanisms could lead to undesirable population growth. Other rationales for population growth are political in geographical areas such as Northern Ireland where relative population sizes may determine the political future of the region. This provides just one more reason for political resolution of the geographical conflicts facing the world today.

We aren't avoiding these subjects because they are more often associated with sociology or politics than with economics. In fact, these topics could readily be explored using economic models and techniques such as game theory and equilibrium analysis – we have already made the point that concepts such as 'institutional racism' are potentially readily understandable using economic analysis. As indicated in the Preface, another book is begging to be written – using the economist's toolbox and approaches – on the social and political factors that have led us to the current (hopefully, temporary) impasse.

We might hope – in a better world – for current generations making decisions to be so concerned for their descendent generations that they would fully weight or even over-weight future well-being compared to current consumption. But, even if that is not going to become the case among the currently dominating generations, there is a difference between issues such as the climate emergency and population growth and issues such as within-generation equity and generational issues such as whether or not Generation Z will be able to buy a house for the next decade or two. Interest rates set too low, under-investment in the infrastructure and in productive capital, as well as in education, and running high government debt are unfortunate policies that benefit the well-off parts of the older generation. They are unlikely to be sustainable, for the reasons we have given. But in and of themselves, they will not destroy the world. The climate emergency will, if not resolved at national and international levels.

9

Universities

Students at the centre

Universities are directly an issue of intergenerational equity, but also provide an outstanding case study of how policy goes badly wrong due to ideology, poor incentives and the failure to pay attention to sustainability. These have left us – in both the US and the UK, although we will concentrate upon the latter – with a needlessly expensive and misdirected higher education system. This is generally financed by the current student generation through student loans. There is over $1.6 trillion in outstanding US Government student loan debt. Students in England are leaving university with a degree and a debt of £60,000. Because of fundamental design flaws in the financing system, and a remarkably powerful lobby for the sector, governments have ended up with a patchwork of proposed fixes – for example, proposed debt forgiveness in the US – rather than engaging in root-and-branch reform.

Before 2012, students in England paid a modest amount towards their fees. The Teaching and Higher Education Act of 1998 introduced £1,000 per annum fees; the Higher Education Act of 2004 allowed for fees up to £3,000; while in 2012, maximum home student fees tripled to £9,000. They have risen modestly to £9,250 since then. A specific exemption in the Equality Act 2010 allows for overseas students to be charged more than local students. Overseas students are typically charged two or more times the home student rate. Ironically, the Liberal Democrat political party had campaigned in 2010 promising abolition of fees. But, as part of the Coalition Government with the Conservatives, the high-fee regime was instituted, partially explaining the near wipe-out of the Liberal Democrats in the 2015 elections.

Students can finance their degree from government student loans, a contingent repayment scheme that has become more complicated, less generous and more inequitable over time (as different repayment rules apply to different generations of students and different levels of study). On the now standard plan for new undergraduate students, they pay a levy of 9% on post-university earnings over £25,000, with their loan balance adjusted by an interest rate based upon the RPI. Loans accrue interest at the beginning of study not on graduation and are related to RPI rather than the more widely used CPI. The loans are written off after 40 years.

Students can gain an extra year of funding for a postgraduate degree or – remarkably – for a Foundation Year for students falling short of standard entry expectations. Universities therefore can expand numbers by getting Foundation Year students, postgraduate students and overseas students, in addition to competing for traditional undergraduates.

The 2012 university funding reforms in England and Wales were designed to provide funding to expand the system without undue reliance on the taxpayer. These reforms followed the review by Lord Browne (2010) which aimed to put 'students at the heart of the system'. David Willetts (2017) makes clear that his primary objective was to expand student numbers. In an earlier book, Willetts (2010) established his concern about equity for future generations and has – in that goal – been fundamental to establishing the Resolution Foundation. Certainly, the reforms – notably the lifting of student number caps and the tripling of the fee rate, mitigated and supported by the income-contingent student loan system – have led to a significant expansion in the percentage of post 18-year-olds eventually attending university, now achieving the 50% figure that seems to have become everyone's target. As with the 2% inflation target arbitrarily adopted by central banks, or the 100% government debt to GDP cap proposed by some economists, there is no theoretical, empirical or strategic reason for a 50% goal.

In seeking to expand university intake, Browne and the government wanted to involve non-traditional students from different ethnicities and backgrounds. The reforms included very robust expectations for widening participation. A substantial amount of the increased income to universities was intended to be spent on increasing attendance and success from non-traditional entrants.

What could go wrong? The unit resource per home student went up by 50%, so there was more than ample funding for a quantum leap in the quality of teaching and research (important for state-of-the-art 'research-led teaching') at universities. Students did not have to pay up-front and would only pay if their incomes were high enough, so students from less traditional and less well-off backgrounds should not be deterred from attendance in the way they would be if fees had to be paid up-front. Universities would compete for well-informed students by offering better programmes, and would largely be expected to have a more diverse group of entrants. The taxpayer would not have to cover these additional costs, since the graduates would, over time, repay their loans from their enhanced earnings.

Nonetheless, virtually all participants (students, universities and the government) are unhappy with the outcome of these reforms.

- Universities UK – what might be viewed as the university managements' lobby group – have written (11 January 2023) on their website: 'The fee system is politically contentious and unpopular with both students and universities.'
- A recent Higher Education Policy Institute (HEPI) report (24 June 2021) shows that, since the tripling of fees in 2012, students have found universities to be relatively poor value for money.
- Research by Alison Wolf and Andrew Jenkins (2021) found sharp growth in managers and professional services, notably in the 'student experience'.
- Because of the write-off feature of the loan system, the taxpayer is contributing over 50% of student fees due to predicted loan write-offs. Decisions from the Office of National Statistics (17 December 2018) mean that these losses are now accounted for in government deficits. The latest changes to the loan system (making it less generous) are predicted to lower the government contribution from about 61% to about 34%.
- The Office for Students (12 May 2022) has expressed its concerns over grade inflation in degree classifications.
- The lack of a cap on fees charged to overseas students has led universities (primarily funded by the British taxpayer) to seek to admit more of these high-fee students, at the expense of places for British students, and to have explicitly lower entry grades required for high-fee students.
- Since universities have gotten full fees for Foundation Year students (but about to be capped for 2024 at £6,000), the number of these students has grown even though this study could be done (taught by experts in level 3 education) at a Further Education College at considerably lower cost to the taxpayer.

A well-intentioned set of reforms has had the intended effect of moderately increasing student participation rates in higher education, but at considerable cost in terms of taxpayer contributions and efficiency, notably as bureaucrats replace teachers and researchers in the university. Our book (Frank et al, 2019) explores in detail how the incentives introduced in 2012 had unintended consequences that were negative for the quality of education. Here we want to focus on broad issues that are important for designing any policy. These include: don't be driven by ideology; don't reward poor performance; make sure that the decision-makers have preferences aligned with the policy goals; and put in mechanisms to ensure that choices and equilibria are sustainable.

Creating a market

Since the Reagan and Thatcher era, policy makers of all stripes have been seduced from time to time by the idea that markets can serve a major role in public provision of goods. In our 'no label' economics world, there is nothing inherently wrong with this idea, provided that the 'markets' that are constructed are done so carefully and are genuine markets rather than effective oligopolies. With universities, there are particular challenges. One is that there are no 'shareholders' so care must be taken in governance to ensure that someone is seeking to achieve efficiency in pursuing desirable (from the government's point of view) objectives. The second is that quality is extremely hard to measure. Information about quality is asymmetric – the provider (the university, in this case) knows a lot more about the teaching standards on its programmes than does a prospective student who reads the National Student Survey (NSS) or various league tables.

There are now remarkably good datasets on, for example, the employment and earnings outcomes following from specific degrees at each university. The Longitudinal Education Outcomes (LEO) data combine education performance and tax and benefits records and can, over time, show the rewards of doing one degree subject over another, and at one university over another. But that information will be historical (perhaps not dissimilar to knowing that COMPAQ led the way in portable computers, information that is not very useful in choosing a computer today), and presents only a very partial picture – employment outcomes – of the advantages of a particular degree. Almost by definition – looking at earnings – it biases in favour of STEM over the humanities, when for many students, pursuing their interests in the arts or literature might be the ideal subject both personally and in their contribution to society. As we have noted, as an economy and a society, we have made remarkable strides in developing and applying technology over the last few decades. We have done remarkably poorly in the social interactions and policies that would turn those technological advances into GDP, much less broader measures of societal well-being.

Economists spend considerable time telling non-economists that what we do is not about money and finance, but about efficiently achieving whatever ends the 'client' desires. In principle, we can design a 'market' for students that encourages universities to provide a first-class liberal arts degree (covering a broad body of knowledge) that prepares students well for postgraduate studies in their chosen field or for graduate employment. Arguably, that is precisely what the US system does, with outstanding liberal arts colleges that, for undergraduates, regularly dominate the big research universities. But even if 'employability' or future earnings were the sole objective, the policy put in place in the UK is extremely inefficient.

In many ways, the 'market' design in the Browne Report was a carefully thought-out one that – with additional tweaking over time, as is always needed – could well have reasonably achieved its aims. Unfortunately, the government made two devastating changes in implementing the report. In Browne's review, universities would compete for a limited total number of students across the sector (limited by a minimum entry standard), who would be 'well informed' in making their choices. The Coalition Government instead eliminated student number caps, and didn't institute minimum entry standards. Further, while in the Browne proposals, the 'standard' fee would be £6,000, roughly the amount needed to cover the cost of educating the student, the Coalition Government set a price cap of £9,000, well above the unit cost of educating a student and thereby creating a mad dash for the now highly profitable students.

Under the old system, there were student number targets set for each university that were largely historical and therefore – with reasonable effort – a university could expect to meet the numbers without undue concern. Universities were penalized if they went (beyond a relatively modest allowable amount) over or under on numbers. Since there could be little competition for numbers of students, there was instead vigorous competition for the best students. Departments put in significant efforts to recruit well-qualified students with Open Days to sell the programmes, and visits to schools. Low-demand departments would have a particular incentive to market their offerings, in order to protect jobs and departmental budgets, and to be able to recruit new or at least replacement staff. If a department could not achieve its targets, another department would pick up the slack. A university did not in general want a high-demand department to expand student numbers at the expense of a low-demand department in this situation where the university's student numbers were fixed. It would lead to a shortage of staff in the high-demand department and a surplus of staff in the low-demand department.

The Browne proposals would have moderately shifted the nature and extent of competition. Although the unit resource (about £6,000) would have been largely unchanged, it directly followed the student and a university could expand (or contract) if that was its chosen strategy. Since at least some of the costs of the university are relatively fixed (existing buildings, much of the administrative staff), a modest expansion would only need to cover marginal costs rather than average costs. While £6,000 just about met the total average costs (including a share of existing buildings and other fixed costs), it exceeded the marginal costs of adding a modicum of students to existing classes. Under the proposals, the government would set the required minimum A-level points tariff needed to be offered a place, and in that way the government largely controlled aggregate student numbers. A moderate expansion in system-wide student numbers would be accommodated by some universities competing for some additional students.

The Coalition Government made two major changes. Let's consider them in turn. It raised the fee level from the proposed £6,000 to £9,000. Suddenly, students were hugely profitable and competition would be ratcheted up. That is not necessarily a bad thing, but it must be recognized that – in this attempt to set up a market – the government was choosing a market price. The market was not setting the price. The higher the price went above the cost of production, the greater the competition for the – in the Browne proposals – fixed numbers of students. The government would have to balance the additional costs of a higher fee against the potential benefits of competition in improved education and, as we will discuss, in research activities.

But then, having pumped up the competition by setting a high fee level above the cost of education, the government let all the air out of the balloon by removing the student cap without introducing – as in the Browne proposals – minimum standards for entry to university. Provided they were willing to lower entry standards, most universities could enrol as many students as they wanted. But in fact, the situation was even worse than that. A mid-level university was no longer competing for better students with comparable or higher ranked universities; it was competing for more students from lower ranked universities. The nature of the competition necessarily changed. A university that previously set a firm BBB admissions standard might now in practice admit at CCC. For Foundation Year students, the entry standard would be set even lower.

As we sub-titled our book, the government created 'markets without competition' (Frank et al, 2019).

An informed market and the nature of competition

The Browne Report regularly uses the word 'informed'. To assist students in making their choices of university and subject, the Office for Students (OfS) funds 'Discover Uni'. This shows, for each programme at each university, the NSS results, entry information (the distribution of A-level tariff points), continuation rates for the course, earnings after 15 months, three years and five years, first destinations (after 15 months), a survey of graduates about their work experiences, and links to the course on the university's website. For the five years on earnings data, the graduating classes of 2012–14 are being reported. Through other sources, students will be able to learn the degree grades awarded.

What there isn't in any of this is an actual attempt to measure the quality of education in the programme in the sense – does the student gain an understanding and knowledge of the subject? This could be measured. The group Reform (21 June 2018) proposes a national assessment for each subject worth up to 10% of the final classification and where the success of its students on the national assessment would determine the proportions of degree classes awardable by a particular institution. The proposed Designated Assessment Bodies would set standards and provide oversight.

Quality control has largely been delegated to individual universities. This is not done at school level, where there are national A-level examinations and schools compete for the best results. There are rigorous inspections for schools and further education colleges by OFSTED (Office for Standards in Education, Children's Services and Skills). External quality control used to be in place for both teaching-orientated institutions (polytechnics) and research-intensive institutions (universities). Although polys could design their own courses, set and mark their own exams, the degree was awarded by the CNAA (Council for National Academic Awards). There was a rigorous external examiner system, as well as institutional inspections. The NAB (National Advisory Body) acted in a similar manner to the UGC (University Grants Commission) and oversaw the work of the CNAA. The CNAA was about providing 'quality control' with a prime focus upon standards reflected in the syllabi, the quality of staff, student–staff ratios, library facilities, external examiners' reports and exam results. Reports were confidential, so could be more honest and effectively warned the director of the poly that, for example, "If you don't appoint a couple more staff your accreditation is in jeopardy".

Even now, there is vigorous competition across the different colleges at Oxbridge (as there used to be at the University of London) in the Norrington and Tompkins tables. Since students sit common university examinations, the league tables reflect the performance of the students at the particular college. This – or some alternative – could be done across the university system, if the government wanted real competition in educational standards.

How does one compete in the absence of objective quality measures? One route – which may or may not be effective – is through the NSS. Stephen Gibbons, Eric Neumayer and Richard Perkins (2015) found that a higher NSS score had a significant, but modest, effect on applications, although this was on data before the 2012 reforms intended to increase competition. The primary route was through league table rankings. Universities have in practice focused upon the 'student experience' reflected in the NSS. While this can involve greater feedback on submitted coursework – something that students invariably complain about – there are other aspects that may be more problematic. One is grade inflation. Students are likely to give your course higher evaluations if they get higher grades than they expected. Another precedes the pandemic, but has been reinforced in custom by the pandemic – students may prefer not to attend lectures and classes. Student unions demanded 'lecture capture' – recording of lectures – under the justification that students would wish to listen multiple times for revision. It is not too cynical – and disengagement of students throughout the sector shows – to think that students would rather sleep in at home than attend the 9 a.m. mathematics lecture. Pot noodles in bed is hardly an inspirational university experience.

A particular problem is that the hierarchy of universities has become more entrenched. We have already discussed the theory of clubs as a way of sustaining privilege. The most successful club in the UK university sector is the Russell Group. This group was formed in 1994. It expanded in 2012, coincident with the new funding regime, adding Durham, Exeter, Queen Mary and York, all of which had previously been in the 1994 group of smaller research-intensive universities. This expansion allowed the Russell Group – fairly or unfairly (and remember, in clubs, you are allowed in not because you want to join, but because it benefits existing members) – to stake claim to being the 'elite' research universities in the UK. It has been a remarkably successful marketing and PR exercise, aided and abetted by the lack of any objective quality measure. It has had unfortunate knock-on effects in schools where they market their 'success' based upon the number of Russell Group places their students secure.

Claiming that the 2012 reforms increased competition among universities is akin to claiming that OPEC increases competition in the oil markets.

What is being subsidized?

When a student takes out a loan for fees and maintenance, they are (from 2023) charged the RPI inflation as interest, pay 9% of their income over £25,000, and have any remaining loan forgiven at 40 years. It is expected that this regime – notably the extended payback period from the previous 30 years – will significantly lower the costs to the government from non-repaid loans.

We have already discussed – in the context of working tax credits – the problems with subsidizing failure. Given that £9,000, when first instituted, more than covered the full costs of university, the entire subsidy goes to students who end up earning less than £25,000. Further, graduates face high marginal tax rates. Instead of the 20% for the general public (including those who went to university before the high fees were instituted in 2012), graduates pay 29% until the loans are repaid. Instead of 40% higher rate, graduates pay 49%. Including national insurance, the marginal rate for basic rate taxpayers with student loans is 41%.

It's hard to see why this system is viewed as being better than a graduate tax that charges all graduates a percentage surcharge on their income tax bill (rather than on their income). Such a system would be progressive at the rate already judged appropriate for income in total. It would provide ongoing funding to universities as well as recognizing the support that graduates have received. It would not be necessary to outsource as is the case with the current loan system, thereby saving considerably on administrative costs which would simply be a few additional lines on the current self-assessment form.

There are issues for individuals who are trained in the UK at taxpayer expense and then move abroad. In terms of collecting 'repayments' on student loans, this would be less complicated than the current system of assessing amounts due, since it could just go through the self-assessment form. Whether the UK should adopt broader coverage of tax on foreign income would be a digression, although it seems illogical that someone can avoid contributing to the exchequer by becoming non-resident (while still effectively spending much of their time in the UK) or non-domiciled. There are in fact large revenues that can be gained by broader coverage of tax liabilities for both individuals and firms.

Under the current system (and indeed under a graduate tax of the sort we have described), a poorly designed and implemented course, that attracts unqualified and indeed potentially disengaged students, attracts the highest subsidies. The system is based upon the idea that students will do the policing, by avoiding such courses. It seems, however, that this is abrogating the government's responsibility to the student and the other stakeholders in the education process. The government has now recognized this to the extent of wanting to crack down on 'low-value' courses. But there is a likelihood that this 'bolt-on' to the poorly designed overall system will be highly inefficient. For one thing, it is important in judging a course to take account of 'value-added'. A course at an advantaged university that attracts highly qualified entrants from advantaged backgrounds who graduate into high-paying jobs may well be adding less to their future earnings than a course at a less traditionally advantaged university that attracts students from less privileged backgrounds. Of course, earnings shouldn't be the only metric – courses that train students for low-income jobs (such as nursing and teaching) that are of high social value are arguably much more worthwhile from a public benefit perspective than business studies and accounting courses. Students who train in humanities and take on low-paid jobs in the public and voluntary sector are similarly contributing more than their incomes might suggest.

The underlying problem – that leads to unproductive courses – is that the 'market' gives both universities and students the wrong incentives. A university that charges the high fees allowed but saves on expensive inputs such as teaching staff makes a profit on students and has an incentive to recruit less successful or even unqualified candidates. But, in our system where Universal Credit for someone (single and without children) under 25 is about £300 a month, the student loan system must seem a remarkably favourable alternative. Fees are paid by the student loans company, and the individual can get up to £8,400 maintenance loans even while living with their parents (who can charge them rent). This hugely and inefficiently tips the scales for 18-year-olds in favour of going to university, even if they have little interest and little intention of devoting themselves to study. Arguably, this was always the case for students of advantaged backgrounds whose parents would fund them to go to university but not on extended gap years travelling around the world. It's not clear that extending this – while starving further education colleges and apprenticeships of funding – is a good use of public funds.

The managerial university

The principal-agent problem is where the person funding the operation and having ultimate power delegates this to an agent or agents. The government, on behalf of the taxpayer, is pouring a very large amount into universities. The Institute for Fiscal Studies estimates that, in 2023, the government is spending £22 billion to educate each university cohort. The OfS has taken over the role of previous arms-length quangos such as HEFCE (the Higher Education Funding Council for England) which in turn replaced the UGC, so in that sense the government could have a much greater influence on university management (note the change or terminology from 'grants' to 'funding' which indicates the first shift towards more government control). But in practice it has been content to have 'more managerial' universities where the VC and senior management dominate decision-making at the expense of academic control through the University Senate.

Adrian Bell, Chris Brooks and Andrew Urquhart (2022: 776) describe the problem with this empowerment of VCs:

> Growing a reputation for excellence in research or teaching from the ground up where it did not already exist is an expensive and prolonged endeavour that would be unlikely to reach fruition during the VC's term in charge, leaving that individual's legacy in doubt and allowing their successor to take the credit. Instead, the establishment of grand ventures and investment in infrastructures financed by borrowing have morphed from a means to providing the structure and facilities needed to strengthen research and teaching into being an end in themselves.

The *Financial Times* (23 June 2016, 'University challenge: the race for money, students and status') also describes the massive increase in debt – both bond-financed and from private equity – in the sector incurred in building programmes. The *Financial Times* raises issues of sustainability of the high debt and notes the role of our old 'friend', the zero interest rate policy pursued by central banks:

> 'We would not have issued [a bond] had it not been for the combination of exceptionally low interest rates and very favourable terms,' says Frank Marshall, estates bursar at University College, Oxford, which raised £40m through a 50-year bond in April last year, at a rate of just over 3 per cent.

Put very simply, the typical VC remains up to ten years, but an ambitious VC – appointed to a smaller or less prestigious university – might hope to attain a Russell Group post in a shorter period of time. This has led to 'prestige' building projects done quickly and other changes that might be viewed as expensive (and counter-productive) fads such as creating 'Schools' in place of 'Faculties' with executive deans rather than existing professors taking up a deanship role as a three-year break in their research and teaching.

For a publicly traded company, the stock market is constantly providing a gauge and indeed one that directly feeds into the chief executive's remuneration through stock options. If academics, through the Senate and other internal committees and departments, are disempowered, the only control left becomes the 'amateur' and non-remunerated governing body, the University Council.

The problem of finding management that aligns with the government's objectives – it is unlikely that the government had in mind that so much of the increase in funding would go into what are often called 'vanity' building projects – was underemphasized because of a belief that students would provide the market discipline. But there would need to be something connecting what students decided with the chief executive's incentives. The government, for example, if they really wanted to exert some influence could have taken over the remuneration determination for VCs, rewarding them if the A-level intake of their students goes up, for example. They could have avoided inflationary excesses in VC and other senior management pay by relating their base salary to some reasonable multiple (the figure '2' is often cited) of professors' salaries.

Otherwise, it was bound – particularly in a zero interest rate world – to get lots of expensive building done at speed. With few exceptions, these buildings have modest architectural interest. Perhaps not surprisingly, even in this race to build, it is the traditionally outstanding academic universities that have produced noteworthy (in a good way) buildings. The 2022 Stirling Prize went to the new library at Magdalen College, Cambridge. A RIBA London award went to the UCL Student Centre and the Zayed Centre for Research in 2021, and to a building on the White City Campus of Imperial College in 2022. The LSE Centre Building, opened in 2019, also won RIBA awards. But – as with academic research and teaching – other universities can, if they put in the effort, succeed. Kingston University's Town House won numerous awards, including the Stirling Prize in 2021, with its architects – Grafton Architects – gaining the Pritzker Prize in 2020.

Sustainability

When fees were tripled in 2012, a prudent university would have started from the point that it could, in principle, keep doing exactly what it was doing, and have – because direct teaching grants were cut when fees were increased – 50% more home student-based revenue than before. This was a huge windfall that could have been spent on hiring more academics, raising the university's research standing and reputation, and lowering the student–staff ratio, the measure of input into the teaching process. A modest expansion of student numbers could have occurred, provided it was within the scope of the existing estate or a modest amount of new building.

We have already described the massive building programmes that were instituted. Concerns about how much value for money taxpayers are getting led to the government commissioning the 2019 Augar Review. In their introduction, the panel of authors (chaired by Philip Augar, a British author and former equities broker) put it plainly: 'For a small but significant minority of degree students doing certain courses at certain institutions, the university experience leads to disappointment' (p 10). They observe and recommend:

> Generous and undirected funding has led to an over-supply of some courses at great cost to the taxpayer and a corresponding undersupply of graduates in strategically important sectors. ... Universities should find further efficiency savings over the coming years, maximum fees for students should be reduced to £7,500 a year, and more of the taxpayer funding should come through grants directed to disadvantaged students and to high value and high cost subjects.

In effect, the 'market for students' was failing, in entirely predictable ways that we have described above – funding was too high and poorly directed. On face value, returning fees to £7,500 a year would take us back to the Browne proposals – and, at the time of publication of the Augar Report, was worth £6,700 in 2012 pounds. Augar further proposed supplementing this with directed funding. The report also was categorical that university foundation years were – except in special cases – 'poor value for money'. It is hard to understand why anyone proposed and instituted that students should attend university for a pre-entry year at full costs when this was part of the bread-and-butter provision of further education colleges at a fraction of the expense.

But having bad policies in place – even over a decade, much less the 40 years we have described elsewhere in this book – leads to inefficiencies set in concrete. Much of the borrowing undertaken by universities on the great building spree engendered by the 2012 reforms is at low, fixed interest rates. Some, however, is on ancillary activities (such as student housing) and is consequently not necessarily reported on balance sheets and may be financed by private equity through giving the 'lenders' ownership of a future stream of student rents – and in some cases having the university take the risk of voids, making it difficult to infer the implicit interest rates (which indeed may be effectively index-linked against inflation). It is hard to see why universities are allowed to borrow on anything other than standard loans, with a clearly demarcated interest rate, or to engage in 'interest rate swaps' or other derivatives, or special purpose vehicles. What is clear is that few universities have the expertise to go head-to-head with the private equity firms on finance issues. Indeed, the NHS experience with the private finance initiative (PFI) indicates the pitfalls on this sort of non-transparent finance.

However, the greater problem is accounting properly for additional non-academic staffing for the new buildings and the depreciation on them. Once you have built an extension to your house, and put a swimming pool in the back garden, you have the additional running costs indefinitely. Universities, in effect, built in higher fixed costs for the future, presumably on the expectation that the government would raise student fees at least in line with inflation, allowing them to cover their additional expenses. VCs indulging in this spree have by and large now left their posts, leaving their successors to inherit their perfectly predictable mistakes and white elephants.

But there is an even more important way that the government over the last decade has budgeted on an unsustainable basis, that applies to universities as well as the NHS, the civil service and indeed the entire public sector workforce. Public sector pay caps and austerity have meant – as the government is currently learning through the strikes running from universities to the NHS to the civil service – that public sector pay is artificially low. The University and Colleges Union calculates that the real-term decline in lecturer pay is over 25%. As with the NHS, it is hard to see how offering pay rates that lead to recruitment difficulties in international markets can be viewed as a sustainable strategy, even if there were not incessant strikes by disgruntled lecturers, nurses and doctors.

Widening participation

The Browne Report also set the objective of widening participation. The objective was that students of all social backgrounds, and of all ethnicities and nationalities, should participate on an equal basis. Universities are expected to devote considerable expenditure from fee income to this objective.

Widening participation was handled, in the 2012 reforms, by a process involving the establishment of an Office for Fair Access (OFFA). In order to charge the £9,000 fees, a university needed to have an access agreement with the OFFA. This agreement contained commitments by the institution to significant expenditures on building a diverse student body. Each university sets its own target and reports each year on its success. With the establishment of the OfS, the OFFA was shut down in 2018, with the responsibilities transferred to the OfS. There is now an on-line dashboard showing widening participation success for each institution. This shows, for example, attainment (measured by first and upper second class degrees) by ethnicity for the institution. The OfS has the Uni Connect programme that invests in a network of hubs to work with secondary education providers and that is funded at about £40 million annually.

Does this work? In terms of, for example, Black participation in universities, the issues were not particularly about overall participation. In 2012, 31.4% of Black students gained a place, compared to 30.6% of White students, for state school educated individuals. But by 2020, this was 47.5% of Black students and 32.6% of White students. The problem is 'matching' – that is, Black students – and other demographics that have been disadvantaged – with outcomes. Put simply, Black students may be going to the wrong universities and doing the wrong subjects, with the wrong results.

From the Dashboard, the sector as a whole shows participation of Black students rising from 6.0% to 7.1% of student entrants. But Cambridge University had only 3.6% Black student entrants in 2019/20, albeit up from 1.4% in 2015/16. The University of Birmingham, in a more diverse setting, went from 4.9% to 6.0%. But Birmingham City (a post-92 university) went from 10.0% to 13.7%. It is hard to believe that Cambridge – being at the front of the line for recruiting students – could not overnight increase its Black representation to at least the national average.

The methodology used by first the OFFA and now the OfS involves what we can call 'essay writing' by universities, rather than direct action. Universities have to prepare plans and submit them. This sort of bureaucratic exercise – as also happens for staff equality initiatives such as the Athena SWAN scheme – simultaneously increases the size of the administration at universities (in place of hiring actual teachers and researchers) and potentially substitutes documents and plans for concrete action and results. Why not just have targets and let the university find the best way to achieve them? If Cambridge was told that it needed to have 7% Black student entry, to match the national average, it would find an efficient way to achieve the target. It could do this by recruiting from less advantaged schools, as well as addressing aspects of the social and academic environment at Cambridge that may be deterring Black and other non-traditional students from applying.

The 'matching' problem has been studied for students of less advantaged socio-economic backgrounds. Stuart Campbell, Lindsey Macmillan, Richard Murphy and Gillian Wyness (2022) have looked at the LEO data (that we discussed earlier, with its comprehensive measures of educational background and workplace earnings). They find that low socio-economic status students are under-matched in their degree programmes, where efficient matching is that the best (based on secondary school achievements) students should be matched into the best programmes (based on the average entry qualifications of students and upon future earnings). In terms of socio-economic background, Cambridge's participation of the lowest quintile went from 3.7% in 2015/16 to 6.6% in 2019/20, while the highest quintile went from 41.3% to 36.7%. At Birmingham City, the lowest quintile went from 38.6% to 45.0%, while the highest went from 13.0% to 11.5%. This is social immobility in action.

How do less advantaged students do at university? One measure is 'good degrees' – obtaining either a first or an upper second. At Birmingham City, the top social group's attainment in this measure goes from 76% in 2015/16 to 90% in 2019/20, while the most deprived goes from 62.4% to 73.5%. At Cambridge, the most advantaged go from 93% to 98% attainment; the least, 89% to 94%.

Looking at first-class degrees only, turning to ethnicity, there is more of a problem. In 2021, the government reported that 38.2% of White students obtain a first compared to 30.3% of Asian students, 33.2% of mixed students, but only 19.1% of Black students.

Addressing the gaps

The US has had more experience than the UK at addressing equality of opportunity for students of diverse demographics. At first, the US relied upon 'affirmative action' where universities had to show progress to be eligible for government funding. As affirmative action became limited by legal decisions (and has now been effectively struck down by the Supreme Court), some states introduced laws that based admissions upon the individual's standing in their secondary school. Students in the top 10% of their school are admitted to the University of Texas, except for the flagship university at Austin, where the constraint is tighter (currently 6%). This sort of admissions standard in the UK would mitigate much of the mis-matching reported in the paper by Campbell et al (2022) described earlier, but also achieve considerable diversity at the top universities. It would have a secondary effect of a greater balance of students across schools – getting into a top state secondary, by fair or foul means, would be less desirable if it cut your chances of getting into a top university rather than – as at present – increased them.

The American experience also can guide us in addressing attainment gaps. The currently popular UK solution of renaming them as 'awarding' gaps is – in itself – rather pointless, but tends to direct attention to the wrong measures. Bureaucrats running universities think that maybe Black students might do better if there was more continuous assessment rather than traditional unseen written examinations. In fact, the argument is likely to go in the other direction – unseen written examinations are anonymous, so discrimination is less likely to occur and would rely upon differential usage of language by different social classes, for example, rather than direct observation of the individual student in a classroom presentation.

The simple economic reality is that students from less well-off backgrounds, or going to less favoured schools, need additional resources to get up to speed at university. Fiddling with examinations or the term timetable, or appointing 'teaching-focused' academics rather than experts researching and publishing in their subject, avoids the expense of giving more individualized teaching and support to students who come in with fewer inherited advantages. The good news from the US experience is that – done properly – the additional resources are of a 'getting up to speed' nature not ongoing. This also means that the student isn't artificially propped up during university, only to suffer in employment when the supports are removed. Although, unfortunately, the university cannot protect the student from future ethnic or social discrimination in the labour market, it can make sure that a student of whatever demography has the same inherent productivity as the most socio-economically advantaged students.

Paul Tough (2019) describes a prototypical programme. He discusses a chemistry lecturer at the University of Texas (Austin) – David Laude – who in 1999 identified 50 first-year chemistry students at risk of failing based on their background indicators:

> [They] were placed in their own, smaller section of Chemistry 301. … Rather than dumb down the curriculum for them, [the lecturer] insisted that they master exactly the same challenging material as the students in his larger section. In fact, he scheduled his two sections back-to-back: identical material, identical lecturers, identical tests. But for the smaller group, he did more, supplementing his standard lectures with extra instruction and dedicated peer mentors and faculty advisors. And it worked. The [at-risk students] … concluded the course that fall with the same grades, on average, as the students in the larger section. They returned for their sophomore year at rates above the average for the university as a whole, and three years later they had graduation rates that were *higher*, on average, than the students in the larger section of Chemistry 301, the ones with [university entrance examination] scores two hundred points above theirs. (Tough, 2019: 212–13)

Unlike fiddling with the assessment system or term structures, or adopting the style of the year in pedagogical constructs, or changing language from 'attainment' to 'awarding', what works is to put in resources in an efficient way. Adding an extra, smaller section of Chemistry 301 is not cheap. There is in this also a reminder of a further lesson – give responsibility and power to the person who cares. A pro-vice-chancellor (Education) will direct administrators to write excellent submissions to the OfS and will tinker with assessment and other structures. Additional bureaucrats (rather than teachers) will be hired, with the supposition that somehow the bureaucrat will know more about teaching than those who labour on the front line. A lecturer who cares will put in the effort and design initiatives that work.

Excellence throughout the hierarchy

I expect we have all worked in organizations seeking excellence, and organizations that are just seeking to get by or have even given up trying. Often, if one stays at a firm, university or other organization for long enough, one will experience excellence and mediocrity at the same place during different time periods. Being involved in a dynamic, progressive institution is one of the most overlooked non-pecuniary benefits of employment.

Prior to 1992, there was a clear hierarchy in higher education. The polytechnics (see McGettigan, 2018) had a clear role as being teaching and industry-focused, under local authority control but with degree-granting powers residing in the CNAA. Within their assigned sphere, the polytechnics could achieve excellence. That universities were meant to have a different mission is clear from the creation of the new universities of the 1960s and 1970s. In 1992, the 'binary divide' was eliminated, but the hierarchy remains. Instead of achieving 'excellence' in the role of a polytechnic, most became 'adequate' universities.

The new universities of the 1960s also had a clear role. East Anglia, Essex, Kent, Lancaster, Sussex, Warwick and York achieved research and teaching excellence commensurate with or exceeding that of the previously established universities. It is often forgotten that – with the exception of Oxford and Cambridge – English universities were a product of the 1800s and 1900s and were not imbued with greater antiquity. This made it easier for a Warwick to overtake the bulk of the existing universities. In addition to the seven universities newly established in the 1960s, a number of others were transformed into universities, and similarly succeeded.

The 2012 reforms put this at risk. The high profit margin on students encouraged the Russell Group to expand its membership (maybe to intentionally weaken the 94 Group) and solidify its position, and for the higher ranked universities to expand their student numbers. They hoovered up students from the next tier of universities (that might not have differed initially, but – if they didn't become part of the Russell Group – lost out in marketing, if nothing else). This is where the information provision in Discover Uni is highly relevant, notably the important provision of the distribution of A-level grades of each university programme's intake.

When there were student number caps at each university, even students with high A-levels could not be sure of a place at the elite universities. They would disperse through the system, reflecting in part their choice of subject. University X might not be in the top ten overall, but might very well be exceptionally good in some subjects. And a strong external examiner system gave reassurance that a degree from any university met a certain shared standard. Almost all universities outside the very top specialized in this way – former polytechnics could still be national leaders in specific areas of research and teaching. Either because of the student's desired subject, or regional preference, or for other reasons, all universities could anticipate a reasonable range of students. Ironically, some of the mis-match we described in the previous section assisted in this – students from a less privileged socio-economic background might go to a local polytechnic or to evening classes at Birkbeck College, or avail themselves of the Open University, both of which have outstanding standards of provision.

With student number caps lifted, and the marketing success of the Russell Group (which extends to job applications after graduation), it is hard to see why a student with good A-levels would go elsewhere (except for specialist subjects such as drama). The publication of A-levels of the intake would make this an equilibrium. If University X has a distribution centred around BCC, with few students obtaining more than BBB, why would a top student with ABB or better go there? This means, on the one hand, that it is hard for a university department to move up – even if the university invests in the department, prospective students still see that the best prepared students go elsewhere. Since much of education occurs between students, rather than in the classroom, this is an entirely rational decision on the part of prospective students. Top students rationally go to the LSE not because they anticipate better teaching at the LSE (and certainly shouldn't anticipate small seminars with the world-leading professors on the staff), but because they will be interacting with other top students (as well as gaining a prestigious label on their diploma). Unfortunately, this situation also means that it is easy for a university department, or for the university as a whole, to go down – certainly in international rankings – if there isn't the desire to maintain excellence.

As with any business, the public and the government can say that a declining university has brought it upon itself. But the taxpayer and students are putting huge sums into university education, and there is an obligation on policy makers to set the right environment where universities are encouraged (and, if possible, induced) to define an appropriate mission and to be excellent at that mission. For the reasons described, the 'market' in higher education has failed to achieve those objectives. The government regularly hints that – as with a failing business in the private sector (although the various bailouts suggest that market discipline is diminished even there) – declining universities will be allowed to go bust. But until that happens (again, as with banks), no VC will take the threat seriously.

While there is no reason for all universities to have the same mission, it is hard to see why all universities should charge the same fees, even if all are – as they should be – good or excellent at achieving their aims. It was never the intention of the 'market' that it would turn out – in the economics student's jargon – to meet 'the law of one price'. Perhaps the best comparison to the UK lies in California. The University of California charges in-state fees of $14,436 for the 2024/25 academic year (although California resident students with household incomes of less than $100,000 have their fees waived). This is roughly equivalent to annual English fee levels, but paid for a four-year degree period. This system of nine research-intensive individual campuses is among the best in the world, serving a state population of 40 million. A student going to one of the top research-intensive universities in England should not feel unfairly treated compared to a Californian.

California, however, has a two-tier university system. In addition to the prestigious University of California, there are the 23 California state universities which charge only $6,084 a year. Until 1992, the UK also had a two-tier system with the former polytechnics under local authority control. It is hard to see why different universities of very different traditions, and very different standards of product quality, should charge the same price to their students.

Research

There is one more piece in the puzzle. At a research-intensive university, which includes most of the pre-1992 universities, a lecturer has traditionally been viewed as spending about 40% of their time on research, 40% on teaching and 20% on administration. The time and effort spent on research is viewed as supporting teaching through the concept of 'research-led teaching'. Would you rather be taught by an expert in the field, or by someone who reads the literature to keep up, or someone who just teaches from the textbooks? There is a continuum, but good universities in the past have viewed active research and publishing as vital to being a good teacher. In the same way, would you prefer your surgeon to be a renowned expert, or at least someone who keeps up with advanced techniques and medicines, or someone who does the basics? Even if the New York stereotype of having to have 'the best doctor' or go to 'the best restaurant' may be extreme, there is something comforting about that level of achievement. In this context, it is surprising that policies have led to considerable growth in teaching-focused posts, where the academic is not required to research and publish in their field. In the US, these posts are typically on much lower pay scales, which makes the calculus different from the UK, where a teaching-focused lecturer is on the same pay scale as a traditional 'research and teaching' lecturer.

Research is – at least to some scale – desirable in its own right. This is however funded separately and not exclusively (or perhaps even predominantly) from student fees. The government's research funding body, UK Research and Innovation, spends about £7.9 billion or about £35,000 per member of academic staff. As we will propose shortly, this is perhaps the ideal route for increased funding at universities, where the amounts disbursed should take account of the potential positive effects on teaching.

An advantage of research is that productivity can be measured at the individual academic level. 'Publish or perish' means that the academic is expected to have concrete evidence of their research output in terms of publications. Either through the grapevine, or through formal rankings of journals (for example, the Chartered Association of Business Schools provides the ABS list of journal rankings in business, economics and related fields), it is easy to evaluate the CV of an academic in terms of quality rather than quantity. Publishing in low-ranked journals is not valued highly, publishing in the very top journals is.

The government – seeking to enhance research productivity across UK universities – introduced the Research Assessment Exercise in 1986. Each subject area in each university was ranked for research. This was superseded by the Research Excellence Framework (REF) in 2014, but the general principles remained the same. Units of assessment, not individual academics, would be evaluated. While some funding would follow, the effect of a good result was more reputational. A highly ranked department would attract good academics and good students. For reasons that are less clear, 'metrics' and using the quality of the journal as a good indicator of the quality of the article were abhorred, and the process has therefore become more expensive (£250 million) than it might be. For political reasons, the measures have also included more and more 'impact' as an element, where 'impact' represents demonstrating the pathway from a published piece of work to affecting outcomes in the 'real world'. This is largely unmeasurable except in special cases (for example, rapid development and introduction of a vaccine for COVID), so defeats much of the purpose of the exercise – to have a clear and valid measure of research productivity at subject level in a university.

Could the same thing be done for teaching? This is more complicated to answer, in part because it requires first a definition of 'good teaching'. We cannot count the number of first-class degrees given, because the university determines the number of firsts. Going on teacher training courses, or becoming a fellow of the Higher Education Academy (or, even more dauntingly, a senior fellow or a principal fellow), may or may not be productive (this is a natural area for research, rather than presumption), but it is not a direct measure of teaching effectiveness. Similarly, student satisfaction (as with the NSS) is a measure of short-run happiness, not the educational value of a course or quality of teaching. The 'customer is always right' is a dangerous principle to apply to teaching.

There are potential measures of teaching effectiveness. The OfS can access LEO data to learn about the background and A-level attainment (or alternative qualifications) of students. In principle, 'value-added' in terms of earnings can be measured and this could be viewed as a reasonable, if imperfect, measure of teaching excellence. This is happening now in academic research and publications, indicating again how research supports teaching.

The Institute for Fiscal Studies has provided a first analysis of the returns to different degrees (Britton et al, 2020). They found that the discounted lifetime return on average to a degree was around £130k for men and £100k for women, a gain of about 20%. However, economic returns vary widely, with high returns for degrees from Russell Group research-intensive universities and for subjects such as medicine, dentistry, veterinary, economics, mathematics and engineering. It is perhaps not exactly a surprise that 'hard' and 'mathematical' subjects gain a premium. But what is important to note is that the vogue for 'vocational' subjects such as business & management or law may be misplaced, and conversely – unless compared to the high-return degrees listed – the winding-down of humanities teaching is not supported.

What the data cannot readily show is the effectiveness of a particular course right now, since the earnings impact takes place over time. Further, as we've emphasized, earnings are not an ideal measure of value-added given that pay in different jobs does not necessarily reflect the public value of the job.

Solutions

We are now coming towards the end of the book, and therefore it's time to start turning our attention to policy solutions.

The post-pandemic inflation has made many problems politically easier to resolve. It would have been politically difficult – dealing with a sector so unified that, even in the midst of industrial activity, the unions and the universities come together in demanding more government funding – for the government to follow the Augar Report recommendation of cutting university fees. Students do not have the same leverage on the fees issue as does the sector, or fees would never have risen to £9,000. But inflation has done Augar's work for the government, real fees have fallen to the levels proposed first by Browne and subsequently by Augar. The government, on that score, can simply stand back and do nothing.

Overseas fees, set by universities (often in conjunction with private recruiting organizations) are already too high and, unlike home fees, are likely to rise with inflation. On the one hand, amending the Equality Act to allow for price discrimination, as has been done in this case, is simply distasteful. The costs of educating an overseas student – if they have the same qualifications as a home student on the course – are little different. There may be modest additional costs in English language and cultural support. Further, since the home fee of £9,250 is (despite the claims of universities) a full cost fee, the taxpayer would not be subsidizing an overseas student if they were charged the same amount. If the government wants to view overseas students as a revenue source, it should (and already does in terms of the charges for visas) charge the students or the agents who recruit them directly at the national level.

Ideally, the money raised could be recycled back to support universities in specific initiatives. While the home student fee covers the teaching costs reasonably ascribable to that student, we have noted that research at the university is funded separately by the taxpayer. That research – through the concept of research-led teaching – benefits students. In that sense, both home students and overseas students are indirectly subsidized by the research budgets. The government could efficiently 'tax' overseas students and put the money raised into research and other university activities such as community engagement.

Having a break-even (now that inflation has eroded the excess value) home fee and an overseas fee that is a multiple of the home fee (and therefore hugely profitable) distorts the system. Even if we weren't concerned about the price discrimination against overseas students – many of whom will be of diverse ethnicities and come from less well-off countries than the UK – the high fees charged distort, in a negative way, the education programme that impacts not only upon overseas students, but upon home students. If the university feels it needs to be focused upon making profits from overseas students and may therefore apply lax admissions standards for those students (assisted by profit-making recruiting organizations), the whole programme will be tilted. Course content will be weakened, and the assessment process will have to be modified to allow students to continue in their programme even if their first-year results are disastrous. There is little gain to removing the excess profit margin – and its distortions – from home students, if it remains in place for overseas students.

Inflation also solves part of the problem of universities that over-built student centres and other similar facilities, provided they financed this with traditional mortgage-type loans at the very low interest rates available in the recent past. The pound sterling repayment amount is devalued in real terms every year with inflation. Universities that entered into more complex arrangements, essentially selling off future streams of student housing revenue, will have made a bad deal but, to be honest, it is hard to understand why they thought they could outsmart the private equity people offering these deals. In any case, inflation hasn't made them worse off, they just haven't gotten the benefits.

Universities do need more funding, but it needs to be rewarding quality. The government has recognized the importance of university research, and – particularly in the UK and US, which have led in IT and pharmaceuticals – universities are fundamental for this endeavour. Further, as we have observed, research productivity is not only measurable, but is being measured in the REF. The rewards for high performance in the REF should be increased, along with research support in general. This is not just a boost to the traditionally excellent universities, but is an avenue for all universities. The very top universities will score highly – and gain funding – in many fields. Other universities will gain funding in a few fields where they typically build on existing strengths.

At worse, if universities merely replicate the current hierarchy, funding will look like California, where the top universities receive high funding and the lesser universities receive lesser funding. But every university has the incentive to become better, if they choose to take advantage of it. As an example, Northumbria University has made very public its research ambitions and has introduced the Vice-Chancellor's Fellowship Scheme. Surely funding should follow this sort of initiative, and not some marketing gimmick devised to attract more students.

David Willetts (2021) has written a report on how to expand higher education without further claims on the taxpayer. He argues for new universities throughout the country and for a diversity of missions for universities. In many ways, the old model of UK polytechnics was a good one. The easiest way to establish technologically focused, innovative and exciting institutions is to set up new ones.

But the new universities need not be more vocational – there has been talk of an 'MIT of the North'. The Robbins Report of 1963 led to the creation of eight new universities and a sense of vibrancy throughout the sector. Well-funded new universities at a stroke invigorate the competition that was sought by government policy but impeded by the sector.

In some ways, the rebalancing of student fees with the actual costs of education – removing the excessive profit margins for home and overseas students – will itself resolve issues of deterioration of student engagement, grade inflation, over-bureaucratization and the 'managerial' rather than 'academic' university. Removing the distorting incentives can remove some of the pressures and, once universities are competing and become clearer in their missions and success, the best staff and students will sort into dynamic universities. Bureaucratic universities will not have the budgets or the environment for success.

Finally, at a sector level, but for the economy as a whole, wages have to rise with inflation. There is no empirical rationale for the real wage deterioration in the public sector, and real wage stagnation throughout the economy, over the last few decades. This will be a major theme of our final chapter on policy.

Student engagement and the pandemic

Even before the pandemic, student unions campaigned for 'lecture capture' and – in the distorted market we have described – universities rushed to accommodate them. Lectures would be recorded and students – instead of sitting in the lecture theatre – could play them back from the convenience of their accommodation. It is hard to understand why anyone thought this a good idea from a pedagogical point of view. In-person theatre tickets cost a significant multiple in price over streamed versions. People in general prefer to travel to Venice than to watch a travelogue. If it was felt that, uniquely, lectures were better viewed on the laptop than in person, there are institutions with skills honed over decades at teaching in this way. The Open University has a process for producing – over a period of years – top quality (first TV and now) on-line materials.

During the pandemic, on-line education became a necessity. But, as with other forms of employment, things are having a hard time returning to what would previously have been viewed as a form of normalcy. Things have become exacerbated by 'commuting students'. *The Guardian* observed that a high proportion of university students were now living at their parental home (Adams, 2023), with a subsidiary article explaining the rationale of students. Of course, if a student lives away from campus and has 'lecture capture', their disengagement from the educational programme – for which they are taking out loans of nearly £20,000 a year – becomes even more extreme.

Here again the funding system has been extremely poorly designed. A student can get a loan for maintenance up to £8,400 if living at home, with a modest uplift to £9,978 if they live away from home (outside London). The extra £1,578 covers at most a few months' rent. Even if a student could afford to live on campus, they have a choice between a relatively comfortable sum of £8,400 living at home versus an extremely difficult £9,978 in student accommodation. For much of the country, the £9,978 is simply inadequate to meet their financial needs, even if they take on (poorly paid) bar or shop work. The situation is even worse if parents – in a cost of living crisis – find the rent paid by the student helps out the family budget and encourage them to stay at home and 'commute'.

Consequently, the lecturer finds the lecture hall nearly empty by the end of term, with a few diehard students paying rapt attention and taking notes.

Further, the disengagement particularly affects students from less well-off backgrounds. We've already described how students who are less privileged, and may have gone to less privileged schools, need to catch up. But, if they are particularly financially impacted by inadequate student funding and stay at home, they get less from the educational programme and gain less from interactions with other students and events on campus, thereby falling further behind.

As with so much in our economy, no new money is needed, just a more efficient use of existing resources. But there is a broader lesson after the pandemic. It is hard to think that home working throughout the economy is all that much different from the experience at universities. Over time, it is likely that we will see productivity of those staying at home fail to develop since they will be missing the 'learning on the job' that represents much of the productivity gains in the economy. Further, it is precisely those who need in-person, team engagement the most, those who need mentoring, that won't be getting it. The privileged student, whose parents support them with additional funding, will live on or near campus and participate fully. They will go to a job with the social skills to succeed, even if a pandemic makes them work from home. The effects, at university and in employment, will further impair social mobility and generational equity.

10

Housing

The battleground

No area of intergenerational disparity is perhaps as contentious as housing. The Resolution Foundation website observed on 20 September 2017 that 'families headed by 30 year olds are only half as likely to own their home as the baby boomer generation was at the same age' and that 40% were in private rented accommodation (compared to 10% 50 years earlier).

I have a flat list of Islington properties from when I was a new lecturer, and a flat cost about £20,000. Today, the average flat in Islington costs about £800,000. Inflation in general has been such that prices have gone up by a factor of five, so there's a lot left there to explain. It certainly cannot be explained on the basis of traditional house price to income ratios of three to one. The average wage in the UK in 1980 was about £6,000, so it is seen that the Islington flat was priced about right on traditional standards. Average full-time earnings in the UK are now about £30,000. Of course, London earnings are higher than the UK average, and Islington has been gentrified. But today's London university lecturer is unlikely – on a salary of about £40,000–45,000 – to find an affordable flat in most of London.

The *Financial Times* wrote an editorial on 13 October 2022 on how the '[h]ousing shortage risks breaking the American dream'. They ascribe the cost of houses to '[d]eclining interest rates … constrained land supply, zoning issues, and over-regulated markets'. In the UK, there has been a constant refrain about the need to build on the green belt to alleviate the 'housing shortage'.

The Department for Levelling Up, Housing and Communities reported (on 31 March 2021) that there were 24.9 million dwelling units in England in 2021, an increase of 216,490 (0.88%) on the previous year. Of these units, 15.9 million were owner-occupied, 4.9 million privately rented and 4.1 million social housing. There were 653,000 vacant units.

The point – as with other asset markets – is that it is the 'stock of housing', not the 'flow', that determines the price. A doubling of house building to a rate of roughly 2% would still have a trivial effect on the total stock of housing. Much more impactful on the supply side is the utilization of vacant dwellings, potential limitations on owning second homes, banning holiday lets, and the density of occupation of a given property. But even then, the 'asset' nature of housing means that the price is predominantly determined by investment criteria. A change in the interest rate operates with a leverage that a change in the flow of housing construction cannot hope to overtake. This is compounded by the introduction of interest-only mortgages which added fuel to price rises and made buy-to-let particularly attractive.

We have earlier described the everything bubble where – because of low and declining interest rates – assets are being priced at a high multiple to the prices of goods and services (that is, incomes). Falling interest rates – over four decades – drove prices higher and higher. For many things – for example, the price of Bitcoin or gold coins, or even Apple shares – it doesn't really matter since the ownership does not directly bring you consumption opportunities. But when house price levels mean that ownership becomes unattainable for new generations (or for the less favoured in older generations), this directly impacts upon their consumption choices. If you are priced out of the house purchase market, you can still obtain 'housing services' in the rental market, but you do not have the opportunity to design your housing to fit your tastes and preferences, and – in the current legal regime – the right to extended tenure. Under 'assured shorthold tenancies' in the UK, a landlord can recover a property (after the initial six-month period) without giving any reason with only two months' notice.

Previous rental regimes in the UK gave tenants greater security and other advantages. Rents were controlled so your rented housing would not suddenly become unaffordable. You had the right to remain there due to 'security of tenure'. Given your anticipated long stay, you might invest in maintenance, renovations and improvements to the property. It might also be the case that you could bequeath your housing rights to the next generation. These rights for tenants also made speculation in property purchase for renting less attractive and so provided a curb on house prices.

It is ironic that those who extol the values just described – sustainability of your housing (provided you took out a long-term fixed rate mortgage, as in the US), security in costs and occupancy, and the ability to improve the property (since you had the right to remain without an increase in the rent) – want to isolate them to owner-occupied housing and not extend those benefits to those in the rental sector, who are not buying a house, either through choice or necessity.

In any case, the one-way bet on house prices (which held for the four decades of declining interest rates) is over. Once interest rates hit zero, they were not going to fall any further and this source of house price inflation would come to an end. While the government could continue to prop up rising house prices by fiscal measures (the tax and benefits regime) – and did so through the pandemic with, among other things, the stamp duty holiday – it would not have the leverage of falling interest rates. Despite the end of the pandemic and record house prices, the government extended the stamp duty holiday (with increased thresholds before payment was required) until 2025. This is a measure of the political strength of the 'house price lobby' in the UK.

In this chapter, we distinguish between the nature of tenure (owner-occupied, private rental, social housing), the quality of housing, and the price of housing. We look for an exit ramp from the political drive for ever-increasing house prices.

The nature of housing tenure

Margaret Thatcher's 'right to buy' programme, introduced in 1980, led to over 300,000 London council properties being sold to sitting tenants at highly discounted prices, eventually reaching a discount of 60% or 70% (for flats). It is estimated that nearly three million properties throughout the UK were handed over to their public tenants. Subsequently, it is estimated by the *Independent* newspaper (Kentish, 2017) that 40% have moved from owner-occupied to the private rental sector.

At a stroke, a large number of public tenants became homeowners. For those fortunate enough to have long tenure (and therefore a 60% discount) on a nice semi-detached brick house with a garden, this was clearly a life-enhancing move. Those who were living in run-down council flats built during the 1960s might, in retrospect, have found the change in status less exciting, particularly since they became liable over time for their share of significant upgrading works.

Leaving aside the issue of discounts (paid for by the taxpayer but – since the funds from selling the property flowed into the government coffers in the first instance, and the lost rents played out only over time – not deemed a matter of great fiscal consequence), this was simply a shift in housing tenure from rented to 'owned', typically under a mortgage. The loss of rental income to local authorities, which had made the original capital investment, naturally had implications for any future building of council houses.

Should we care about the nature of housing tenure? Certainly, Margaret Thatcher saw it as creating a 'property-owning democracy' that might be more inclined to vote Conservative. Over 60% of households own their home in the UK, with a comparable rate in the US. Owning your home gives you security of tenure (provided you have not suffered a large calamity leading to repossession or a forced need to sell), but so do strong rent laws that have in the past applied in the private rental sector in the UK. Home ownership, if one has taken out a long-term fixed interest rate mortgage as is common in the US, also largely fixes your housing costs. Various local and national governments have sought to extend that to the private rental sector through rent control.

Kirsty Lang in the *Financial Times* (2022) describes the virtues of the rental market in Vienna, where 60% of the population live in 'high-quality subsidised housing, including middle-class families and young professionals'. The average monthly rental of a good-sized flat is €767. There is, therefore, clear empirical support that there is an alternative to having a high-cost, private sector dominated housing market. It is not necessary that social housing should carry a stigma. Importantly, though, good maintenance is vital for either social or private rental properties. One of the complaints expressed by many council tenants has been that they could not maintain their property themselves. Councils wanted to control maintenance for understandable reasons (particularly in a block of flats, poor maintenance could be a danger to adjacent tenants), but were believed to often fail to provide adequate maintenance to tenants through inefficiency or financial pressures. An irony was that many tenants were/are in the building trade and could readily do the work.

It was observed, after right to buy, that one could recognize privatized houses or flats on a former council estate by the individual doors fitted by the occupants. But this is not about the nature of tenure – there is nothing that precludes a local authority or other social (or private) landlord from offering the tenant a choice of doors. And, in well-off conservation neighbourhoods, or with listed property, homeowners perceive a benefit to imposing limits on the changes and developments that can be made by their neighbours. They specifically limit the right of neighbouring owners to change their doors.

What is different in practical terms in home ownership compared to even long-term rentals is that one can 'monetize' any improvements made to the property. Capital gains can arise not just because of house price inflation, or the gentrification of the neighbourhood, but alternatively as a return to refurbishment and improvements. In the US, where capital gains on main residences are taxable, costs of improvements can be deducted. On selling the property, one gets back the costs of most renovations and extensions in a higher selling price (but not, apparently, for building a swimming pool in England).

This efficiency advantage of a system dominated by home ownership can be over-stated. Under security of tenure and low fixed or regulated rents, a private or public tenant has the incentive to undertake property repairs and improvements. If they are going to live in the property indefinitely, they can fit a new door (if the landlord agrees) and gain the benefit for years or decades. This is precisely what happens with commercial leases of shops and cafes, often on ten-year leases.

Arguably, private housing leads to over-development. Adding a storey to your house, either open to the skies on a new upper floor, or buried mole-like under the ground in a basement extension, crowds the neighbourhood and puts greater demand on services such as traffic and parking. Your cellar extension takes months if not years to complete, disrupting the quiet enjoyment your neighbours are entitled to in their own homes. For those who live in gentrifying neighbourhoods, planning permission proves of limited protection from these externalities, although your neighbours' renovations may well increase the value of your own property as partial compensation.

The quality of housing

There is nothing in economics that requires social housing to be low quality. Nonetheless, council estates that started off as desirable places to live became centres of crime – such as the Heygate Estate in Southwark featured in that way in the film *Harry Brown*. The only perceived solution was to tear it down. But this may have more to do with issues of segregating housing by social class, and the lack of provision of youth support services than about the design and nature of tenure of social housing. Problems compounded with years of failures to maintain estates in good condition and invest in improvements. On the positive side, it is because it was a large council estate, and not privately owned flats, that the regeneration plans could be developed and implemented by the authorities in a relatively direct way.

At the extreme, the Grenfell Tower calamity exposed the devastatingly poor quality of the UK housing stock in both the public and private sector. Nearly 500 buildings have been found to have the same cladding, while nearly 1,000 have dangerous cladding. Government reports in 2019 showed 167 public buildings and 175 private sector residential buildings with aluminium composite cladding systems, along with 60 student residences and 31 hotels. Dangerously poor housing is not the sole province of the public sector and extends even to student residences where one might have hoped for more of a duty of care.

We have already discussed how, for education in the university sector, public provision need not be low-quality provision. The University of California at Berkeley is one of the dominant academic institutions in the US. It is also a public university. Princeton, on the other hand, is private and also a dominant academic institution. There is no reason why one form of organization has to lead to higher quality of provision than another. Further, both ration their supply and turn down the majority of applicants for student places. With respect to technology developed away from the university sector, the role of the public sector has been emphasized by Mariana Mazzucato (2013). The US Advanced Research Projects Agency has been generally credited with the development of much modern electronic (and other) technology. In the UK, publicly funded research labs (such as the NPL or Porton Down) have and can provide high-quality curiosity driven research which feeds into the commercial sector.

A well-regulated and run public authority can provide first-rate affordable housing, and a well-regulated and run private sector can provide first-rate affordable housing. As in our discussion of universities in the previous chapter, a 'market' – without full specification of its operation and regulation – does not ensure an efficient result, while the absence of a 'market' – without full specification of the system's operation and regulation – does not ensure an equitable result.

Affordable housing and poor doors

When a development proposal is approved, or if a piece of land is given planning permission, there is a potentially very large planning gain created. It is hard to see why a government (local or central) would not wish to claim a large part of the windfall for itself. One way is to require that a proportion of the new development be 'affordable' – under Ken Livingstone as Mayor of London, the target was that 50% should meet that criterion. However, this was not necessarily low-cost 'socially rented' housing, but included 'affordable rent' of up to 80% of market levels, as well as rent-to-buy and part-ownership properties that went to people with incomes up to £74,000 in the 2011 London Plan.

An alternative way of collecting planning gain would be to extract a windfall tax on the premium resulting from planning permission. The revenues could, in principle, be hypothecated (usable only) for high-quality public housing. There are two practical issues that might make on-site affordable housing a better way of putting planning gain to a public purpose. One is that hypothecated revenue streams can be undone if the authorities simply cut other funding currently put into social housing, keeping the total budget unchanged.

The other potential gain from requiring that the affordable housing component be on-site gets at the issue of segregation by social class. Not only does this avoid 'sink estates' but provides a natural bound on the quality of the provision – a new development with expensive flats would be harder to sell if the associated affordable housing provision was of clearly low quality. Even then, however, the developers would typically have 'poor doors', different entrances for the affordable and the full-price housing, and there were regular stories in the press of children in the affordable housing being excluded from the otherwise communal play areas.

A perceived problem (though rarely stated explicitly) with providing high-quality social housing is that, if it is very attractive, people of all sorts of income levels will want to live there. This is not necessarily a bad thing. As in Vienna, there is no particular reason (ideology aside) to think that a well-regulated public sector cannot be as efficient in provision as a well-regulated private sector. In either case, it is necessary to design carefully the public or private allocation system and the quality of provision, notably the safety of the housing. An unregulated private sector, or a bureaucratic public sector, will each be highly inefficient in its own way. Further, a public sector can provide different qualities (or even the same quality) of provision at different prices – rents can be set as a percentage of income. Depending upon one's architectural tastes, comparing the mid-century modern (or historical) social housing (designed by architects such as Goldfinger's Trellick House, Hodgkinson's Brunswick Centre or even the much-derided Barbican) to the modern developments in prime riverfront space near the new US Embassy and the repurposed Battersea Power Station leaves no clear dominance for the private sector. What the developers did achieve in these recent developments, by bargaining with the local council, was the diminution of the on-site affordable housing down to derisory levels.

Timothy Besley and Stephen Coate (1991) make the point that the state can provide private goods such as housing as a way of redistributing income. But the redistribution only occurs if the goods, at a subsidized price, are targeted at the less well-off. This can be done by limiting the 'quality' in different ways – there might be small rooms or poor fittings. Repairs might be time-consuming to organize. There is a trade-off, with the potential quality rising with the intended percentage of the population taking advantage of the provision.

In our work (Frank and Smith, 1996) we gave an alternative approach to rationing that we see in practice but also that allows simultaneously for reasonably high public sector provision in general. Suppose the subsidized housing rental sector contains low-quality housing and high-quality housing. By instituting a seniority system where individuals start out in low-quality housing but, over time, move into better accommodation, the well-off are deterred. This phenomenon is very familiar to academics who wait for their colleagues to retire or find jobs elsewhere so that they can move into better offices. Traditionally, student housing was allocated in this way – first-year students were given the least desirable rooms, while finalists were first in the queue for the best rooms.

If publicly provided housing takes the form of low-quality council estates, devoted only to the 'most vulnerable in society', the quality of provision may well deteriorate to low levels. Tenants may find themselves in dangerous and crowded housing, with poor repairs carried out only after badgering the bureaucracy day after day, week after week. Segregation by social class may provide an opportunity for gangs to develop and take over, making the estate a nightmare. As has been observed by Hastings and Matthews (2012), the 'sharp elbowed' middle classes can get better access to local public services.

Megan Baynes (2021) describes the experiences of a council tenant who has since gone on to be an activist. There's not much to add, other than – as we have done every so often – reminding the 'progressives' that calling for government provision, regulation or intervention in itself is meaningless without having a clear proposal for effective provision, regulation or intervention. Providing the less well-off with cockroach-infested properties is not really a 'progressive' policy.

Getting your boiler serviced

Anyone renting in the private sector, paying a high rent for a 'luxury flat', will have their own nightmare stories to relate. Let's work through a relatively innocuous issue, energy efficiency.

Everyone is advised to have their boiler serviced annually, for safety, efficiency and avoiding breakdowns, but neither homeowners nor private landlords are required to do so. Private landlords are required to get a 'gas safety check' every 12 months, but there does not seem to be pro-active enforcement of this regulation. If you are a private tenant, and in unsafe property or one without a safety certificate, you can contact your local authority to seek assistance, but with clear indications that this will not be an immediate resolution. Ed Magnus (2021) reports on a survey of renters by Plentific, an on-line 'property technology' company. Half of private renters report that they do not have a gas safety certificate or a carbon monoxide alarm.

In contrast, the government enforces the MOT on cars by requiring it in order to tax the vehicle for on-road use, and in turn enforces taxation of vehicles by the standard legal remedies. Automatic number plate technology is used to locate untaxed vehicles, with first modest but then stiff fines or impoundment following. That this is not done for gas safety is a choice – it doesn't mean that private renting should be banned, any more than sink estates mean that social housing should be truncated.

The price of natural gas in the UK has, on the wholesale markets, quadrupled in the post-pandemic period. The government regulations operate a price cap so that consumer tariffs rise slowly in response to such rapid increases. Nonetheless, on 1 April 2022, the price cap was scheduled to rise such that an average consumer would see their annual bills go up from £1,277 to £1,971, rates that are fairly unaffordable for the typical household.

Inefficient boilers are, therefore, significantly more costly to run than before. In my street, vans of boiler installers were parked in front of nearly every house as homeowners rushed to replace their old boilers. The homeowner pays the gas bill for their house, and has an incentive to achieve efficiency. The landlord only does so if the rental market is sufficiently efficient that an inefficient boiler leads to a lower rent attainable, on a pound-for-pound basis. But, almost by definition, the rental market cannot achieve the first-year student's 'law of one price' since every flat is different.

The government has sought to address this with its 2018 'Minimum level of energy efficiency standard'. Landlords already were largely expected to obtain an 'energy efficiency certificate'. As of April 2020, they had to improve the property up to Band E, up to an expenditure of £3,500. Band E involves insulation (with indicative costs given by the government suggesting that only loft insulation comes within the cost cap).

Insulate Britain blocked the M25 and engaged in other demonstrations to get the government to provide insulation, heat pumps and other energy efficiency measures. The externalities from doing so – including the impact on climate change but, as has become extremely clear, on aggression and warfare from belligerent hydrocarbon producing countries – are great. But it's clear that – as with many issues to do with the private rental sector – these things will happen only if there are government subsidies or regulation.

Due to perceived abuses, the government regulates everything from the nature of rental contracts (how long they last, and how you can be evicted during or after the term) to the handling of deposits in the 'tenancy deposit protection' scheme. As we have said, the issue is not so much whether rented housing is social or private, but whether it is 'effectively regulated' in either sector, and the rights and obligations in either framework. Private rentals can be at a regulated rent with security of tenure, while public rentals can be on a month-to-month 'market rent'.

Ownership

Ownership of a house comes with its own obligations and benefits. That 'ownership' and 'rental' are not clearly defined opposites is shown by the UK concepts of 'long leasehold' and 'freehold'. With a long leasehold flat, one 'owns' the flat – with obligations to maintain the structure and pay a modest ground rent – but it reverts to the freeholder after the lease of up to 999 years. There are dangers to this, and freeholders managed on occasion to reclaim the property on the basis of some – even modest – lapse in meeting the lease requirements. Consequently, the law became more and more involved, with rights to extension of the lease and purchase of the freehold. Even owners of a freehold property have legal obligations ranging from building regulations and planning to limitations imposed by the private sector to gain insurance and a mortgage.

Functionally, what one has gained by buying a house depends upon the lending norms and the tax regime. In the US, one typically gets a 30-year fixed interest rate repayment mortgage – in effect the rent one pays (the mortgage payment) is fixed for 30 years and then goes to zero. One has the right to sell the property but not the attached mortgage – if interest rates have gone up, the new owner has a higher 'rent' to pay if the price of the house is the same as you paid. In the US, your home (and second home) mortgage interest is deductible when calculating your federal income tax (if you itemize deductions), but only in full if the mortgage was taken out before 1987 and subsequently subject to a dollar value limit. If you sell your primary residence, a capital gain up to $250,000 ($500,000 for married couples) is federal tax exempt. The different states have different rules on their additional income taxes. Of course, while you've fixed your rent for 30 years (and then it goes to zero), your maintenance and other costs rise with inflation.

In the UK, one typically gets a variable rate mortgage or a mortgage with a few years fixed rate. On a primary residence, one does not get mortgage interest tax relief (abolished by the Thatcher government) but you typically do not pay capital gains tax if you sell. On a buy-to-let property, since the laws changed in 2020 you get a tax credit of 20% of the interest rather than a deduction, so only 'basic rate' tax is removed, and you are liable for capital gains tax. Because the interest rate may change, under a typical UK mortgage you have not 'locked in' the 'rent' for 30 years, as in the US.

To see the relationship between interest rates and house prices, consider the following scenario. Households choose whether to rent or to buy a house. Assume that there is no inflation in rents and that you can obtain a perpetual mortgage (that you never repay) at a permanently fixed interest rate. Ignore the other costs (maintenance, depreciation, insurance and so on) that you might incur as a homeowner but not directly as a renter.

Then the interest payable on the house price is your permanently fixed 'implicit rental'. If you buy a house for £500,000 at an interest rate of 2% (on offer until recently), then this is £10,000 per annum. If this is significantly less than rent levels, there is a strong incentive to buy the house. There are issues to do with timing (if you think house prices will fall, and there are high costs in buying and selling houses, you might wait). In general, however, house prices adjust to bring these figures – the interest rate carrying cost of the house versus rents – into alignment. Consequently, if rents remain the same and interest rates double from 2% to 4%, the balancing house price falls in half. Since this is the sort of interest rate movement we've recently seen, there is nothing out of experience in this sort of occurrence in terms of interest rate moves. We'll come back to why house prices haven't adjusted to this extent. Indeed, a lot of the balancing in the last year or two has been in rentals rising rather than house prices falling.

In practice, over the last 40 years – as we've described in earlier chapters – interest rate movements have largely been a one-way bet. Downwards. House prices (measured for houses that actually change hands) for the US have, as a result, gone up regularly, with the exception of the rising interest rate period preceding the financial crisis and the actual housing crisis in the

Figure 10.1: US House Price Index

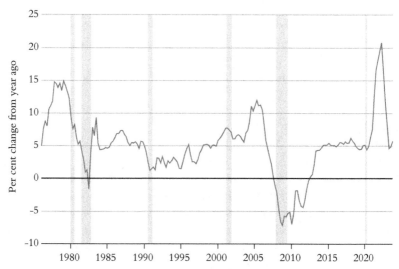

Source: US Federal Housing Finance Agency, All-Transactions House Price Index for the United States [USSTHPI], retrieved from FRED, Federal Reserve Bank of St Louis; https://fred.stlouisfed.org/series/USSTHPI, 27 February 2024.

Great Recession (see Figure 10.1). Note how house prices in the US did not even fall during the severe recession of the early 1980s.

Underlying rents

We've looked at house ownership as a financial market decision, where arbitrage is the guiding principle. Rents on houses are the underlying 'value', which is intermediated by interest rates in determining the capital value of a house bought as a primary residence, a second home or a buy-to-let property. Indeed, for the buy-to-let property, the connection between underlying rents and property price seems direct. Buy-to-let only makes sense if the rents received and anticipated capital gains cover the cost and leave a suitable profit margin. Watching an episode of *Homes under the Hammer* will make that clear! Over the last decades, it is the anticipated capital gains – from the everything bubble caused by consistently falling interest rates – that have driven the buy-to-let sector.

Normally, there is not a lot of volatility in rents. They move in a constrained way over time as guided by supply and demand. The Office for National Statistics has recently provided an experimental measure of private sector rents (see Figure 10.2).

During the period of fairly full employment and robust economic activity in the mid-teens of this century, rentals – even in London – had modest

Figure 10.2: UK annual private rents inflation rates

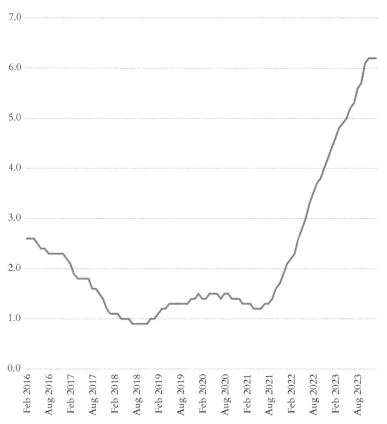

Source: Index of Private Housing Rental Prices from the Office for National Statistics.

inflation. If there was an underlying shortage of housing stock, it didn't show up in rapidly rising rents. This is one reason why the idea of building our way out of house price unaffordability is likely looking in the wrong direction. This is partially because of the modest amount of new housing – even a multiple of the current rate of building will be a small proportion of the existing stock of housing.

In England and Wales, the Department for Levelling Up, Housing and Communities (13 January 2022) reports that 800,000 properties sold in 2021. There were an estimated 27.8 million households. Roughly 200,000 new properties become available in England each year. To gauge the effect on rents and house prices, the proper comparison is not the 1 to 4 ratio of new properties to selling properties, but the 1 to 100 ratio of new properties to the housing stock. Even if two million new houses were built a year, so that the housing stock grew by 10%, the impact on prices would depend upon the 'elasticity of demand' – how much would prices have to fall to get people to consume 10% more housing? Most people – particularly in the small flats of central London – would love to have more room, and much of the increased building would go into more space rather than lower prices.

The conventional view has shifted from adulation of the central banks and low interest rates to some critiques of the pandemic and post-pandemic years. This is 'balanced out' by others who worry about the post-pandemic rises in interest rates to 4–5% as being likely to cause a recession. But, even with the rise in interest rates, it is hard to see that the central banks are doing anything other than following their easy money policies of the last four decades. The last serious inflation period was in the late 1970s/early 1980s. Inflation in the UK in 1980 was about 18%. Towards the end of 1979, the bank rate hit 17%. Inflation in the US in 1980 was about 12%. The Federal Funds rate peaked at 20%. By the 'Volcker' playbook – after Paul Volcker, then Chair of the Fed – interest rates in the post-pandemic inflation of over 10% were way too slow to rise and too low at their peak. Arguments now to lower rates quickly have more to do with the political imperative to sustain house price capital gains than with economics.

Sustainability of house prices

According to data from the Office for National Statistics (22 March 2023), the ratio of median house price to income in the UK has risen from 3.55 in 1997 to 7.69 in 2020. In London, it has gone from 4.00 to 11.78.

The average monthly rent in England, according to the Office for National Statistics, is £795 (between April 2021 and March 2022). For London, it is £1,450. Average property prices are £290,000 in England (January 2023, ONS), and £534,000 in London. Put differently, for both England and London rents are about 3.3% of the price of a house. Given that financing costs for a mortgage are already at that level, and there are significant maintenance and other costs to property ownership, buying a house for occupancy or for buy-to-let can only make sense if the purchaser expects significant capital gains or derives a significant benefit to ownership and the rights contained therein, or if there is no alternative investment perceived as safe with a higher return. This held when bank deposits paid an interest rate very little above zero.

For the last 40 years, home ownership – and indeed the ownership of almost any asset – proved to be a profitable investment because central banks kept lowering interest rates, each year driving up asset values even more. Further, central banks made clear that they intended to forestall any recession by further lowering interest rates. Capital values would consistently go up with falling interest rates, and there would be no risk since central banks were prepared to do 'whatever it takes' if there were any setbacks in asset prices such as the sub-prime mortgage crisis leading to the Great Recession.

This process has largely come to an end, although the post-pandemic rise in interest rates to 5% allows for one 'last hurrah' if central banks go back towards zero. Even if they do so, there are problems on the fiscal side – governments are reconsidering their fiscal deficits.

In the UK, as we've observed, the tax benefits to buy-to-let have been cut significantly. The very large subsidies to first-time buyers, who rely upon one government scheme or another (or their parents), are costly. In the UK, we have the 'First Homes Scheme' which provides a discount of 30% to 50% that must be passed on to the next owner. There is the Lifetime ISA, which gives a 25% bonus on savings. There is the 'Help to Buy' equity loan or mortgage guarantee.

What there isn't is a significant policy to bring down the price of housing, for a very simple political reason – existing homeowners would suffer a fall in their home equity. Any sustainable policy relies on somehow finessing this political constraint, as we now discuss.

Generational equity, entrenched politics and policy

Earlier generations in the UK had access to council housing, rent control and security of tenure in private rentals, and realistically priced owner-occupied housing. A combination of more recent policies has worked to the detriment of the younger generations.

Thatcher's 'right to buy' allowed tenants in desirable council housing to buy the property, at a massive discount. As we've observed, many of these properties are now privately rented. We have reiterated throughout this book that, as economists, our job is not to judge the preferences of individuals and politicians. A democratically elected (and re-elected again and again) government chose to hand out publicly owned property in this way, to benefit a proportion of the current population at the expense of future generations. In the same way, they privatized at low prices numerous state-owned companies such as British Telecom, British Gas, British Airways, British Rail, and so on. Unless the funds were used to pay off the national debt (and they weren't), this was transferring wealth from future generations to the present ones.

Fiscal and monetary policies, over the last 40 years, have driven the price of housing up and up, to the point of clear unaffordability. This benefits some in the older generations – who are sitting on massive capital gains – at the expense of the younger generations. However, we have argued that this is unsustainable. The UK house price to income ratio of 8 to 1 will have to fall to a more traditional level of 3 (or at most 4) to 1, unless one believes that the economy will return to and remain at zero interest rates. Even conventional thinking recognizes that maintaining a zero interest rate economy – with a zero interest rate effective floor – means that the central banks will have difficulty in the second foundational element of elevated house prices, the zero risk provided by central banks 'doing whatever it takes' in a 'financial crisis'.

There are two ways (or a combination of the two) to restore balance. One is for house prices to fall and the other is for incomes (salaries and wages) to rise. Note that we are talking about a 50% fall in house prices, if that is the sole adjusting factor. Consider the angst that would ensue among homeowners and its political repercussions, even though few arguments can be made that the current situation is either fair or efficient. The ONS reports that about three-quarters of people over 65 own their home outright, 5% with a mortgage and about 20% are in the social (15%) and private (5%) rental sectors. Given the high rate of outright ownership, it is hard to see that people in this age bracket will suffer hardship by a fall in house prices. *Today's Conveyancer* (Lennox, 2022) reports that homeowners are 'sitting on £2.6 trillion in equity'. Despite the generational (and within-generation) fairness benefits from allowing a substantial fall in house prices, and the limited impact on the well-being of the older generations, it would be a brave government or central bank that sought a substantial fall in nominal house prices.

Ironically, much of this goes back to parents wanting to keep their children out of the fray for resources that may – in the absence of strong policy changes now – be the future lot of the younger generations, even in wealthy countries, as the bad policy effects of the last four decades (particularly in population and the climate) take hold. The politics of home ownership among seniors was seen clearly in the election of 2019. Theresa May, then the Conservative prime minister, proposed a new way of paying the ever-growing bills for senior social care, putting more of the burden on those receiving the care. The plan would extend the existing charges on nursing home care to care-in-the-home, where the individual's home would count in their assets to be used to pay for the social care. They would not have to sell their homes, since the funds could be claimed from their estate. Nonetheless, seniors (and perhaps, more realistically, their children) were up in arms over the effect on inheritances, and the proposal was labelled the 'dementia tax' and had a profound negative effect on Theresa May's campaign.

Economists (and others) too often think of ideal policies without considering the political constraints. Equity and efficiency both argue that homeowners sitting on massive capital gains in their house, through no special effort on their own part but merely benefitting from the timing of their birth and the location of their residence, should hand the money back to some better use. But any significant house price fall will be politically infeasible. House prices, even in the most serious financial downturns, fall by maybe 20% – this is less an economic limit than a political one, being the point at which governments and central banks 'do whatever it takes'.

The alternative policy to house price falls is to let inflation in wages and salaries carry the adjustment burden. A few years of even 5% inflation would start to address this imbalance, in the same way as – in the previous chapter – inflation has brought university fees back to a more efficient level. Rather than claiming that the 2% inflation target is going to be achieved in the next few years, central banks would be better off adopting a 5% (or more) target in the short term. There is a proviso to this. Central banks are right in wanting to anchor expectations. In fact, they are doing the opposite with their current policies that predict interest rates returning to very low levels in the relatively near future. Based upon experiences from the 1970s, central banks are committing to 'stop-go' policies that will cause inflation to cycle upwards. A realistic interest rate projection for the medium term at the traditional level of 5% – or higher, to take account of the investment needs in infrastructure and the green economy – will more realistically anchor future expectations.

Importantly, the inflation needs to be in wages and salaries to address the house price to incomes imbalance. Recent data from the US (BLS Beta Labs, 2023) shows real hourly wages rising by 1.1% (although hours went down, so that overall real incomes remained constant). This rise in wages is exactly what is needed to rebalance the economy, not just for housing, but in terms of the share of income going to workers and that going to firms in profits. In the UK, annual growth in pay to June 2023 is 8.2% in nominal terms and 0.5% in real terms. But for the UK Government's misguided incomes policy for the public sector (to the point of creating costly recruitment difficulties in, for example, the NHS), this would be an accidental landing on the right policy. Our discussion on the labour market in Chapter 7 suggests that the gap between where real wages should be and where they have been constrained in the last four decades suggests a much higher real wage increase is warranted. As we have argued, laws that rebalance power between labour and firms will lead to both greater equity and greater efficiency in restoring desirable long-term employment relationships.

But this rebalancing will only work if interest rates are high enough to stifle any resurgence in house price inflation, or if some other fiscal element is applied to keep a lid on prices. For example, interest-only mortgages could be banned, and stamp duty could be raised rather than lowered. Ironically, we need to reverse the extraordinary subsidization of home ownership (through both monetary policy of low interest rates and through fiscal subsidies) in order to make home ownership affordable for younger generations.

Certainly, the idea of building on the green belt – which, for the reasons we've described, will have little effect on the price of housing – in order to supposedly help the younger generations that are focused upon a green future, is a level of irony that is only surpassed by Tom Lehrer's famous line 'When Kissinger won the Nobel Prize, satire died'.

11

Let the Good Times Roll

Just not that into you

Dynamic programming is a method for working out the best route to a destination. An economist can help you – if you have defined preferences – both with the issue of choosing your endpoint and the route there.

Suppose you are about to enter the Sixth Form and have decided that you want a career in the literary world. You do some research – and get advice – and decide that getting an undergraduate degree in English Studies at Durham University is your first ambition. You look at their website and see that a standard offer is A*AA including English literature. You now need to choose your A-levels and your strategy of achieving the requisite grades. The Russell Group has a planner called 'informed choices' to help you in this decision-making. For English literature, it advises you to do the A-level in that subject, but also History and Religious Studies.

While this seems straightforward enough, two points quickly follow. One is that going to Durham is only a starting point for what universities are now calling 'the student journey'. In this one case, the current jargon might actually be accurate. You will show up with your newly purchased bed linen and dishes and start off on what your childhood reading might have labelled 'an adventure'. Going to Durham to read English is not a stationary outcome – your interests and knowledge develop over the three years of your degree. But it is a plan – you go through the three years, get your degree and seek to find a job in the literary sector.

You may have to recalibrate all along the plan, both the part of the plan of getting to Durham and the journey that follows thereafter. You may fail to achieve A*AA and find you have to go to your insurance choice of university or enter clearing. We regularly advise 18 year olds that clearing is not a disaster – they will find a good programme and (provided they put in the effort they may not have done at A-level stage) they will succeed. After completing your first-class degree, you may still find that getting a job in the literary world is too difficult an ambition, and may decide to follow a different career. University degrees are 'general human capital' which will be valuable even if you don't follow strictly within the field of study. This is one reason why degrees in the humanities are valuable, even if the bulk of graduates will end up working in totally different areas.

Now consider a more consequential road map. The Paris Agreement was adopted at the end of 2015 and committed countries to limiting global warming to 2 degrees, with efforts to limit this to 1.5 degrees. The target of 1.5 degrees is viewed as sustainable in the sense that – provided it is maintained over time – the world is unlikely to go into a 'journey' of continued deterioration and potential eventual extinction. We have already mentioned recalibration – more and more scientific evidence is developing that climate change is occurring faster than anticipated, and the impacts of even 1.5 degrees are greater than previously thought. That represents no great planning problem – we simply accelerate the move to carbon neutrality, in the same way as you put in more studying if your mock exams indicated you weren't on track for A*AA.

In the university choice example, the student could alternatively just give up on Durham, or on going to university at all. People without degrees can have productive and fulfilling lives. But, with respect to global warming, giving up or lowering our ambitions is a much more problematic choice. Some politicians seem to argue implicitly that they are content with a sustained decline in the habitability of the world, where populations move further and further from coastal and floodplain areas, where forest fires destroy cities and where biodiversity decreases as species become extinct. Things just get worse and worse and potentially lead to human extinction. They talk of mitigating the effects.

The Stern Review (2007: 23) on climate change observes: '[q]uestions of intra- and inter-generational equity are central. Climate change will have serious impacts within the lifetime of most of those alive today. Future generations will be even more strongly affected, yet they lack representation in present-day decisions'.

There was a romantic comedy in 2009 entitled *He's Just Not That Into You*. In Chapter 3, we explored how maybe in effect your parents are just not that into you, and could perfectly rationally choose to maximize their own well-being (and you, as part of their family, during their lifetime extolling 'family values') at your cost a few decades down the road. Governments and central banks (that ultimately report back to governments) can maximize the well-being of those who are voting today rather than the hypothetical voters down the road.

We have observed that many of the guardrails that limited this sort of equilibrium have been removed. Central banks have felt able to print extraordinary amounts of money and set interest rates at remarkably low levels. There is no interfering gold standard or Bretton Woods structure for international exchange rates. Governments have felt able to limit investment in infrastructure and to limit regulations that should be in place to ensure safety and to achieve some semblance of equity and social mobility. Government debt has dramatically risen and the Conservatives who previously called for balanced budgets started calling for tax cuts instead.

The story we've just told about figuring out where you want to go and mapping out how to do it, is straightforward. In the old days, one would go into the American Automobile Association office and they would take out maps of your proposed journey and mark them up for you with the best route. This is now done more quickly on the computer or – indeed – you might decide to rely on your electronic navigator to simply tell you what to do at each junction. But what happens when things start to go off course? There are regular stories in the press of the individual who finds themselves driving into a lake by following the satnav, or a bus or lorry that becomes stuck under a low bridge.

Unfortunately, there is no guarantee in our world that things automatically stabilize. When you are following the satnav into the river, nothing necessarily redirects you onto a more secure route. The bus driver discovers the error in their route only when the top of the bus has been shaved off and they are stuck in place.

Central banks observed that the 2007/08 housing mortgage crisis could potentially lead to another Great Depression. As we observed earlier, however, during the actual Great Depression a significant number of automatic stabilizers were built into the system, such as depositor insurance at banks, social security and unemployment insurance. It is entirely possible that the financial crisis of 2007/08 was limited not by the central banks, but by these automatic stabilizers. In fact, the zero interest rate policies adopted by central banks may have destabilized the system and given us the high post-pandemic inflation.

Much of the instability may be political in nature. With housing, as (we would argue due to low interest rates) prices became unaffordable, governments stepped in with policies that made things worse by subsidizing house purchase, thereby driving up prices further. In the same way, it appears that the climate emergency does not have automatic stabilizers – indeed, the reverse. Wild fires directly add to the carbon in the atmosphere and the trees are no longer there to perform carbon capture. Hotter summers lead to greater use of air conditioning.

The stabilization then, for most of the things that have gone askew – and there are a lot of things that have gone askew – is to have concrete policy responses. This requires political stabilization; something changes the balance of forces such that climate change becomes the mandate, rather than keeping the price of petrol low. We have to move more quickly to electric cars, to public transport, to insulated houses, to less travel, to less wasteful production and consumption.

But first the political battles need to be won. Partially the balance automatically shifts as Generation Z becomes of voting age. But the urgency of climate change, and the extent of the changes necessary, are such that something more is needed in the same way as the suffragettes (and not so much the 'peaceful' suffragists) took direct action to secure the right to vote. We have made the point that an equilibrium persists because the beneficiaries either directly support its maintenance or don't do anything to change the situation. The tobacco companies did not rush to stop producing cigarettes once the scientific evidence for the link with health issues became clear in the 1940s and 1950s. Los Angeles did not aggressively address smog – first experienced in 1943 – until the 1960s. From the end of the Civil War in the 1860s, it took nearly a century for the US to begin to address legal racial disparities, much less the social and economic disparities. Fifty years after the Equal Pay Act in the UK, the gender pay gap persists. That which is too slow a pace for health, for pollution, for racial and social equity, becomes a glacial pace when extinction is a possibility. Of course, even the metaphor of 'glacial pace' for 'slow' is becoming less and less pertinent as the glaciers melt throughout the world.

Public well-being, individualism and independence

Twenge's (2023) study of generations presents a continuous history of the post-war period, as well as descriptions of the discrete characteristics of the different generations that inhabit this space in time. Twenge describes a continuous motion of direction towards individualism. After a discrete break in socio-economic philosophy in the 1980s, there has also been a continuous travel towards 'individual self-interest' and 'materialism'. Individualism is not the same as 'individual self-interest' and can be expressed in a unique style of dress or dancing, or in political expression rather than in selfish behaviour or consumerism.

Individualism is also not the same as independence, and there are worries about whether millennials and zoomers have been encouraged – or even allowed – to develop sufficient independence to organize their own lives and contribute to society. Generation X was the last to wander the neighbourhood freely after school. Millennials and zoomers were raised with what can be considered either 'due caution' in a dangerous world or 'over-parenting'. The irony is that technology shifted the threats facing younger people from those out in the real world to those in the internet world. Zoomer children might well have been safer getting up to unsupervised adventures in the real world than being restricted to what seems the much more dangerous virtual world.

It is hard to tell a university lecturer sitting with an (electronic) stack of essays to mark that individualism is a bad thing. What is the point of 100 identical essays that could have been written by even an early version of AI? We are now being told to introduce 'authentic' assessment that allows students to express their individualism; as with many of the currently fashionable education 'reforms', new labels are being given to precisely what a good lecturer has sought to do from the beginning of Socratic dialogue.

In the 1960s and 1970s, there were regular cartoons showing a group of hippies pointing out the uniforms (suits and ties, for the men) of the commuters on their way to the office, and the commuters pointing out the uniforms (long hair, tie dye shirts and beads) of the hippies smoking something in the park. The truth is that, within the confines of a suit and tie, you can explore your identity by colours, patterns and shapes – narrow 1950s' tie, perhaps, or a 1970s' wide kipper? The musical *Hair* provides individual characteristics, and costumes, for numerous members of the hippie tribe.

Individualism and independence seem unreservedly good characteristics, in the same way that 'self-interest' and 'materialism' seem unreservedly bad. Should anyone be surprised that – after 40 years of extolling self-interest (often in its particularly concentrated and dangerous form of 'family values') and materialism – we've ended up with a ravaged environment, huge inequalities within a nation and throughout the world, low productivity growth, inadequate housing stock, poor infrastructure and democracy-threatening political discord? Can you imagine a family, a business or any other organization founded on 'individual self-interest and materialism' that would be anything other than an abject failure?

Boomers have arguably overstayed their welcome on the playing field. Even with advances in medical treatment, they will of necessity be giving way to the next generations of leaders. Concerns about the poorly understood Generation X may have explained in part why the remaining silent generation and boomers have been so slow to leave the field. More or less no one wants to see the (at the time of writing) anticipated rematch between Trump and Biden for the presidency, but it seems so hard to move on. Ultimately, the sands in the hourglass come to an end.

There is a real worry, however. An overlooked feature of 'passing the torch to a new generation' is that the next leaders will have largely grown up under 40 years of the common political and economic framework of 'greed is good'. They won't have seen, in the workplace, traditional firms where workers and managers formed a long-term productive relationship – they've seen only the gig economy. They will only have seen 'yah-boo' politics that has become more extreme over time. While most people would like to see the people smugglers put out of business, and there can be reasonable disagreements on immigration, it remains distasteful to base political campaigns on slogans like 'stop the boats' or 'build the wall'.

In major political shifts, such as the one we clearly need right now, we rely on the enthusiasm of youth to drive the change. It is the Greta Thunbergs who have focused the intensity, not the Al Gores, despite the importance of what he and other boomers have done. Yet, hope is possible as Twenge observes about the zoomers:

> It may seem counterintuitive that a generation with high depression rates would be politically active … Gen Z's general sense of negativity about the world and their own lives, fueled by their anger and disappointment, may be the spark that ignites a new youth movement for social change. Their power has not been fully tapped, and older generations underestimate Gen Z at their peril. (Twenge, 2023: 438)

'The great moderation'

The last four decades have been described as 'the great moderation'. Ben Bernanke (2004) explores the roles of structural change, improved macroeconomic policy and good luck. This book has a simpler explanation in mind for what happened over the last four decades – we borrowed from the future to smooth out and generally increase our consumption. Instead of building up the 'rainy day' fund, we drew down from it whenever it was convenient, and failed to replenish the fund on days when the sun was shining. The simplest example, perhaps, is monetary policy – interest rates were consistently on a downward path from the early 1980s. When the dot-com bubble burst, when the mortgage bubble burst in the financial crisis, when the pandemic struck, we borrowed and printed money. Interest rates went down, but never went back up again.

In this book, we have deviated from the current conventional wisdom in a number of ways. One is on the role for 'shocks', which we see as largely blaming the dog for eating our homework. The major 'shocks' were entirely predictable and indeed predicted. We knew we were in a dot-com bubble, we knew we were in a housing bubble, we even knew that a pandemic was likely to occur at some point (and, some would say, we even knew it was likely – from the experiences with the 2002 SARS and the 2012 MERS – that it would be a coronavirus pandemic). The invasion of Ukraine was similarly predictable and predicted. In any case, as observed by Stephen King (2023): 'The roots of the post-pandemic rise in inflation lies in this world of monetary complacency, not in Russia's invasion of Ukraine in 2022 or China's ongoing Covid lockdowns.'

The biggest 'shock' of all was positive not negative – the remarkable technological boom over the last four decades arising from massive investment (often for military reasons) in electronics, computing, aeronautics and rockets, and nuclear energy. The development of microcircuits leading to mobile phones and laptop computers, the internet and essentially unlimited computing power (including AI) may be technological progress of a scope unprecedented in human history. Going forward, there has been remarkable progress in cost-cutting in the production of batteries and solar panels. Medical progress, seen in the rapid production of effective COVID vaccines and recently in pharmaceutical treatment for Alzheimer's disease, is another area where we have been benefitting from the work of scientists and engineers. While each of these represents its own challenges – although, for example, the concerns about AI seem over-stated – productivity in both economic and social terms should have been already hugely enhanced, with extraordinary potential for future gains.

Yet, in almost every dimension, we see practical variants of the Solow paradox, described in the *Financial Times* article 'Why don't computers work?' (Elder, 2022). Robert Solow observed in 1987 that 'You can see the computer age everywhere but in the productivity statistics'. As Elder (2022) puts it, 'as technology gets faster, people get slower'. Medical technology has been amazing, but the cost has risen – and keeps rising – to potentially unsustainable levels. We don't know how to provide social care for an ever-growing elderly population, something that Theresa May discovered to her cost when her proposals were labelled a 'dementia tax'. That the Silicon Valley Bank has just failed in 2023 and had to be bailed out by the authorities, shows the stark contrast between the success of the technology scientists of Silicon Valley and the limitations to the financial sectors even that geographically close to the success stories.

Scientists developed COVID vaccines in record time, while the fiscal and monetary authorities wasted public funds on one daft scheme or another to prop up the economy. If you read Donald Trump's *The Art of the Deal* (1987), it becomes discomfortingly clear that Trump does at least understand how good business should work (even if his own business career doesn't seem to follow the principles in the book). Trump deserves credit for the successful 'Operation Warp Speed' to develop COVID vaccines. Meanwhile, the impeccably pedigreed (Goldman Sachs and Stanford MBA) UK Chancellor Rishi Sunak came up with 'Eat Out to Help Out' – encouraging social mingling in the midst of a pandemic – and the remarkably poorly designed furlough scheme. The UK Government came up with the unbelievably expensive (estimated at £37 billion) 'Test and Trace' scheme about which Meg Hillier, the Chair of the Public Accounts Committee, said (UK Parliament Committees, 2021): 'Yet despite the unimaginable resources thrown at this project Test and Trace cannot point to a measurable difference to the progress of the pandemic, and the promise on which this huge expense was justified – avoiding another lockdown – has been broken, twice.'

As we approach the challenges of the next four decades – when the stakes have risen by the potential prospect of climate extinction – economic and social policy will need to catch up with scientific success. The scientists have given us the tools to deal with our problems, and will continue (subject to sufficient government funding and institutional support – those who ascribe the progress to the 'private sector' rather than universities and defence research have simply not been paying attention) to develop technology at an amazing rate. But whether or not it is used effectively to deal with the climate emergency, to alleviate poverty and achieve a fairer and more productive economy, and to improve the welfare of the populace, rests with the economic and social practitioners and policy makers who will have to up their game.

As universities adopt the fashion of the day in shutting humanities departments and making staff redundant, it's important to note the role of 'culture'. David Brooks writes in the *New York Times* (25 January 2024): 'I confess I still cling to the old faith that culture is vastly more important than politics or some pre-professional training in algorithms and software systems.' We have made the point in this book how novels and films can enhance our understanding of how not only society, but the economy works. For devising policies, as well as for engaging the underlying politics that determines what policies will be adopted, it is necessary to have a broader understanding and empathy with the people who preceded us and shaped our institutions, with the people who share our time on Earth and will be part of the current political calculus, and with the people of the future whom we impact upon.

'The firm'

The Royal Family, in the 20th century, adopted the moniker 'the firm' showing that a family could be a business. On occasion through this book, we have teased our fellow economists who insist that the reverse does not hold, that the economy is not like a household. In fact, it is exactly like a household or firm, but with two additional – and quite important – powers. The government and the central bank, between them, can raise taxes and print money. These are not unrelated powers – indeed, some theories of the value of money observe that ultimately printed money is valuable because the government accepts its own currency in the payment of taxes.

These powers are not unlimited. The Laffer curve famously observes that, at a certain point, high taxation is self-defeating since there is no activity left to tax. Monetarists have observed that massive (think of wheelbarrows) printing of money necessarily leads to hyper-inflation. Since these describe extremes of policy, it's not clear how helpful these observations are to 99% of economic scenarios.

The real problem is that political influences have so constrained both tax and money (or, the opposite side of the same coin, interest rates) policies in the West to the point where they are clearly – to this author anyway – suboptimal. The government runs deficits not because of any Keynesian macroeconomic imperative, but because it seems unable to summon the willpower to set budget-balancing tax rates even during a boom. The central banks set zero interest rates and view 5% – the historical average – as so radical that it must be a temporary response to 10% inflation and – as soon as inflation falls a little bit – quickly lowered. It is simply not plausible that, for four decades of near full employment or over-full employment, the economy has needed the stimulus of continued interest rate cuts and large government deficits.

While proponents of this largesse to the current generation in the US and Europe cite 'the global savings glut', they have two logical problems. One is that 'the global savings glut' driven from some countries (China) is observationally equivalent to 'the global consumption glut' (the US). For accounting reasons, world expenditure must equal world income. This has been achieved by US over-expenditure balanced out by China's under-expenditure. Put differently, China supplies the goods on credit that the US wants to consume but is no longer producing. So, which came first, US over-consumption or Chinese over-saving?

The other logical problem is that, even if there was a 'global savings glut', it could have been used to power investment rather than consumption. In fact, China did exactly this domestically. An example that is highly pertinent to the climate crisis is that China now has built 25,000 miles of high-speed railways, much of this within the last five years. In contrast, the UK has 71 miles of high-speed railways and is finding it an impossible challenge to build High Speed 2 linking London, Birmingham and Manchester (having given up on Leeds entirely). The US has 375 miles of medium-speed rail, but – as one of the nascent signs of the US waking up to the needs of the future – has allocated $170 billion for rail improvements in the 2021 Infrastructure Bill (which hopefully will be spent more efficiently than a similar sum now anticipated for HS2).

There is some reason to believe that the political inability to tax the well-off and corporations may be coming to an end. The 2021 OECD/G20 Inclusive Framework on Base Erosion and Profit Shifting (BEPS) starts to move to a minimum 15% global tax rate on corporations. The Labour opposition in the UK has pledged to address some of the more egregious tax-avoidance in the tax code, notably the 'non-dom' status where the very well-off pay a relatively modest charge of £30,000 or £60,000 to shield their overseas income despite being UK residents.

Conservatives used to argue for a 'flat tax'. In 2016, the Institute of Economic Affairs (IEA) published a paper on 'Taxation, government spending and economic growth'. This critiques the existing tax system and proposes: a flat rate of 15% on income above £10,000 and on distributed profits; VAT at 12.5% with exemptions eliminated; a housing consumption tax on rents and imputed rents of 12.5%; a land value tax; and a reduced fuel duty. It is noted that conservatives – on either side of the Atlantic – no longer argue for 'flat taxes' with much energy, perhaps because the tax system is now so complicated and so regressive (at least at the top percentiles of income and wealth) that conservatives no longer have much enthusiasm for reform. It is less clear why progressives end up – in both fiscal and monetary policy – supporting policies designed by and for the wealthy. Ironically, the conservative IEA proposals in 2016 would be highly redistributive towards the less well-off today and contain important efficiency gains.

We therefore now turn to the political battles that lie ahead. The non-negotiable debates that must be won concern the prevention of extinction, a priority to hit net zero on carbon far sooner than the Paris Accord date of 2050. We don't need to devote much space in this book on how to reach net zero, since other sources (notably the Stern Review) staked out much of the territory nearly two decades ago. Stern makes the case for addressing carbon emissions as soon as possible, and that the costs represent perhaps a 1% fall in GDP. In his article a year later (Stern, 2008: 26), he notes policies of carbon taxation, of quotas that might be tradable in markets, regulation and R&D in technologies. In our no label economics, we have tended to emphasize direct 'quantity' measures such as regulation, technology and public and private investment in infrastructure. In Chapter 9, we discussed the huge inefficiencies generated by the desire to have 'markets' in higher education, and markets to limit carbon – such as the EU Emissions Trading System have not been without drama.

There should already have been high-speed charging networks for electric vehicles throughout the UK, there should already have been high-speed rail throughout the country, there should be low-cost or free bus transport. It's inconceivable – but sadly observable in reality – that the UK Government in 2015 put an effective ban on new onshore wind turbines. The Conservatives are moving towards a campaign in the next election based on slowing our progress to net zero (required for 2050), notably with a potential delay in implementing the ban on petrol car sales (planned to take effect by 2030) and on the recent announcement of new North Sea oil and gas licences. The Labour opposition has, in response, weakened its commitment to green investment from its original pledge of £28 billion a year.

One of the troubling features of the political economy of the last decades is the degree of tribalism and the loss of compromise and negotiation. We have argued, for example, that population growth – at this point in time – is simply wrong. Most of the population of child-bearing age has tended to agree, and fertility rates have fallen sharply in developed countries. How then do we address issues such as the two-child limit for benefits in the UK (one of our analogues to the historical Chinese one-child policy)? Arguably, since the relevant benefit averages about £50 a week, a sense of proportion might indicate that it isn't worth the risk of child poverty to sustain the principle that having additional children should not be encouraged in any way. In the same way, the 'bedroom tax' applied to households on government benefits who are deemed to have a 'spare bedroom' in their social housing seems petty, even if it has a desirable aim of freeing up scarce larger housing properties. Each side of the debate on these issues has a legitimate point, and righteous anger by those who emphasize the well-being of the households affected and those who are focused exclusively on the efficient use of the housing stock is unhelpful.

At the moment, some of the politics verges on the extreme, not just in Washington DC on the 6 January 2021. The 2023 by-election in Ealing was won by the Conservatives, fought on a campaign against the Ultra Low Emission Zone (ULEZ). Given the importance of combatting air pollution in the capital, Mayor Sadiq Khan reacted to the political imperative not by compromising on the extension of ULEZ to the outer boroughs, but on the scheme for grants to switch to a newer model of automobile meeting the emissions standards, with everyone (and not only the less well-off) eligible for a £2,000 grant. It is hard to understand the motivation of those who destroy the cameras that enforce ULEZ, and parts of the press and political establishment that almost seem to be encouraging them. We have already referred to the cynicism of the current government that has sought to mobilize the pro-(petrol)-car lobby for short-term political gain.

Don't 'whip inflation now'

If the policy imperatives on climate change are immediate and obvious, particularly for the generations that will live through the effects of inaction, the generational impacts of fiscal and monetary policy may be less clear. We have argued that the low interest rate, low tax, low investment and high debt regime of the last few decades benefitted the older generations, as did the low wages resulting from the gig economy. The better-off members of the more established generations owned the assets, notably housing, that benefitted from the everything bubble. The high public debt incurred over the last decades is being handed on to future generations. The profound impact of interest rate policy on generational equity is largely unexplored in the economics and policy literature, and represents a major theme of this book. Further, it cuts across historical divisions of political identification. Traditional conservatives would have opposed the expansion in government debt and the high growth in the money supply that allowed the current generations to consume at the expense of the future.

We have argued for monetary policies that have a different destination (recalling dynamic programming) than the conventional wisdom – in particular, we should return to a normalcy of 5% interest rates – and have a very different pathway – we should get there by running high inflation for the next few years. Instead of the current central bank policy in the

US and UK of predicting a return to low interest rates starting as soon as inflation is seen to allow for it, the authorities (fiscal and monetary) should anchor the economy to a normal – not a 'global savings glut' or 'secular stagnation' – equilibrium with high investment. The government has fiscal and regulatory tools that allow for high investment even if interest rates are at a more normal level than the near zero of the last decades. Investment can be increased if financial engineering, such as share buybacks, is eliminated, and by other uses of the tax system. If corporate tax rates go back up, then allowing investment to be offset against profits has a bigger bang. In the same way, if labour law encourages unions and higher wages, investment (in AI and robots) will raise the productivity of labour to match their wages. In 1962, President Kennedy followed the advice of his Keynesian economic advisers and adopted a 7% investment tax credit as the most efficient way of achieving a higher growth economy. If there is an aggregate demand shortage that leads to unemployment, fiscal policy can be used to sustain jobs. Every first-year economics student is exposed to the 'balanced budget multiplier' – by shifting the tax burden from high consuming lower and mid-income households to well-off households, aggregate demand goes up without increasing the deficit.

The government and the central banks have a lot of clubs in their golf bag, and can use them to achieve multiple targets – higher wages, higher investment, lower unemployment – simultaneously. They can also use these tools to determine the rate of inflation. After the pandemic, inflation in the US and UK jumped. Faced with a similar situation in 1974, President Gerald Ford announced the 'whip inflation now' programme – complete with badges emblazoned 'WIN'. While we don't at the moment have badges to wear, there was a general consensus that inflation must be beaten back and the central banks have significantly raised interest rates, albeit to 5% and not the double-digit levels that were seen in the Volcker Fed of the early 1980s. Now that inflation has returned to levels of 3–4%, commentators want the central banks to declare victory and start lowering interest rates, almost irrespective of the pathway for inflation.

At the time of writing, the UK January 2024 CPI (consumer price) inflation rate is 4.0% (over the past year) and bank rate is 5.25%. The February 2024 Bank of England Monetary Policy Report anticipates that inflation will fall to 2% during the year. They judge bank rate as likely to be 3.9% at the beginning of 2025, based upon forward market rates. In the US, the PCE price inflation is 2.9% in December 2023 and the Federal Funds rate is about 5%. The Fed publishes a 'dot chart' of member predictions on future interest rates – this shows a median 'guess' of about 3.5% in 2025 and 2.5% in the 'longer run'. With either confidence or bravado, they anticipate that inflation will be at the 2% target in the 'longer run'.

It's unclear whether the central banks really think that we will in a few years return to the Goldilocks economy that held (in between the dot-com bubble crisis, the financial crisis and the pandemic crisis) for the last few decades. Assuming that long-run interest rates will return to 2.5% is like assuming that the Earth's temperature will return to temperate levels. Even if the 'global savings glut' description was true for the 40 years preceding the pandemic, which is not at all clear, it is unlikely to hold for the next period of time. This is partially because combatting the climate crisis will require immense amounts of investment in the infrastructure, in insulation and updating housing to be energy efficient, in new modes of manufacture, in robots and in AI. The continued demographic decline in population growth (except for countries such as India that are making the political decision to perpetually impoverish their people) means that the working population will be smaller and there will be fewer savings for their pensions. China will wish – even if for some unfathomable reason it continues to deprive its people of democracy and continues to threaten Taiwan – to devote more of its output to home consumption, rather than continuing to lend to the West to enhance their consumption. As with climate change, there remains a high level of denial about the reality of the effects of four decades of 'greed is good'. In the current allocation of responsibilities, the central banks are targeting inflation, not interest rates. But the discourse of the monetary and fiscal authorities can shift, and can adopt 5% interest rates as a sensible medium-term outcome.

We argue for adopting 5% interest rates as the target, rather than 2% inflation, since the economy needs to be rebalanced. Central banks should send the message that the party is over, and that we need to invest rather than consume. Asset prices in particular, rather than funding a continued consumption boom through the everything bubble, need to be brought into balance with incomes. The particular asset price we focus upon is housing. By promising realistic interest rates for the next decades, the central banks anchor expectations and house prices. The current median ratio of house prices to income of 8.3 needs to be restored to affordable, traditional levels of 3–4. Interest rates need to be high enough to keep house prices from rising further. The cumulative inflation of the post-pandemic period has already brought real house prices down by perhaps 20%. Inflation would continue to eat away at the affordability ratio, without causing the capital losses that would create political dispute. As with the 'bedroom tax' on less well-off households, there needs to be a civil balance between the interests of current householders with aspiring newer generations, and between owners and renters.

The house price to incomes ratio then falls as wages go up. The government has a slew of measures to shift from the low-wage gig economy, to a high-wage economy. Some of this involves high-class education and training. Some of it involves union power, the minimum wage, and statutory redundancy, maternity and other interventions. As we argued in Chapter 7, the 'flexible labour market' was not particularly flexible (workers don't have the skills, the housing market and the job security to invest in productive employment relationships) nor efficient. The gig economy, with its pretence that workers and firms benefitted by zero-hours contracts and other transitory relationships, rather than long-term investments in productive employment, was always a fiction devised for political reasons. In the same way, investment in productive technology and equipment raises the productivity and wages of workers. A combination of productivity increases in wages, and a shift in bargaining power from profits to wages, will help to restore the asset to household incomes ratios in the economy. Inflation can play its part – if house prices are capped by higher interest rates, then inflation in prices and incomes restores balance and affordability.

Laissez le bon temps rouler

The 2023 American Economic Association (AEA) meetings were held in New Orleans, the first in-person event since 2020. After Hurricane Katrina hit in 2005, the population of New Orleans fell nearly in half, and has subsequently recovered to being 25% down on its peak. The hurricane was responsible (US Census Bureau) for 1,833 deaths and $150 billion in damage. Visiting the city is in some ways a sobering experience, since the diminution of the population and the financial impacts remain apparent. As the climate emergency proceeds, New Orleans is an example of the costs of natural calamities, but also that a recovery process can occur. Occasionally, economists and other policy-influencers maintain that it's better to be cautious about confronting the climate emergency, since we can mitigate the effects. New Orleans is an example of the actual nature of the costs on human life and suffering, but also on the inefficiencies of postponing repairs to our environment. As an old advertisement for oil filters intoned, 'You can pay me now … or you can pay me later'.

Advance registration for the AEA meetings was down by 50% from pre-pandemic levels. Partially this was due to the separation of the job market activity from the conference. Changing social norms means that the uncomfortable practice of interviewing in hotel rooms is, thankfully, ended. But there were ways to address that by providing dedicated interview rooms that maintained face-to-face interactions. Throughout the economy, firms and organizations are finding it difficult to convince individuals to come into the workplace. At the same time, it is hard to find an industry leader who doesn't feel that – particularly for new entrants to the labour market and specifically to the firm – this makes it nearly impossible to learn the corporate culture, to develop working relationships and generally to gain from 'on-the-job' training. These humanizing interactions may well be more important to people from diverse backgrounds – it has been observed that support for LGBT+ rights (including marriage equality) rose sharply as family members 'came out' and even the most socially conservative individuals were softened by realizing it was their own family that was involved.

In the same way, the US Civil Rights legislation was grounded in the public demonstrations led by Martin Luther King and others. Martin Luther King adopted non-violence, but that does not mean that he was content to sit back and wait until segregationists and others who would not stand up to them responded to calm and reasoned argument. Rather, non-violence was a tool and a weapon: 'Nonviolent direct action seeks to create such a crisis and foster such a tension that a community which has constantly refused to negotiate is forced to confront the issue' (King, 1963). The result was that the Civil Rights Act of 1964 was passed in the US Senate (albeit after a filibuster from diehard segregationists) by a vote of 73–27. The Martin Luther King holiday was passed in the Senate by 78–22 in 1983.

In 'The Population Bomb Revisited' (2009), Paul and Anne Ehrlich consider what they got right and wrong in their 1968 book. They make clear that the publisher chose the somewhat incendiary title, they would have preferred the much more academic *Population, Resources, and Environment*. I have no such let out, I came up with the title for this book at an Extinction Rebellion event.

The main 'positive' reality, compared to what could have been as seen in the Ehrlichs' book, was that mass famine and starvation was avoided by the Green Revolution. But this has only delayed the effects seen from climate change, worldwide pollution and disease. The authors seem truly prescient in their anticipation: 'It is not inconceivable that we will, one of these days, have a visitation from a "super flu," perhaps much more virulent than the famous killer of 1918–1920' (Ehrlich and Ehrlich, 1968: 70). But even there, we have done better than the Ehrlichs anticipated: 'It would be impossible for vaccines to be produced and distributed in time to affect the course of the epidemic in most areas.' The technology we have developed over the last decades exceeds almost any predictions that could have been made.

But over the last half-century since the Ehrlich book, there have been successes. Mankind has not been without victories:

- population growth declines and eventually actual population declines in developed countries associated with greater gender equality;
- marriage equality;
- banning of DDT;
- pollution limited in developed economies;
- ozone layer restored by worldwide action on CFCs;
- lead removed from petrol;
- mileage standards adopted to force manufacture of more efficient cars;
- HIV/AIDs arrested by treatments and prevention.

There were 40-degree days in London, for the first time ever, last summer. One way forward is for us all to buy air conditioners, and set us further on a downward trajectory as we respond to the heat. There is no guarantee that the world, the economy, the political environment all have built-in stabilizers that restore tranquillity. In past times of calamity, such as the Great Depression, economic and political stabilizers were built into the system – we have argued that those stabilizers served the purpose that economics textbooks anticipated, and that they – rather than central bank actions – limited the impact of the financial crisis. The events of 6 January 2021 showed both that we still had political stabilizers, but also that they had reached a point of fragility. Generation Z is noted for its amiability, and it may fall upon them to start bringing civility back to public discourse. But this doesn't mean that they or us should be silent. As we have observed, the examples of Martin Luther King and Nelson Mandela show the impact of the combination of forceful expression and inherent decency.

This is an economics book, and we have hopefully made the case for the strength of the subject in its logical coherency as a remarkable set of tools that can be applied. The economics of incentives, of the interactions of individuals and households, along with producers, in reaching equilibrium, and policy measures that can shift that equilibrium, even under an environment of intense uncertainty, can address most of our political economy issues, and indeed many of our sociological ones. We don't need – like Holmes and Moriarty – to be fighting at the Reichenbach Falls, when we are facing an extinction equilibrium.

It was with a degree of irony that I titled this chapter 'let the good times roll', but there is an underlying positivity. Richard Brooks' novel *The Brick Foxhole* was written in 1945 and eventually was adapted for the film *Crossfire*. While the novel was notable for the storyline of a murder of a gay man (later changed to a Jewish man for the film), it was really about the frustrations of the soldiers in barracks in the US (nicknamed 'brick foxholes'), neither in the war nor out of it, and the underlying commercialism and bigotry of society. The 'greatest generation' came of age in the war. There was no guarantee that America would enter the war, that Britain would hold. A character in James Baldwin's *Another Country* (1962: 334), observes: 'Maybe nothing can be stopped, or changed … but you've got to *know*, you've got to know what's happening.' Generation Z, analogously, is coming of age in a highly flawed society in a necessary war against extinction, but one where they will be far better off individually and as a group if they are on the front lines, and not in the barracks, and if they 'know what's happening'.

References

Acemoglu, D. and P. Restrepo (2020). 'Robots and jobs: evidence from US labor markets', *Journal of Political Economy*, 128(6): 2188–2244.

Adams, R. (2023). 'One in three of England's university starters "may live at home" this year', *The Guardian*, 10 August. (www.theguardian.com/education/2023/aug/10/one-in-three-of-englands-university-starters-may-live-at-home-this-year?ref=biztoc.com). Accessed 23 May 2024.

Akerlof, G. A. and R. E. Kranton (2010). *Identity Economics: How Our Identities Shape Our Work, Wages, and Well-being*. Princeton University Press: Princeton.

Augar, P. (2019). *Independent panel report: post-18 review of education and funding*. HM Government. www.gov.uk/government/publications/post-18-review-of-education-and-funding-independent-panel-report. Accessed 23 May 2024.

Bailey, A. (2020). 'Bank of England is not doing "monetary financing"'. *Financial Times*, 5 April. (www.ft.com/content/3a33c7fe-75a6-11ea-95fe-fcd274e920ca). Accessed 3 March 2024.

Baldwin, J. (1962). *Another Country*. Dial Press: New York.

Baynes, M. (2021). 'Tenant left in "cockroach-infested" and "rotten" council housing in south London for three years', *Evening Standard*, 25 May. (www.standard.co.uk/news/uk/cockroach-rotten-council-housing-mitcham-merton-council-b937056.html). Accessed 8 June 2024.

Bell, A. R., C. Brooks and A. Urquhart (2022). 'Why have UK universities become more indebted over time?', *International Review of Economics & Finance*, 82(C): 771–83.

Berman, J. M. (2020). *Anti-Vaxxers: How to Challenge a Misinformed Movement*. MIT Press: Cambridge.

Bernanke, B. S. (2002). *Remarks by Governor Ben S. Bernanke at the conference to honor Milton Friedman*. The Federal Reserve Board. (www.federalreserve.gov/boarddocs/speeches/2002/20021108/). Accessed 3 March 2024.

Bernanke, B. S. (2004). *Remarks by Governor Ben S. Bernanke at the meetings of the Eastern Economic Association*. The Federal Reserve Board. (www.federalreserve.gov/boarddocs/speeches/2004/20040220). Accessed 22 May 2024.

Bernanke, B. S. (2015a). 'The Taylor rule: a benchmark for monetary policy?' Brookings Institution, 28 April. (www.brookings.edu/artic les/the-taylor-rule-a-benchmark-for-monetary-policy). Accessed 3 March 2024.

Bernanke, B. S. (2015b). *Why are interest rates so low, part 3: the global savings glut.* Brookings Institution, 1 April. (www.brookings.edu/blog/ben-bernanke/ 2015/04/01/why-are-interest-rates-so-low-part-3-the-global-savings-glut/). Accessed 3 March 2024.

Bernanke, B. S. (2015c). *The Courage to Act: A Memoir of a Crisis and its Aftermath.* W. W. Norton & Company: New York.

Besley, T. and S. Coate (1991). 'Public provision of private goods and the redistribution of income', *American Economic Review*, 81(4): 979–84.

BLS Beta Labs (2023). 'Beta news release', August. (www.bls.gov/beta/ nextgen/realer/real-earnings-2023-09-13.htm#:~:text=Real%20average %20weekly%20earnings%20for%20all%20employees%20increased%20 0.3%20percent,percent%20in%20the%20average%20workweek). Accessed 8 June 2024.

Bogel, J. C. (2008). *Enough: True Measures of Money, Business and Life.* Wiley: Hoboken, NJ.

Bohnet, I. (2016). *What Works: Gender Equality by Design.* Harvard University Press: Cambridge, MA.

Booth, A. L. and J. Frank (2008). 'Marriage, partnership and sexual orientation: a study of British university academics and administrators', *Review of Economics of the Household*, 6(4): 409–22.

Booth, A. L. and G. Zoega (2003). 'On the welfare implications of firing costs', *European Journal of Political Economy*, 19(4): 759–75.

Boyle, C. (2019). 'Robinson Crusoe at 300: why it's time to get rid of this colonial fairytale', *The Guardian*, 19 April. (www.theguardian.com/books/ 2019/apr/19/robinson-crusoe-at-300-its-time-to-let-go-of-this-toxic-colonial-fairytale). Accessed 2 March 2024.

Bristow, J. (2019). *Stop Mugging Grandma: The 'Generation Wars' and Why Boomer Blaming Won't Solve Anything.* Yale University Press: New Haven.

Britton, J., L. Dearden, B. Waltmann and L. van der Erve (2020). 'Graduate outcomes: the impact of undergraduate degrees on lifetime earnings', IFS, 29 February. (https://ifs.org.uk/publications/impact-undergraduate-degrees-lifetime-earnings). Accessed 7 June 2024.

Brooks, D. (2024). 'How to save a sad, lonely, angry and mean society', *New York Times*, 25 January. (www.nytimes.com/2024/01/25/opinion/ art-culture-politics.html). Accessed 6 March 2024.

Brooks, R. (1945). *The Brick Foxhole.* Harper & Brothers: New York.

Brooks, R. (1948). *The Boiling Point.* Harper & Brothers: New York.

Browne, J. (2010). *Securing a sustainable future for higher education: an independent review of higher education funding & student finance.* HM Government: Department for Business, Innovation and Schools. (https://assets.publishing.service.gov. uk/government/uploads/system/uploads/attachment_data/file/422565/ bis-10-1208-securing-sustainable-higher-education-browne-report.pdf). Accessed 8 June 2024.

Campbell, S., L. Macmillan, R. Murphy and G. Wyness (2022). 'Matching in the dark? Inequalities in student to degree match', *Journal of Labor Economics*, 40(4): 807–50.

Card, D. and A. B. Krueger (1994). 'Minimum wages and employment: a case study of the fast-food industry in New Jersey and Pennsylvania', *American Economic Review*, 84(4): 772–93.

Card, D. and A. B. Krueger (1995). *Myth and Measurement: The New Economics of the Minimum Wage.* Princeton, NJ: Princeton University Press.

Carmichael, L. (1988). 'Incentives in academics: why is there tenure?', *Journal of Political Economy*, 96(3): 453–72.

Chancellor, E. (2022). *The Price of Time: The Real Story of Interest.* Penguin Books: London.

Clark, W. V. T. (1940). *The Ox-Bow Incident.* Random House: New York.

Coase, R. (1975). 'Marshall on method', *The Journal of Law & Economics*, 18(1): 25–31.

Conger, K. and K. Browning (2021). 'A judge declared California's gig worker law unconstitutional. Now what?'. *NYTimes*, 23 August. (www. nytimes.com/2021/08/23/technology/california-gig-worker-law-explained. html). Accessed 3 March 2024.

Das, S. (2016). 'Look what happened when the Fed raised rates in 1936'. *Independent*, 19 January. (www.independent.co.uk/news/business/comment/ look-what-happened-when-the-fed-raised-rates-in-1936-a6820346.html). Accessed 3 March 2024.

Defoe, D. (1938). *The Life and Strange Surprizing Adventures of Robinson Crusoe of York, Mariner.* Penguin: London.

Dobbin, F. and A. Kalev (2018). 'Why doesn't diversity training work? The challenge for industry and academia', *Anthropology Now*, 10(2): 48–55.

Dowland, S. (2009). '"Family values" and the formation of a Christian right agenda'. *Church History*, 78(3): 606–31.

Drury, A. (1959). *Advise and Consent.* Doubleday & Company: New York.

Ehrlich, P. R. and A. H. Ehrlich (1968). *The Population Bomb.* Sierra Club/ Ballantine Books: New York.

Ehrlich, P. R. and A. H. Ehrlich (2009). 'The population bomb revisited', *The Electronic Journal of Sustainable Development*, 1(3): 63–71.

Elder, B. (2022). 'Why don't computers work? A neat theory to explain the productivity puzzle 2.0', *Financial Times*, 18 May. (www.ft.com/content/ 0a87229a-0c21-4994-a3ec-d62fb28b0b27). Accessed 6 March 2024.

El-Erian, M. (2023a). 'Fed policy needs to get out of the muddled middle'. *Financial Times*, 21 March. (https://link.gale.com/apps/doc/A742158163/STND?u=rho_ttda&sid=bookmark-STND&xid=3820810d). Accessed 3 March 2024.

El-Erian, M. (2023b). 'Investors should still expect a bumpy road ahead'. *Financial Times*, 1 August. (www.ft.com/content/c9ff97b9-c485-494e-9474-6bb5507be554). Accessed 3 March 2024.

Elliot Major, L. and S. Machin (2018). *Social Mobility: And its Enemies*. Pelican Books: London.

Favara, G., C. Minoiu and A. Perez-Orive (2021). 'U.S. zombie firms: how many and how consequential?'. *FEDS Notes*, Board of Governors of the Federal Reserve System, 30 July. (www.federalreserve.gov/econres/notes/feds-notes/us-zombie-firms-how-many-and-how-consequential-20210730.htm). Accessed 3 March 2024.

Fazzari, S., R. G. Hubbard and B. Petersen (1988). 'Financing constraints and corporate investment', *Brookings Papers on Economic Activity*, 19(1): 141–206.

Fetzer, T. (2022). 'Subsidising the spread of COVID-19: evidence from the UK's Eat-Out-to-Help-Out Scheme', *The Economic Journal*, 132(643): 1200–17.

Frank, J. (1986). *The New Keynesian Economics: Unemployment, Search and Contracting*. Prentice Hall/Harvester Wheatsheaf: London.

Frank, J (2014). *The Responsible Economy*. Routledge: Abingdon.

Frank, J. (2020). 'The persistence of the gender pay gap in British universities', *Fiscal Studies*, 41: 883–903.

Frank, J. and E. Smith (1996). 'Seniority seating at the Royal Opera House', *Oxford Economic Papers*, 48(3): 492–98.

Frank, J., N. Gowar and M. Naef (2019). *English Universities in Crisis: Markets Without Competition*. Bristol University Press: Bristol.

Friedman, M. (1962). *Capitalism and Freedom*. University of Chicago Press: Chicago.

Friedman, S. and D. Laurison (2020). *The Class Ceiling: Why it Pays to Be Privileged*. Policy Press: Bristol.

Galbraith, J. K. (1958). *The Affluent Society*. Houghton Mifflin: Boston.

Gibbons, S., E. Neumayer and R. Perkins (2015). 'Student satisfaction, league tables and university applications: evidence from Britain', *Economics of Education Review*, 48(C): 148–64.

Golding, W. (1954). *Lord of the Flies*. Faber and Faber: London.

Graetz, G. and G. Michaels (2018). 'Robots at work', *The Review of Economics and Statistics*, 100(5): 753–68.

Hammond, G. (2022). 'Help to Buy has pushed up house prices in England, says report', *Financial Times*, 10 January. (www.ft.com/content/19236eef-abed-4401-a6b1-25c1035ab095). Accessed 8 June 2024.

Hastings, A. and P. Matthews (2012). 'The middle-class enjoy definite advantages in public service provision: more critical and extensive research is needed', LSE Blog, 10 April. (https://eprints.lse.ac.uk/44045/1/__Lib file_repository_Content_LSE%20Politics%20and%20Policy%20Blog_April%202012%20to%20be%20added_blogs.lse.ac.uk-The_middleclass_enjoy_definite_advantages_in_public_service_provision_More_critical_and_extensive_res.pdf). Accessed 7 June 2024.

Higgins, E. (2021). 'Not getting vaccinated to own your fellow libs'. *The Atlantic*, 22 September. (www.theatlantic.com/ideas/archive/2021/09/what-do-lefty-anti-vaxxers-do-now/620092). Accessed 2 March 2024.

Institute of Economic Affairs (2016). 'Taxation, government spending and economic growth'. (https://iea.org.uk/publications/taxation-government-spending-and-economic-growth/). Accessed 6 March 2024.

IPCC. (2021). *Climate change 2021: the physical science basis.* (www.ipcc.ch/report/sixth-assessment-report-working-group-i/). Accessed 7 March 2024.

Kaser, M. (1999). 'Escape routes from post-Soviet inflation and recession'. *Finance & Development*, 36(2). (www.imf.org/external/pubs/ft/fandd/1999/06/kaser.htm#:~:text=They%20could%20not%20have%20anticipated,and%204%2C735%20percent%20in%20Ukraine). Accessed 3 March 2024.

Kentish, B. (2017). 'Forty percent of homes sold under Right to Buy now in the hands of private landlords, new analysis reveals', *The Independent*, 8 December. (www.independent.co.uk/news/uk/politics/right-to-buy-homes-sold-private-landlords-latest-figures-rent-a8098126.html). Accessed 8 June 2024.

Keynes, J. M. (1936). *The General Theory of Employment, Interest and Money.* Macmillan: London.

King, M. L. Jr (1963). 'Letter from a Birmingham Jail', 16 April. African Studies Center, University of Pennsylvania. (www.africa.upenn.edu/Articles_Gen/Letter_Birmingham.html). Accessed 8 June 2024.

King, S. (2023). *We Need To Talk About Inflation: 14 Urgent Lessons From the Last 2,000 Years.* Yale University Press: New Haven.

Koo, R. C. (2003). *Balance Sheet Recession: Japan's Struggle with Uncharted Economics and Its Global Implications.* John Wiley & Sons: Hoboken, NJ.

Kuhn, T. S. (1962). *The Structure of Scientific Revolutions.* University of Chicago Press: Chicago.

Landers, R. M., J. B. Rebitzer and L. J. Taylor (1996). 'Rat race redux: adverse selection in the determination of work hours in law firms', *American Economic Review*, 86(3): 329–48.

Lang, K. (2022). 'Lessons from Vienna: a housing success story 100 years in the making', *Financial Times*, 30 December. (www.ft.com/content/05719602-89c6-4bbc-9bbe-5842fd0c3693). Accessed 8 June 2024.

Lennox, J. (2022). 'Nation's homeowners sitting on £2.6 trillion in equity', *Today's Conveyancer*, 24 June. (https://todaysconveyancer.co.uk/nations-homeowners-sitting-2-6-trillion-equity/). Accessed 6 March 2024.

MacAskill, W. (2022). *What We Owe the Future*. Basic Books: New York.

Magnus, E. (2021). 'Landlords fall behind on gas safety checks in nearly half of rented homes, figures suggest – while quarter of tenants are waiting on repairs', Thisismoney.co.uk, 9 April. (www.thisismoney.co.uk/money/buytolet/article-9423065/Landlords-fall-gas-safety-checks-nearly-half-rented-homes.html). Accessed 8 June 2024.

Manning, A. (2003). *Monopsony in Motion: Imperfect Competition in Labor Markets*. Princeton University Press: Princeton, NJ.

Marshall, A. (1890). *Principles of Economics*. Ebook available from https://books.googleusercontent.com/books/content?req=AKW5QafODKlzLsSbRO-UUY0uvtLVg4PSOn4SyDpVbosyPDStTUZKv-O1I0dhmdc28gyXltq_fsxlSW3HfnYdPy9mDJv2FjIqSf8La8fsAKm-Zvu5jWVPiNQf4PUWgtvzcpXHdlOuUZtuiP1xFB4ojL4z1bZUC5L_w10KUtI9HIugv3fhlkvA97WiBFnlezobXFfP-FLcyfBBYvUDsrdPFJKXhCeMmfMi_8fbEOZc27kTJQKEpk75I9X39vJCLtVVSbmjIAQO2-tDCAc9cxTlCl4SMYJ59Ml6Bw

Mazzucatto, M. (2013). *The Entrepreneurial State: Debunking Public vs Private Sector Myths*. Anthem Press: London.

McCarthy, J. (2022). 'Same-sex marriage support inches up to new high of 71%'. Gallup, 1 June. (https://news.gallup.com/poll/393197/same-sex-marriage-support-inches-new-high.aspx). Accessed 2 March 2024.

Mcgettigan, A. (2018). 'Whatever happened to the polytechnics, Parts 1 and 2', *Critical Education*, 27 February. (https://andrewmcgettigan.org/2018/02/27/whatever-happened-to-the-polytechnics-part-1/). Accessed 7 June 2024.

Moore, E. (2014). 'UK to repay tranche of perpetual war loans'. *Financial Times*, 31 October. (www.ft.com/content/94653f60-60e8-11e4-894b-00144feabdc0). Accessed 3 March 2024.

Morris, W. (1892). *News from Nowhere*. Kelmscott Press: London.

NOAA. (2024). *Global average surface temperature*. (www.climate.gov/media/12885). Accessed 1 March 2024.

Okun, A. (1973). 'Upward mobility in a high-pressure economy', *Brookings Papers on Economic Activity*, 4(1): 207–62.

Oluo, I. (2020). *Mediocre: The Dangerous Legacy of White Male America*. Seal Press: New York.

Orwell, G. (1934). *Burmese Days*. Victor Gallancz: London.

Phillips, A. W. (1958). 'The relation between unemployment and the rate of change of money wage rates in the United Kingdom, 1861–1957', *Economica*, 25(100): 283–99.

Pigou, A. C. (1933). *The Theory of Unemployment*. Macmillan: London.

Reich, R. (2021). 'Win the Amazon union fight and we can usher in a new Progressive Era'. *The Guardian*, 21 October. (www.theguardian.com/commentisfree/2021/mar/21/amazon-union-fight-warehouse-bessemer-alabama). Accessed 3 March 2024.

Reinhart, C. M. and K. S. Rogoff (2010, May). 'Growth in a time of debt', *American Economic Review: Papers and Proceedings*, 100: 573–8.

Robinson, J. (1962). *Economic Philosophy*. C.A. Watts & Co: London.

Romer, P. (2016). *The Trouble with Macroeconomics*. (https://paulromer.net/the-trouble-with-macro/WP-Trouble.pdf). Accessed 2 March 2024.

Sainato, M. (2022). 'Workers denounce Starbucks over union contract negotiations: "They don't treat us like human beings"'. *The Guardian*, 17 November. (www.theguardian.com/business/2022/nov/17/starbucks-union-fight-delays). Accessed 3 March 2024.

Sanders, L. (2021). *Nine in ten Americans have a positive view of Martin Luther King Jr.* YouGov, 14 January. (https://today.yougov.com/topics/politics/articles-reports/2021/01/14/positive-view-martin-luther-king-jr). Accessed 2 March 2024.

Sandler, T. and J. T. Tschirhart (1980). 'The economic theory of clubs: an evaluative survey', *Journal of Economic Literature*, 18(4): 1481–1521.

Small, M. L. and D. Pager (2020). 'Sociological perspectives on racial discrimination', *Journal of Economic Perspectives*, 34(2): 49–67.

Sommer, J. (2024). 'IBM reopens its frozen pension plan, saving the company millions'. *New York Times*, 9 February. (www.nytimes.com/2024/02/09/business/ibm-pension-plan.html). Accessed 3 March 2024.

Steinbeck, J. (1945). *Cannery Row*. Viking Press: New York.

Stern, N. (2007). *The Economics of Climate Change*. Cambridge University Press: Cambridge.

Stern, N. (2008). 'The economics of climate change', *American Economic Review*, 98(2): 1–37.

Sternberg, J. C. (2019). *The Theft of a Decade: How the Baby Boomers Stole the Millennials' Economic Future*. PublicAffairs: New York.

Thaler, R. H. (2021). 'More than nudges are needed to end the pandemic'. *New York Times*, 5 August. (www.nytimes.com/2021/08/05/business/vaccine-pandemic-nudge-passport.html). Accessed 2 March 2024.

The Guardian (28 November 2021). 'Sappy ending: Canada digs deep into strategic reserves to cover maple syrup shortage'. *The Guardian*, 28 November. (www.theguardian.com/world/2021/nov/28/sappy-ending-canada-digs-deep-into-strategic-reserves-to-cover-maple-syrup-shortage). Accessed 3 March 2024.

Tobin, J. (1966). *National Economic Policy: Essays*. Yale University Press: New Haven and London.

Tough, P. (2019). *The Years that Matter Most: How College Makes or Breaks Us*. Houghton Mifflin Harcourt: Boston & New York.

Troianovski, A. and A. Satariano (2021). 'Google and Apple, under pressure from Russia, remove voting app.' *New York Times*, 17 September. (www.nytimes.com/2021/09/17/world/europe/russia-navalny-app-election.html). Accessed 2 March 2024.

Trump, D. with T. Schwartz (1987). *The Art of the Deal*. Random House: New York.

Twenge, J. M. (2023). *Generations: The Real Differences between Gen Z, Millennials, Gen X, Boomers, and Silents – and What They Mean for America's Future*. Atria Books: New York.

UK Department of Transport (2020). *Smart Motorway Safety*. (https://assets.publishing.service.gov.uk/government/uploads/system/uploads/attachment_data/file/936811/smart-motorway-safety-evidence-stocktake-and-action-plan.pdf). Accessed 3 March 2024.

UK Parliament Committees (10 March 2021). 'Unimaginable cost of Test & Trace failed to deliver central promise of averting another lockdown'. (https://committees.parliament.uk/committee/127/public-accounts-committee/news/150988/unimaginable-cost-of-test-trace-failed-to-deliver-central-promise-of-averting-another-lockdown/). Accessed 6 March 2024.

Wallis, P. (2018). 'Guilds and mutual protection in England', *LSE Economic History Working Papers* no. 287.

Wilder, T. (1967). *The Eighth Day*. Harper & Row: New York.

Willets, D. (2010). *The Pinch: How the Baby Boomers Took Their Children's Future – and Why They Should Give it Back*. Atlantic Books: London.

Willets, D. (2017). *A University Education*. Oxford University Press: Oxford.

Willets, D. (2021). *Boosting higher education while cutting public spending*, HEPI (Higher Education Policy Institute) Report 142. (www.hepi.ac.uk/wp-content/uploads/2021/09/Boosting-higher-education-while-cutting-public-spending.pdf). Accessed 7 June 2024.

Wolf, A. (2013). *The XX Factor: How the Rise of Working Women Has Created a Far Less Equal World*. Crown Publishers: New York.

Wolf, A. and A. Jenkins (2021). *Managers and academics in a centralising sector: the new staffing patterns of UK higher education*, The Policy Institute, King's College London and the Nuffield Foundation.

Wolf, M. (2023). 'The Bank of England must have the courage of its conviction'. *Financial Times*, 25 June. (www.ft.com/content/83026a79-2ac9-40e8-94e7-efee443e8d8d). Accessed 7 March 2024.

Yellen, J. (2019). 'Former Fed Chair Janet Yellen on why the answer to the inflation puzzle matters'. Brookings Institution. (www.brookings.edu/articles/former-fed-chair-janet-yellen-on-why-the-answer-to-the-inflation-puzzle-matters/). Accessed 3 March 2024.

Index

References to figures appear in *italic* type.

2001: A Space Odyssey 137–8
2021 OECD/G20 Inclusive Framework
   on Base Erosion and Profit Shifting
   (BEPS) 194

A

abortion 32, 34, 42, 143
Acemoglu, Darin 137
Adams, John 102
Advanced Research Projects Agency,
   US 174–5
Advise and Consent (Drury) 28–9
AEA (American Economic Association) 199
aeroplane analogies 110–11
affirmative action, US 133, 159
Affluent Society, The (Galbraith) 44, 82
Affordable Care Act 2010 (US) 10
Afghanistan
   GDP per capita 129
   war 4, 10
African National Congress 30
aggregate demand management 112
AI (artificial intelligence) 2, 6, 18, 46, 113,
   131, 192, 197
   and pensions 137–8
Al-Qaeda 4
Amazon 117–18
American Baseball, 'reserve clause' 118–19
Another Country (Baldwin) 201
Anti-Vaxxers (Berman) 61
Apple 56, 127
apprenticeships 27, 40, 112, 126,
   132, 154
Arab Spring 4
architectural awards, university building
   projects 155
arts, the, and diversity 135–6
asset prices 14, 82, 85, 86, 89–91, 171, 198
asset values 16–17, 86, 88, 89, 182
'assured shorthold tenancies' 171
Athena SWAN scheme 158
Augar Report, 2019 8, 112, 156

Australia, climate change impact xi, 1
autarky 15, 21

B

baby boomers (1946–1964) vii, 4, 5–6, 11,
   15, 16, 18, 190, 191
Bailey, Andrew 84
'balance sheet recession' 86
'balanced budget multiplier' 70, 197
Baldwin, James 201
Bank of America 83
Bank of England xiv, 14, 84
   inflation targeting 11, 12, 13, 75, 76, 86,
     97, 110
   interest on reserves 66, 79, 80
   interest rate policy 81–2, 85, 86, 89, 93,
     95, 97, 98–9
   Monetary Policy Committee 108
   Monetary Policy Report, February 2024 197
   money supply policy 71, 73, 74
   post-pandemic inflation 43
   price stability 75
   'soft landings' 110
   and the Truss budget 91
Bank of Japan 75–6
banks 72, 80, 82–3, 127
   bailouts 4, 107
   see also central banks
Barber Boom 42, 140
bargaining 52, 119
   see also employment relationship;
     trade unions
Basel II 72
batteries xii, 192
Bayesian statistics 61
Baynes, Megan 177
'bedroom tax' 196, 198
'beer milkshake' 81
Bell, Adrian 154
BEPS (2021 OECD/G20 Inclusive
   Framework on Base Erosion and Profit
   Shifting) 194

Berman, J. M. 61
Bernanke, Ben 10, 42, 43, 65, 69, 88, 94, 102, 104, 191
Besley, Timothy 125, 176
bias
  'implicit bias training' xiii, 7
  'subconscious bias training' 141–2
Biden, Joe 31, 190
Bill of Rights, UK 26
Birmingham City University 158
Birmingham University 158
Bitcoin 83
'Black Live Matter' movement 5
Black people, US 29
Black students 158, 159
Black Wednesday, UK 98–9, 104
Blair, Tony xiii, 10
Blanchflower, David 108
Bleak House (Dickens) 21
Bogel, John 138
Bohnet, Iris 142
Boiling Point, The (Brooks) 29
bond vigilantes 96–9
bonds 90, 102
  index-linked 92, *93*
  inflation risk 92, *93*
  interest rate risk 91–2, 93
boomers *see* baby boomers (1946–1964)
Booth, Alison 123, 142
Bounce Back Loan Scheme 45, 107
Boyle, Charles 48–9
branded clothing 9, 21
Brazil 27
Bretton Woods, 1944 83, 103, 187
Brexit 5, 11, 31, 34, 39–40, 108, 112, 134–5
Brick Foxhole, The (Brooks) 201
Bristow, Jenny 6, 141
'British overseas citizen' status 132
Brooks, Chris 154
Brooks, David 193
Brooks, Richard 29, 201
Brown, Gordon 10
Browne Report 86, 146, 148–9, 156, 157, 165
building projects, universities 155, 156, 157, 166
Bundesbank 65, 83–4
Bureau of Labor Statistics, US 117
Burmese Days (Orwell) 133, 135
Bush, George 10
Bush, George W. 10
business loans, UK 44–5, 107
buy-to-let property 19, 96, 102, 171, 179, 180, 182, 183

C

California xi, 1, 118
  universities 163, 167
Callaghan, James 103

Cambridge University 133, 151, 161
  Black students 158
  Magdalen College 155
  widening participation 158
'Camelot' 29
Campbell, Stuart 158–9
Canada 1
Cannery Row (Steinbeck) 81
capital gains 1, 19, 88, 90, 92, 97, 121, 140
  and housing xi, 9, 85, 86, 89, 96, 100, 173, 179, 180, 182, 183, 184
capital punishment 42
car analogies 111–12
Card, David 37, 119
career progression 120, 121
Carmichael, Lorne 121–2
cars
  electric 143, 195
  MOT certification 177
cartels 122–3
Casey Report 141
Catholic Church 42
central banks 188
  discretionary policies 49, 50
  government debt holdings 99–100
  inflation targeting 74–6, 185
  interest on reserves 66, 79–80, 91
  monetization of debt 84
  quantitative easing 13, 64, 70, 80, 81, 91, 94, 99, 108
  regulatory powers 82–3
  'soft landings' 110–11
  zero interest rate policy 6, 21, 64–6, 66–7, 84–5, 96–7, 98, 102, 108–10, *109*, 138, 154, 171, 183, 188, 194, 197
Chancellor, Edward 6, 43, 64
change, political promises of 31
charity 132
child poverty 125
children 131
  see also population
China 5, 81, 82, 198
  COVID-19 pandemic 57
  GDP per capita 129
  integration into world trade framework 12
  manufacturing 23
  one-child policy 129, 130, 195
  railways 194
  rise of 101, 102
  setting of interest rate 69–70
  trade relationship with US 12, 194
CHIPS and Science Act 2022 (US) 12
Churchill, Winston 111
Citizens United 31
Civil Rights Act 1964 (US) 14, 29, 200
civil rights movement, US 58, 61
Clark, W. V. T 128
Clean Air Act (US) 14, 29

climate change x–xi, xii, xiii–xiv, 1, 5, 6, 29–30, 41–2, 127, 188, 198, 199
  Paris Agreement 187, 195
Climate change 2021: the physical science basis (IPCC) 5
Clinton, Bill xiii, 10
Clinton, Hillary 31
clubs 131, 133–4
  universities 151–2
CNAA (Council for National Academic Awards) 151, 161
Coalition Government x, 145, 149–50
Coase, R. 38
Coate, Stephen 125, 176
colonialism 56
  colonial citizens 132
competition
  universities 149, 150–2
consol bonds 90
consumption *see* Robinson Crusoe economics
continuity, assumption of xi–xii
'conventional wisdom' 44, 82
'convexity' 51
Corbyn, Jeremy 27, 31, 124
Coronavirus Business Interruption Loan Scheme 45, 107
Coronavirus Larger Business Interruption Loan Scheme 45, 107
corporate taxation 1, 138, 194, 197
corporations xiii–xiv
  deference to 127
  political donations, US 31
  public support for large corporations over workers 126–8
cost of living crisis 45–6
  see also energy cost of living crisis
'Cost of Living Payment,' UK 124
Council for National Academic Awards (CNAA) 151, 161
COVID-19 pandemic 4, 7, 17, 45, 46, 57, 65, 94, 105, 111, 123, 127, 191, 198
  change in working patterns 131
  government policy response 8, 43–4, 45, 107, 124, 192
  and homelessness 20
  mask-wearing 33
  monetary base expansion 71, 79
  post-pandemic inflation 6, 43, 45, 64, 66, 82, 85, 97, 100, 102, 106, 165, 188, 198
  post-pandemic interest rate rise 183
  social isolation 46
  student engagement 167–9
  truck driver shortage 134
  vaccination xii–xiii, 9, 22, 33, 57, 60–1, 164, 192
CPI (consumer price inflation)
  UK 11, 43, 76, 78, 197
  US 11, 43, 75, 104
crafts 129

criminal records, young people 56, 63
'critical race theory' 30
Crossfire 201
culture
  and population issues 143
  role of 193

D

debt *see* government debt
Deese, Brian 134
defence research 193
Defoe, Daniel 56, 57
Delta Airlines 60
'dementia tax' 184, 192
'demographic crisis' 18
  see also population
Department for Business, Energy and Industrial Strategy 44–5, 117
Department for Levelling Up, Housing and Communities 170, 181
Department of Transport 111
Dickens, Charles 21, 51
'difference-in-difference' 37
direct action 32, 33
disability, differential outcomes 141
discount rate 16, 49, 53–4, 57, 58, 62, 67, 68, 102, 106, *106*
'Discover Uni' 150, 161
discrimination
  by clubs 133
  as evidence of a system 'working as planned' 7, 141–2
  'institutionalized' 141–2
  see also gender inequality; racial inequality
divorce rates 34
Dobbin, Frank 141–2
doctors, employment practices 122
dot-com bubble 4, 7, 82, 94, 100, 106, 191, 197–8
Dow Jones Industrial Average 88, 107
Dowland, Seth 59
drug overdose deaths 127
Drury, Allen 28–9
Durham University 186, 187
dynamic programming 186, 196

E

Ealing by-election, 2023 196
earned income tax credits 41, 125
East Anglia University 161
'Eat out to Help Out' policy 8, 43–4, 192
economic efficiency 25, 26, 32
economists, as barristers 39–42
'ecstasy economics' 9
education 1, 112
  and the COVID-19 pandemic 20
  inclusive xiv
  quality control in schools 150–1
  see also further education; universities

Ehrlich, Anne 129, 200
Ehrlich, Paul 129, 200
Elder, B. 192
electoral systems 31
electric vehicles 143, 195
electronic currencies 83
El-Erian, Mohamed 79, 105
Elliot Major, L. 6
empirical methods in economics 22–3, 24
employment
    disadvantaged and discriminated against
        groups 112
    'formal hiring and promotion criteria' 141
    impact of robots on 137
    new entrants, employment practices
        121–2
    non-financial benefits of 41
    working from home 45, 122, 168–9
    see also labour market; unemployment;
        work, future of
employment legislation 115
employment relationship 121–2
    see also gig economy
energy cost of living crisis 20
    EPG ('energy price guarantee') 22
    financial support for households 124
    price cap 177
energy efficiency, in housing 177–8
Enough (Bogel) 138
Environmental Protection Agency, US 14
EPG ('energy price guarantee') 22
Equal Pay Act 1970 (UK) xiii, 2, 14, 189
Equality Act 2010 (UK) 145, 165
equilibrium x
    and sustainability 33–4
ESG (environmental, social and governance)
    standards 33
Essex University 161
ethnicity
    differential outcomes 141
    see also racial inequality
EU (European Union)
    Emissions Trading System 195
euro 17, 83
European Central Bank 65, 75, 76, 83
European Court on Human Rights 26
European Monetary Union 98–99, 104
exam boards 49–50
Exchange Rate Mechanism 140
exchange rates, fixed 17, 69, 103–4, 187
Executive Suite 24
extinction x–xi, 1, 2, 15, 32, 35, 48, 143,
    187, 189, 192, 195, 201
    and family values 58–9
extinction equilibrium 7, 16
    Robinson Crusoe economics 51, 57–8
    role of science and policy in prevention
        of 62–3
Extinction Rebellion 58, 83

F

Facebook 126
facial recognition 137
Fair Housing Act 1968 (US) 14
Fair Sentencing Act (US) 63
'fallacy of composition' 91
families, passing on of wealth within 56, 63
family disputes, in law courts 21–2
family firms 35–6
family values 58–9, 190
'family-friendly' policies 142
Fazzari, Steven 139
Federal Election Fund 31
Federal Funds rate 197
federal government debt, US 12
Federal Reserve, (Fed), US 10, 14, 38,
    83, 101
    electronic currency 83
    inflation policies 16, 75, 76, 97
    inflation targeting 110
    interest on reserves 66, 79, 80
    interest rate policy 16–17, 65–6, 69–70,
        81–2, 85, 89, 93, 97, 103, 104,
        105–7, 106
    money supply policy 13, 71
    'soft landings' 110
feminism
    and trans people 62
    see also gender inequality
Fetzer, Thiemo 43–4
films, as a methodology 24, 28, 193
financial crisis, 2007/08 xii, 2, 4, 7, 43, 65,
    66, 71, 79, 82, 94, 100, 106, 107, 108,
    124, 188, 191, 198
    see also Great Recession
Financial Times 22, 86–7, 90, 140–1, 154,
    170, 173, 192
Finland 26
First Step Act (US) 63
fiscal drag 86
fiscal policy 1, 4, 6, 10, 42, 71, 76, 84, 195,
    196, 197
fixed exchange rates 17, 69, 103–4, 187
'flat tax' 194, 195
flooding xi
Florida xi
Floyd, George 5
focus groups, research methodology 23, 24
'follow the science' 59–60
food banks 22
football players 38–9
Ford, Gerald 197
'formal hiring and promotion criteria' 141
forward guidance 12, 14, 64, 66, 70, 81, 101
fossil fuels 143
free trade x, 68
Friedman, Milton ix, xiii, 10, 56, 65, 77,
    105–6
Friedman, S. 6

friendly societies 132
FTSE 500 4
furlough scheme, UK 4, 8, 44, 124, 192
further education 112, 147, 151, 154, 156

G

Galbraith, John Kenneth ix, 44, 82, 123
Garland, Merrick 28
Garrick Club, London, women
  members 133, 134
gas safety checks 177
GDP (gross domestic product)
  measurement of 55
  UK 12–13, 109, 125, 146, 195
  US 12, 71, 109, *109*, 129, 139
gender identity, differential outcomes 141
gender inequality xiii, 141
  in marriage premiums 142
gender pay gap 189
  British universities 38–9, 142
Generation X (1965–1980) vii, 18, 58,
  119, 190
Generation Z (1997–2012) vii, 1, 2–4, 3, 7,
  11, 16, 33, 43, 53, 143, 189, 191, 201
  challenge for 4–5, 14–15
  housing affordability 2, 19, 144
  political power 189
gentrification 173, 174
Gibbons, Stephen 151
gig economy 6, 41, 85, 118, 121, 126,
  198, 199
'Gillick competency,' UK law 33
Glastonbury 14
Global average surface temperatures (NOAA) 5
'global saving glut' 12, 42, 70, 81, 84, 85, 97,
  194, 197, 198
global warming *see* climate change
gold standard 17, 69, 102–3, *103*, 187
Goldilocks economy 197–8
Golding, William 56
Google 56
Gore, Al 191
government debt 12–13
  debt overhang 86
    zero interest rate policy 108–10, *109*
  monetization of 84
  see also bonds
Gowar, Norman 7
Graetz, Georg 137
Great Depression 65, 102, 106, 107, 124,
  127, 188, 201
'great moderation' 191
Great Recession 4, 43, 65, 66, 102, 108,
  180, 182
  see also financial crisis, 2007/08
'greatest generation' vii, 201
Green Revolution 200
Greenspan, Alan 10, 88, 90, 94, 138
Grenfell Tower 174

groupthink x, 9, 15, 36
Guardian, The 22, 48–9, 117–18, 123, 168
guardrails xiii, 17, 26, 30, 35, 36, 65, 66–9,
  75, 80, 91, 92, 104, 105, 140, 187
  golden 102–3
  restoration of 112
guilds 131–3

H

Hair 190
hard policies 142–4
Harry Brown 174
Harvard University 133
Hastings, A. 176
HEFCE (Higher Education Funding Council
  for England) 154
HEPI (Higher Education Policy
  Institute) 147
He's Just Not That Into You 187
Heygate Estate, Southwark 174
'high powered money' 71
higher education *see* universities
Higher Education Act 2004 (UK) 145
Higher Education Funding Council for
  England (HEFCE) 154
Higher Education Policy Institute
  (HEPI) 147
Hillier, Meg 192
hippies 14, 190
holiday lets 171
homelessness
  and the COVID-19 pandemic 20
  see also housing
'Homo economicus' 46
homosexuality 61–2
Hong Kong residents, right to settle in the
  UK 132
'honour killings' of family members 59
House of Commons Library 43, 44
House of Commons Treasury
  Committee 108
housing x–xi, 6, 19, 90, 95–6, *96*,
  113, 125
  affordable 175–7, 188
  as asset for social care payment 184
  bailouts 6
  buy-to-let property 19, 96, 102, 171, 179,
    180, 182, 183
  capital gains xi, 9, 85, 86, 89, 96, 100, 173,
    179, 180, 182, 183, 184
  cladding issues 174
  current situation 170–2
  energy efficiency 177–8
  first-time buyer help 8, 95, 183
  'freehold' 178
  generational equity, politics and
    policy 183–5
  gentrification 173, 174
  holiday lets 171

home ownership 99, 172, 178–80, *180*, 182, 184
house prices xi–xii, xiii, xiv, 95, 97–8, 99, 171–2
  house price to income ratio xi, 1–2, 8, 12, 14, 19, 34, 86, 100, 112, 170, 182, 183, 198
  and interest rates 95–6, 179–80, 182
  and monetary policy 19
  sustainability of 182–3
  US 179–80, *180*
housing market equity x, xi
housing stock 170–1
housing tenure 172–4
impact of zero interest rate policy 84–5
and inflation 183, 185–6
insulation 22
intergenerational inequalities 100
'long leasehold' 178
new building 170–1, 181, 186
planning gain 175
quality of 174–5
rental sector 19, 95, 171, 172–3, 177–8, 182, 184
  affordable rent 175
  underlying rents 180–2, *181*
rent-to-buy 175
'right to buy' policy 95, 172, 173, 183
second homes 171
shared ownership 175
social segregation 175–7
stamp duty 172, 185
student housing 176
sub-prime mortgage crisis, 2007/08 19
underlying rents 180–2, *181*
vacant properties 171
see also mortgages
Hubbard, Glenn 139
human capital, investment in 116–17
  see also education; universities
humanities 14, 24, 148, 153, 165, 187, 193
Hungary 5
hurricanes xi, 1
hybrid working 122
hyper-inflation 83, 193

I

IBM 121
identity 59–61
Idiocracy 27
IEA (Institute of Economic Affairs) 194–5
IMF (International Monetary Fund) 103, 140
Imperial College 155
'implicit bias training' xiii, 7
income distribution 26–7, 30
independence 189, 190
Independent 172
index funds 138
index-linked bonds 92, *93*

India 5, 129–30
  population growth 129–30, 198
individualism 189–90
inflation xiv, 11–12, 13, 16, 42, 182, 196–7, 199
  and bonds 92, *93*
  controlled higher rate 13–14, 18, 85–6, 105
  CPI (consumer price inflation) 11
    UK 11, 43, 76, 78, 197
    US 11, 43, 75, 104
  and housing 183, 185–6
  hyper-inflation 83, 193
  inflation targeting 74–6, 185
  and money supply 73
  politics of 84–7
  post-COVID-19 pandemic 6, 43, 45, 64, 66, 82, 85, 97, 100, 102, 106, 165, 188, 198
  and stocks 93–4
  Taylor rule 104–5
  WIN ('whip inflation now') programme 197
  see also Phillips curve
Infrastructure Bill 2021 (UK) 194
Infrastructure Investment and Jobs Act 2021 (US) 12
inheritance 25–7
Institute for Fiscal Studies 154, 165
Institute of Economic Affairs (IEA) 194–5
institutional racism 141, 143
Insulate Britain 178
insurance
  friendly societies 132
  social welfare programmes 132–3
interest on reserves 66, 79–80, 91
interest rates 1, 13–14, 16–17, 43, 89, 99, 102, 105, 123, 171, 191, 196–7
  asset prices 90
  bonds 91–2, *93*
  declining 88–9, *89*, 96–7
  disequilibrium 6
  generational inequality 196
  house prices 95–6
  money supply 72–3
  politics of 84–7
  post-pandemic rise 183
  setting of 69–70
  Taylor rule 17, 104
  zero interest rate policy 6, 17, 21, 64–6, 66–7, 84–5, 96–7, 98, 102, 108–10, *109*, 138, 154, 171, 183, 188, 194, 197
intergenerational equity 5–7, 25–7
International Monetary Fund (IMF) 103, 140
internet service providers 126
investment 197, 198, 199
  and population 138–41, *139*, *140*
investment channels 116
investors, private 98

IPCC (Intergovernmental Panel on Climate Change) 5, 48
Iraq wars 4

J

Japan 24, 121, 130
Jenkins, Andrew 147
Jim Crow laws 31
job security 122–4
'jobs for life' 6, 121
John Deere 119
John Lewis Partnership 115
Johnson, Boris 27, 31, 113
Johnson, Lyndon B. 29
journals, publication in ix, 164
    see also REF (Research Excellence Framework)

K

Kaley, Alexandra 141–2
Kaser, Michael 100
Kennedy, J. F. 29, 197
Kennedy, Robert 14, 29
Kent University 161
Keynes, John Maynard ix, 9–10, 76, 99
Keynesian economics 2, 9–10, 13, 30, 47, 71, 72, 76, 77, 78, 79, 99
Khan, Sadiq 196
King, Martin Luther 14, 29, 32–3, 200, 201
King, Stephen D. 6, 191
Kingston University 155
Koo, Richard 86, 108, 109
Krueger, Alan B. 37, 119
Kwarteng, Kwasi 84

L

Labour Government 107
labour market 40, 85, 113
    'flexible' 114–15, 199
    labour shortages, UK 108, 134–5
    see also employment; work, future of
Labour Party 142, 194, 195
labour theories, Marx 130
Laffer curve 193
Lancaster University 161
Landers, Renee 122
Lang, Kirsty 173
Laude, David 160
Laurison, D. 6
law courts, family disputes in 21–2
law firms, employment practices 122
Lawrence, Stephen 141
Lawson Boom 42, 140
'lecture capture' 22, 45, 122, 151, 167–8
'legacy admissions,' universities 133
Lehrer, Tom 185
LEO (Longitudinal Education Outcomes) data 148, 158–9, 164
'levelling up' policies 11, 132

LGBT+ rights 200
LGBTQI+ people, US 29
liberal arts colleges 148
Liberal Democrat party 145
life expectancy at birth, US 127
living wage 41
Livingstone, Ken 175
lone parent households 34
Longitudinal Education Outcomes (LEO) data 148, 158–9, 164
'long-term relationship' model of employment 121–2
Lord of the Flies, The (Golding) 56
LSE (London School of Economics) ix, 155, 161, 162

M

MacAskill, William 6, 48, 131
Machin, S. 6
Macmillan, Lindsey 158–9
Macpherson Report 141
macroeconomics, methodology of 42–3
Macron, Emmanuel 31
Magnus, Ed 177
Mandela, Nelson 30, 201
Manning, Alan 119
maple syrup cartel 122–3
'marginal productivity' 116
markets
    in public provision of goods 147–8
    universities 147–50, 153, 156, 162–3, 195
marriage 34
    same-sex 32, 34
Marshall, Alfred 20, 35–6, 38, 39
Martin, William McChesney 38, 104
Marx, Karl 130
'materialism' 189, 190
mathematics, role of 38–9
Matthews, P. 176
'maximising shareholder value' xiii
'max-min' approach 57
May, Theresa 184, 192
Mazzucato, Mariana 174
McCarthy, J. 28
'me too' movement 5
medical technology 192
Medicare Trust Fund, US 132
Medicare, US 29
'mediocre white males' 7, 9, 142
Meet the Press, 14 November 2021 134
Metropolitan Police, institutional racism 141
Michaels, Guy 137
Middle Ages, guilds 131–2
migration 134–6, 143, 190
millennials (1981–1996) vii, 5–6, 11, 18, 119, 120, 143, 189
'millennium bug' 4
minimum wage 10, 37, 40
minority ethnic people, US 29

MIT 75
'MIT of the North' 167
monetarism 2, 10
monetary base 71–3, *72*
monetary policy xiv, 1–2, 4, 6, 9, 10–11, 13, 14, 16–17, 17–18, 19, 35, 37, 42, 64–5, 64–6, 69, 70, 71, 74–5, 76, 77, 81, 82, 83, 84, 85, 97, 101, 104–5, 110, 112, 116, 123, 139, 191, 195, 196
monetary theory 71–2
money, quantity theory of 13, 71–2, 76, 77
money supply
  explosion of 71–3, *72*
  source of 73–4, *74*
  see also quantitative easing
moon landing 14
'moral hazard' 60, 107–8
Morris, William 129
mortgages 12, 95–6, 171, 172–3, 184, 185
  sub-prime mortgage crisis, 2007/08 19, 106, 108, 182, 188, 191
  UK 18, 179
  US 178–9
  see also housing
motorways, smart 111
Murphy, Richard 108, 158–9

N

NAB (National Advisory Board) 151
Naef, Michael 7
national insurance rates, UK 132, 133
National Oceanic and Atmospheric Administration (NOAA) 5
National Student Survey (NSS) 148, 150, 151, 164
National Union of Mineworkers 117
'negative income tax' 10
neoliberalism 10–11
'nepo babies' 53
'net neutrality' 126
net zero xiii, xiv, 5, 195
Neumayer, Eric 151
New Keynesian economics 75
New Orleans 199
New York City 1
New York Times 118, 193
New Zealand, COVID-19 pandemic 57
News from Nowhere (Morris) 129
NHS (National Health Service) 34, 38, 112
  and the COVID-19 pandemic 20
  doctors' employment practices 122
  PFI (private finance initiative) 157
Nikkei average 88
Nixon in China (Adams) 102
Nixon, Richard 102, 103
no label economics 9–11, 51, 99, 148, 195
no logo clothing 9, 21, 22–3
NOAA (National Oceanic and Atmospheric Administration) 5

'non-dom' tax status 194
non-financial business debt, US 12
non-fungible tokens 83
non-profits debt, US 12
non-violence 200
Norrington table 151
North Sea oil and gas 195
Northern Ireland, population issues 143
'Northern powerhouses' 40
Northumbria University 167
novels, as a methodology 24, 28, 37, 193
NPL 175
NSS (National Student Survey) 148, 150, 151, 164
nuclear war 4, 14, 28, 29–30
'nudge' 62

O

Obama, Barack 10, 28, 31, 107
Obergefell V Hodges 32
Occupy movement 4
OFFA (Office for Fair Access) 157, 158
Office of the US Trade Representative 69
OfS (Office for Students) 147, 154, 157, 158, 164
  'Discover Uni' 150, 161
  Uni Connect programme 158
OFSTED (Office for Standards in Education, Children's Services and Skills) 151
oil prices 79
Okun, Arthur 108
Olou, Ijeoma 7, 9, 141, 142
on-line education 168
open market operations 73, 79
Open University 168
'Operation Warp Speed' 192
opioid crisis 127
Orwell, George 133, 135
overseas students 145, 146, 147, 165–6, 167, 194
Ox-Bow Incident, The (Clark) 128
Oxford University 133, 151, 161

P

Pager, D. 141
pandemic *see* COVID-19 pandemic
Pareto-efficiency 62–3
Paris Agreement 187, 195
Parliamentary select committees x
parliamentary system, power in 26
pension funds 91, 97, 120–1
Pension Regulator, The 120
pensions 2, 119, 120–1
  defined benefits pensions 121
  defined-benefit schemes 6
  final salary pension schemes 120
  and population trends 130, 136–7
  and robots/AI 137–8
  state pension, UK 6, 34, 132

Perkins, Richard 151
Peterson, Bruce 139
PFI (private finance initiative) 157
Phillips curve 16, 76–9, 77, 78, 81,
    82, 110
Phillips loops 78, 78
Pigou, Arthur ix, 75
Poland 5
policy
    economists' influence on ix–x
    hard policies 142–4
    role in prevention of extinction
        equilibrium 62–3
    sustainability of 11–14
political donations, US 31
political economy challenges 4–5
political impasse 31–2
'poll tax' 30
polytechnics 151, 161, 162, 163, 167
    see also universities
'poor doors' 175
population 195, 198, 200
    clubs 131, 133–4
    'generation gap' 136
    guilds 131–3
    and investment 138–41, 139, 140
    migration 134–6
    population bomb 129–31
    population growth 2, 18, 46, 112, 113,
        129, 136, 143
    and labour supply 130–1
    Robinson Crusoe economics 55–6
'Population Bomb Revisited, The' (Ehrlich
    and Ehrlich) 200
Population Bomb, The (Erlich and
    Erlich) 129
Porton Down 175
poverty, government support payments 125
Princeton University 174
principal-agent problem 154
Principles of Economics (Marshall) 20, 35–6
private equity model 109–10
private finance initiative (PFI) 157
privatization, of state-owned companies 183
productivity 116, 117, 199
Professional Air Traffic Controllers
    Organization 117
property rights, Robinson Crusoe
    economics 48, 52, 56, 63
protest 30, 62
Public Accounts Committee 192
public sector pay 157, 167
Puerto Rico, full US citizenship 132
Putin, Vladimir 4–5

Q

quantitative easing 13, 64, 70, 80, 81, 91, 94,
    99, 108
quantity theory of money 13, 71–2, 76, 77

R

racial inequality xiii, 29, 30, 189
    household wealth 141
racism
    institutional 141, 143
railways 194, 195
Ralph Lauren 9, 21, 23
randomized double-blind controlled
    trails 37
Reagan, Ronald xiii, 10, 27, 65, 115,
    117, 147
Rebitzer, James 122
recessions 81, 99, 109–10
    'balance sheet recession' 86
    see also Great Recession
redistribution 26, 176
redundancy pay 115, 123–4
REF (Research Excellence Framework) ix–x,
    164, 166–7
Reform 150
refugees 135
regional variations, labour market 40
regulatory policy 84
regulatory powers 82–3
Reich, Robert 117–18
Reinhart, C. M. 109
religion
    and family values 58–9
    and population issues 143
    'replacement theory' 30
Republican Party, US 27–8
research
    universities 163–5, 166, 174–5, 193
Research Excellence Framework (REF) ix–x,
    164, 166–7
reserves, interest on 66, 79–80, 91
Resolution Foundation 146, 170
Restrepo, Pascual 137
'right to buy' policy 95, 172, 173, 183
risk-aversion, Robinson Crusoe
    economics 57
Robbins Report, 1963 167
Robinson Crusoe (Defoe) 56, 57
Robinson Crusoe economics 15–16, 48–9,
    50–1, 61, 62, 63, 67–9
    Adam Smith 51–3
    extinction equilibrium 57–8
    fall of the coconuts 56–7
    family values and extinction 58–9
    John Smiths 55–6
    Junior (Crusoe's son) 53–4
    population growth 55–6
Robinson, Joan ix
robots 2, 18, 46, 113, 131, 197
    and pensions 137–8
Roe v Wade 32, 143
Rogoff, K. S. 109
Romer, Paul 43
Royal Family 193

'running the economy hot' 17, 38, 77–8, 79, 85, 99, 104, 108, 112, 113, 116
Russell Group 152, 155, 161, 162, 165, 186
Russia 4–5, 56, 100
   invasion of Ukraine 4, 10, 20, 105, 191

S

same-sex marriage 32, 34
Sandbanks, Dorset 9
Sandler, Todd 133
schools, quality control in 150–1
science 59–60
   role in prevention of extinction equilibrium 62–3
   see also technological advances
scripts 61–2
second homes 171
Second World War 45, 109, 111
'secular stagnation' 42, 81, 84, 85, 97, 197
'self-interest' 189, 190
Senate, US 27–8
sexual harassment 5
sexual orientation, differential outcomes 141
share buybacks 140–1, 197
share prices 90
shocks 2, 3, 4, 11, 12, 17, 34, 47, 102, 105, 107–8, 123, 191
'silent generation' vii
Silicon Valley Bank 91, 97, 107, 127
'skilled worker' visas, UK 135
skills shortages, and Brexit 134–5
slavery xii, 3
Small, M. L. 141
'smart motorways' 111
smartphones 111–12
Smith, Adam 52
   see also Robinson Crusoe economics
social capital 27–30
social care system 1, 192
   housing as asset for payment 184
social class, housing segregation 175–7
social mobility, lack of 6
Social Security Trust Fund, US 132
social welfare provision, as 'insurance' programmes 132–3
sociology, research methodology 23, 24
'soft landings' 110–11
solar panels xii, 192
Solow, Robert 192
Sony Aibo robot dog 137, 138
Soros, George 104
South Africa 129
Soviet Union 100
stakeholders, beneficial outcomes for xiii–xiv
stamp duty 172, 185
Starbucks 118
'statistical discrimination' 141
Steinbeck, John 81
Stern Review 187, 195

Sternberg, Joseph C. 6, 64
stocks 90, 97–8, 102
   returns and risks 93–4, *94*
Stop Mugging Grandma (Bristow) 141
strikes, public sector 157
structured interviews, research methodology 23, 24
students see universities
'subconscious bias training' 141–2
sub-prime mortgage crisis, 2007/08 19, 106, 108, 182, 188, 191
suicide rates 3, 127
Summers, Larry 42
Sunak, Rishi 87, 124, 192
'supply side' economics 112
Supreme Court, UK 26
Supreme Court, US 26, 28, 31, 32, 119, 133, 143, 159
survival, housing market, England x, xi
Sussex University 161
sustainability
   and equilibrium 33–4
   of house prices 182–3
   housing market, England x, xi
   intergenerational equity 6
   of policy 11–14
   universities 155–7
Swensen, David 138
'swinging sixties' 14, 29

T

talking to people 23, 24–5
'taper tantrum,' 2013 94, 107
'taste for discrimination' 141
tax credits 41, 125, 152
Tax Cuts and Jobs Act 2017 (US) 84
taxation 193
   corporate 1, 194, 197
   fiscal drag 86
   'flat tax' 194, 195
   'negative income tax' 10
   progressive xiii
   stamp duty 172, 185
   of the wealthy 194, 195
   windfall tax
      energy cost of living crisis 20
      on planning gain 175
Taylor, John 104
Taylor, Lowell 122
Taylor rule 17, 103–5
Teaching and Higher Education Act 1988 (UK) 145
technological advances xii, 2, 18, 34, 45, 191–3
'tenancy deposit protection scheme' 178
'Test and Trace' scheme 8, 192
Thaler, Richard 62
Thatcher, Margaret xiii, 10, 27, 30, 95, 115, 117, 147, 172, 179, 183

theory, in economics 23–4
Theory of Moral Sentiments, The (Smith) 52
Thunberg, Greta 190
Tobin, James ix, xiii
Today's Conveyancer 184
Todd, Chuck 134
Tompkins table 151
Tough, Paul 160
trade unions 116, 117–19, *118*, 120, 126
trans people 62
'trickle-down' economics 2, 9, 62
  left wing 107–8
truck driver shortage, COVID-19
  pandemic 134
Trump, Donald 5, 27, 31, 63, 77, 84, 94,
  138, 190, 192
Truss, Liz 84, 91, 93
Trussonomics 73
Tschirhart, John 133
Twenge, J. M. 1, 11, 189, 191
two-child benefits cap, UK 195–6
two-tier society 124–6

U

Uber 118, 121
UCL 155
UGC (University Grants
  Commission) 151, 154
UK
  CPI (consumer price inflation) 11, 43, 76,
    78, 197
  electoral system 31
  GDP (gross domestic product) 12–13, 109,
    125, 146, 195
  government debt 108
  home ownership rate 99
  mortgages 18, 179
  racial disparities in household wealth 141
  railways 194, 195
  wages 108, 113, *114*
  wind energy 195
UK Research and Innovation 163
Ukraine, Russian invasion of 4, 10, 20,
  105, 191
ULEZ (Ultra Low Emission Zone) 196
unemployment 4, 10
  Taylor rule 104–5
  unemployment benefits 123
  see also employment; Phillips curve
Uni Connect programme 158
United Airlines 60
United Auto Workers 119
universal basic income 125
universal benefit 10, 18, 20, 51, 124
Universal Credit 34, 44, 125–6, 153
universal services 124–5
universities x, 7–8, 186–7
  2012 reform 146–7, 152, 157, 161
  academic tenure 121–2

addressing the gaps 159–61
Athena SWAN scheme 158
'awarding gaps' 159
Black students 158, 159
Browne Report 86, 146, 148–9, 156,
  157, 165
building projects 155, 156, 157, 166
clearing 186
'commuting students' 168
competition 149, 150–2
diversity 135–6
entry requirements 150
excellence throughout the hierarchy 161–3
fees 5, 7–8, 18, 86, 145, 147, 149–50
Foundation Years 146, 147, 150, 156
gender pay gap 38–9
grade inflation 151
graduate tax 152, 153
hierarchy of 151–2, 161
'lecture capture' and remote learning 22,
  45, 122, 151, 167–8
'legacy admissions' 133
'low-value' courses 153
managerial 154–5
market 147–50, 153, 156, 162–3, 195
'marketization' of 27
NSS (National Student Survey) 148, 150,
  151, 164
overseas students 145, 146, 147, 165–6,
  167, 194
pension scheme 120, 121
policy solutions 165–7
postgraduate degrees 146
quality control 150–1
REF (Research Excellence
  Framework) ix–x, 164, 166–7
research 163–5, 166, 174–5, 193
Research Assessment Exercise, 1986 164
'research-led teaching' 163, 166
Robbins Report, 1963 167
Russell Group 152, 155, 161, 162,
  165, 186
solution 165–7
student engagement and the
  pandemic 167–9
student housing 176
student loan system 6, 8, 19, 25, 49–50,
  145–6, 147, 152, 153
student number cap 146, 149, 161, 162
subsidies 152–4
sustainability 155–7
teaching effectivemness, measurement
  of 164–5
'teaching-focused' academics 160, 163
US 145–7, 159–60
'value added' 153, 164–5
VCs (Vice-Chancellors) 154–5
widening participation 8, 146, 153,
  157–9, 162

Universities UK 147
University and Colleges Union 157
University Council 155
University Grants Commission
   (UGC) 151, 154
University of California 163
University of California at Berkeley 174
University of Essex 142
University of London 151
University of Texas 159
University of Texas (Austin) 159, 160–1
Urquhart, Andrew 154
US 3, 12–13
   civil rights legislation 14, 29, 200
   civil rights movement 58, 61
   climate change impact xi, 1
   corporate taxation 138
   electoral system 31
   GDP (gross domestic product) 12, 71, 109,
      109, 129, 139
   GDP per capita 129
   government debt 98, 109, *109*
   healthcare system 26, 29
   home ownership rate 99
   house prices 179–80, *180*
   industrial strategy 12
   inflation 13
      CPI (consumer price inflation) 11, 43,
         75, 104
      PCE price inflation 197
   investment and corporate profits *139*,
      139–40, *140*
   mortgages 178–9
   racial disparities in household wealth 141
   railways 194
   social welfare provision 132–3
   trade relationship with China 12, 69, 194
   unemployment 104
   universities 145–7, 159–60
   wages 113, *115*
US Congressional Committees x
US Constitution 32
US dollar 69, 83, 103

V

vaccination, COVID-19 pandemic xii–xiii,
   9, 22, 33, 57, 60–1, 164, 192
VCs (Vice-Chancellors) 154–5
Veblen, Thorsten 21
velocity of money 72, 73
Vienna, rental market 173
Vietnam war 29, 42, 136
Volcker, Paul 76, 81, 182, 197
voter suppression 31
Voting Rights Act 1965 (US) 14, 29

W

wages
   above inflation wage settlements 14

back-loading of 119–20
determinants of 114–17
minimum wage 10, 37, 40
public sector pay 157, 167
raising of 17, 116, 184, 185, 197,
   198, 199
stagnation of 2, 17, 113, *114*, *115*, 138,
   139, 167
UK 108, 113, *114*
US 113, *115*
Wallis, Patrick 131–2
Warwick University 161
waste 26
wealth
   distribution of 26–7, 30
   passing on within families 56, 63
Weimar Republic 83
white nationalism 30
Whitelaw, Willie 27
widening participation, universities 8, 146,
   153, 157–9, 162
wildfires xi, 1, 188
Willetts, David 5, 146, 167
Wilson, Harold 103
WIN ('whip inflation now') programme 197
wind energy 195
windfall tax
   energy cost of living crisis 20
   on planning gain 175
Winnie the Pooh books 134
Woilder, Thornton 2–3
Wolf, Alison 142, 147
Wolf, Martin xiv
women
   professional 142
   US 29
   see also gender inequality; gender pay gap
Woodstock 14
work, future of 17–18
   declining working week 131
   employment relationship 121–2
   future generations 119–21
   hybrid working 122
   job security 122–4
   present situation 113–14
   public support for large corporations over
      workers 126–8
   trade unions 117–19, *118*
   two-tier society 124–6
   wages, determinants of 114–17
   working from home 45, 122
   see also employment; labour market
working from home 45, 122, 168–9
Working Tax Credit, UK 125
World Trade Center attacks 4
Wyness, Gillian 158–9

X

XX Factor, The (Wolf) 142

Y

Yale University 133, 138
Yellen, Janet 10, 77–8, 108
yield curve control 64
York University 161
young people
  criminal records 56, 63
  employment 112
  'Gillick competency,' UK law 33
  non-financial benefits of employment 41
  not in education, employment or training 3
YouTube 126
yuan 83

Z

zero interest rate policy 6, 17, 21,
  64–6, 66–7, 96–7, 98, 102, 138,
  154, 171, 183, 188, 194, 197
  debt overhang 108–10, *109*
  and housing 84–5
Zero Population Growth movement
  129
zero-hours contracts 85, 199
  see also gig economy
Zoega, Gylfi 123
'zombie' firms 110
zoomers *see* Generation Z